HTML
Web Magic
Second Edition

HTML
Web Magic
Second Edition

BY RAYMOND PIROUZ

HTML Web Magic, Second Edition

International Standard Book Number: 1-56830-475-7

Library of Congress Catalog Card Number: 98-85794

Printed in the United States of America

First Printing: July 1998

00 99 98   4 3 2 1

This book was produced digitally by Macmillan Computer Publishing and manufactured using computer-to-plate technology (a film-less process) by GAC/Shepard Poorman, Indianapolis, Indiana.

Trademarks

Warning and Disclaimer

Executive Editor
Alicia Buckley

Acquisitions Editor
Laura Frey

Development Editor
Juliet MacLean

Software Development Specialist
Adam Swetnam

Project Editor
Kevin Laseau

Copy Editor
San Dee Phillips

Technical Editor
Rick Luna

Cover Designer
Aren Howell

Book Designer
Gary Adair

Production
Michael Henry
Linda Knose
Tim Osborn
Staci Somers
Mark Walchle

iv

About the Author

Raymond Pirouz is an author, instructor, product developer, designer, and Senior Partner at R35 LLC (http://www.r35.com) and R35 direct (http://www.r35.com/direct), which markets Web design tools, hardware, and software for an Internet audience.

Author of *click here* [ISBN 1562057928], (http://www.rpirouz.com/click), Raymond has been at the forefront of developing content targeted toward the Internet audience.

While art director at Rubin Postaer Interactive, he quickly established himself as an expert in the field of advertising on the Net, creating award-winning campaigns for major clients including American Honda, Cathay Pacific Airlines, and American Century Mutual Funds.

At R35 LLC, Raymond's clients have included Rubin Postaer Interactive (American Honda, Cathay Pacific, and iBank), Virgin Records, California Institute of Technology (Caltech), NASA/JPL/States Of Art, and THINK NEW IDEAS INC. (Panasonic/Monty Python), among others.

As an honors graduate of the prestigious Art Center College of Design in Pasadena, Raymond was granted the World Studio Foundation award for design and advertising excellence and has since won numerous awards for interactive Web design and advertising.

With a strong foundation in the use of traditional media, Raymond has taught an advanced Web design course for UCLA extension and is currently teaching online classes at R35 edu (http://www.r35.com/edu).

Raymond has appeared on numerous radio talk-shows including "Digital Village" on KPFK, "Real Computing with John Dvorak" on NPR, "Floppy Talk," and nationally syndicated "Craig Crossman's Computer America Show."

Pirouz has spoken at numerous book signings and events including the Web '97 and Web '98 conferences along with the New Media '98 conference in Toronto, Canada.

Dedications

For my inspiration, partner, and wife—Dante Monique Pirouz.

Contents at a Glance

Part I: Introduction
    Basic Web Design Tips .2

Part II: Magic with First Impressions
    Using the <Meta> Tag to Get Listed 18
    Creating a Slide Show with META Refresh 24
    Designing a Splash Page with META Refresh 30
    Eliminate Browser Offset 34
    Determining Your Visitor's Browser and
        Platform 42
    Detecting Specific Plug-Ins 50
    Designing an Alternate Page for Older
        Browsers 54
    Make Descriptive Links 58

Part III: Magic with Images
    Create Colorful GIF Rules and Frames 64
    Create White Space 72
    Make Images Appear Magically 76
    Animate a Portion of a Large Image 82
    Serve PNG Format Graphics 86
    Create Image Maps .88
    Design JavaScript Rollovers 92
    Design Image Map Rollovers 98
    Create Rollover Animations 106
    Develop Multiple Rollovers 110

Part IV: Magic with Tables
    Define White Space 116
    Color Table Data Cells 120
    Layer Typography and Images 126
    Design Invisible Linking Cells 134
    Align Images and Text 140
    Create Nested Tables 148
    Resize Tables Dynamically 158

Part V: Magic with Frames
    Create a No-Frames Option 164
    Create a Single-Frame Site 170
    Force Frames 174
    Design Frames Within Frames 180

Create Border Graphics by Using Frames 190
Design Frames for Navigation 198
Target Multiple Frames with JavaScript 202

Part VI: Magic with Windows
Open New Windows with HTML TARGET 208
Open and Close Windows with JavaScript . . .212
Design a Launch Pad Home Page 218
Open Remote Navigation Windows 222

Part VII: Magic with Type
Specifying Fonts with HTML 226
Specifying Fonts with Cascading Style
    Sheets 232
Position and Layer Type with CSS 238
Creating Nonunderlined Text Links with
    CSS 242
Wrap Type Around Images 246
Create Lists by Using Graphics Instead of
    HTML Bullets 252
Create Structured Type by Using Columns . . .258

Part VIII: Magic with Forms
Incorporate Color and Graphics into
    Forms 268
Align Forms with Text and Images 274
Create a Visual Submit Button 276
Create Wrapping Text Fields 278
Design Pull-Down Menus with JavaScript 282

Contents

Part I: Introduction   1

   Basic Web Design Tips 2

       Basics of Web Design 2

       Basic HTML Coding Tips 3

       HTML 4.0 Quick Reference Chart 3

       A Word About JavaScript 15

Part II: Magic with First Impressions   17

   Using the <META> Tag to Get Listed 18

   Creating a Slide Show with META Refresh 24

       Creating a Loop .24

       See the Slide Show in Action 25

   Designing a Splash Page with META Refresh 30

       Using the META Refresh Function 30

   Eliminate Browser Offset 34

       The Invisible Border 34

       Specifying Invisible Margins 35

       Tinkering with JavaScript 36

       Browser Offset Resources 40

   Determining Your Visitor's Browser and
   Platform 42

       Sending Browsers to Specific Pages 42

       Discriminating Between Browsers 44

       Determining the Platform 47

   Detecting Specific Plug-ins 50

       Writing the Code 50

   Design an Alternate Page for Older Browsers . . .54

       Using the <NOSCRIPT> Tag 54

       Design Tips 56

   Make Descriptive Links 58

       Integrating Descriptive Links 58

Part III: Magic with Images   63

   Create Colorful GIF Rules and Frames 64

       Creating GIF Rules 64

       Putting It Together in the Browser 67

       Designing a Frame 68

   Create White Space 72

       Using Spacer GIFs 72

ix

Make Images Appear Magically 76
   Creating the LOWSRC Effect 76
   Creating a Mini-Animation for a
   Splash Page .78
Animate a Portion of a Large Image 82
   Sectioning the Image 82
Serve PNG Format Graphics 86
   The Benefits of PNG Graphics 86
   Creating PNG Files 87
Create Image Maps .88
   Working with Image Mappers 88
Design JavaScript Rollovers 92
   Designing the Rollover Images 93
   Creating the Rollover Effect 94
   Putting It All Together 96
Design Image Map Rollovers 98
   Creating the Single Image Map
   Rollover 99
   Creating the Multiple Image Map
   Rollover 100
Create Rollover Animations 106
Develop Multiple Rollovers 110
   Writing the Code 111

Part IV: Magic with Tables   115
Define White Space 116
   Create Your Site Skeleton 116
   Labeling Your White Space 118
   Placing Your Elements Within the
   Structure 118
Color Table Data Cells 120
   Attract Your Viewer 120
   Speed Up Image Loading 123
Layer Typography and Images 126
   Create Layered Typography 126
   Cropping Animated GIFs 132
Design Invisible Linking Cells 134
   Creating Image Maps 134
Align Images and Text 140
   Creating a Table 140
Create Nested Tables 148
   Creating a Simple Nested Table 148
   Creating Multiple Nested Tables 150

Controlling Type Placement and Flow . .153
Creating a Bordered Structure 155
Resize Tables Dynamically 158
Using Percentages 158

Part V: Magic with Frames   163

Create a No-Frames Option 164
Creation Options 164
Forwarding Users to an Alternative
Page 164
Creating the Page 167
Create a Single-Frame Site 170
Hide Your Site's Directory Structure . . .170
Eliminate Browser Offset 171
Force Frames 174
Avoid Getting Framed 175
Limiting Access to Framed Pages 176
Design Frames Within Frames 180
Basic Frames Layout 180
Nesting Frames 185
Create Border Graphics by Using Frames 190
Get Creative! 190
Design Frames for Navigation 198
Using a Two-Frame Structure 198
The Navigation Without Frames 200
Target Multiple Frames with JavaScript 202
Updating Multiple Frames 202

Part VI: Magic with Windows   207

Open Windows with HTML TARGET 208
HTML Versus JavaScript 208
Coding the HTML 209
Open and Close Windows with JavaScript . . .212
Open New Windows 212
Close Windows 217
Design a Launch Pad Home Page 218
New Windows on Demand 218
Auto-Loading New Windows 220
Open Remote Navigation Windows 222
Making the Remote Control Appear
Automatically 222
Coding and Using the Remote
Control Page 224

Part VII: Magic with Type   225

Specifying Fonts with HTML 226

Specifying Size .226

Specifying Fonts 228

Specifying Fonts with Cascading Style
Sheets 232

Creating Styles .232

Position and Layer Type with CSS 238

Layering Typographic Elements 238

Create Nonunderlined Text Links with CSS . .242

Applying Styles 242

Wrap Type Around Images 246

Typographic Layout Limitations of
Conventional HTML 246

Using Tables to Enhance Layout 247

Create Lists by Using Graphics Instead
of HTML Bullets .252

HTML's Restrictive <UL> and
<OL> Tags 252

Creating Graphically Enhanced Lists 253

Create Structured Type by Using Columns . . .258

The Nonbreaking Space ( ) 258

Creating the Columns Template 260

Filling in the Columns 262

Part VIII: Magic with Forms   267

Incorporate Color and Graphics into Forms . .268

Designing Forms 268

Align Forms with Text and Images 274

Designing Forms 274

Create a Visual Submit Button 276

Designing the Submit Button 277

Inserting the Submit Button 277

Create Wrapping Text Fields 278

Using WRAP Property 278

Design Pull-Down Menus with JavaScript 282

Define the Function 283

Create the Pull-Down Menu 283

Who Needs HTML?

HTML (Hypertext Markup Language) is one of the oldest Web-development technologies around. In fact, it can be considered a dinosaur in Web years. Why write a book about such a seemingly outdated subject?

As the foundation upon which all Web sites are built, HTML initially limited many developers to a set of simple tags that often yielded unsophisticated, boring results. Over the past five years, Web designers have learned to tweak and master HTML along with its many idiosyncratic tags to achieve very specific results—or effects. Web sites that employ these effects engage their audiences like magic when compared to the many dull, lifeless sites that litter the Internet.

At the time of this writing, HTML has evolved to a 4.0 specification as endorsed by the W3C (World Wide Web Consortium at `http://www.w3c.org`). Every Web developer/designer interested in creating engaging Web sites should be familiar with HTML and how it can be used to achieve special effects for Web sites.

What About WYSIWYG Tools?

The current alternative to mastering and tweaking HTML is to allow a WYSIWYG (what-you-see-is-what-you-get) tool to design Web sites for you. Here are some of the most popular WYSIWYG tools:

- Adobe PageMill 3.0 (`http://www.adobe.com`)
- GoLive CyberStudio 3.0 (`http://www.golive.com`)
- Microsoft FrontPage 98
  (`http://www.microsoft.com/frontpage`)
- Claris HomePage 3.0 (`http://www.claris.com`)
- NetObjects Fusion 3.0 (`http://www.netobjects.com`)
- Macromedia Dreamweaver
  (`http://www.dreamweaver.com`)

Although WYSIWYG tools save time and are generally easy to use, they can quickly leave you at the mercy of their limitations. As an astute Web designer, you should master HTML and all its idiosyncrasies to achieve an expert understanding of the language, while keeping up with its steady evolution. In conjunction with HTML coding, you can utilize WYSIWYG tools to ease some of the repetitive and tedious aspects of Web site development.

Get Ready to ROCK!

Web designers have brought HTML a long way from the days of gray backgrounds, dithered images, and hypertext links. At present, you can use simple HTML to achieve a unique variety of magical effects that will leave your visitors clicking for more.

This book is designed and written for people with a general knowledge of HTML who are ready to take their designs to the ultimate level—adding sophisticated touches that will creatively communicate their messages to target audiences.

The World Wide Web is in a constant state of metamorphosis, continuously outgrowing its limitations. These are truly exciting times for Web designers and visual communicators who are willing to take the *HTML Web Magic* challenge to create better, more interactive, compelling sites that make users click with enthusiasm.

Using This Book

Ideally, you should be reading this book in front of your computer with your favorite HTML text editor and Internet browser engaged (4.0+ version preferred). You will learn a lot more if you accomplish a task rather than simply read about it, so it's a good idea to type the HTML techniques on your editor and test them in your browser as they are presented. If you have not taken the time to visit the book's companion site at `http://www.rpirouz.com/html`, do so now and visit it frequently while you read the book, as it reinforces many of the techniques within the pages to come.

Getting Organized

This book is organized in eight parts to help you become an HTML Web Magician. These parts are clearly marked with colorful tabs throughout the book and are summarized here:

- **Part I**   Introduction

  Reviews some basic Web design and HTML tips and provides an HTML 4.0 Quick Reference Chart and a word about JavaScript as it relates to this book.

- **Part II**   Magic with First Impressions

  Describes how to use the <META> tag and covers other techniques such as eliminating browser offset, determining your visitor's browser/platform, detecting specific plug-ins, and designing an alternate page for visitors with older browsers or no plug-ins.

- **Part III**   Magic with Images

  Explores colorful GIF rules and square shapes, white space, using LOWSRC, animating a small portion of an image, and using PNG, image maps, and JavaScript rollovers.

- **Part IV**   Magic with Tables

  Delves into the art of coloring table cells, adding background images to cells, making tables invisible, aligning images and text within cells, creating nested tables, resizing tables dynamically, creating white space with tables, and designing "fake" image maps by using table cells.

- **Part V**   Magic with Frames

  Shows how to eliminate browser offset by using frames, send a framed page to its parent, lay out frames within frames, use tags within frames, create a NOFRAMES option, use frames to create border graphics, design frames for navigation, target framed content, target multiple frames with JavaScript, and develop a JavaScript rotating frame.

- **Part VI**   Magic with Windows

  Covers opening new windows with HTML and JavaScript, opening a JavaScript remote control, and closing windows with JavaScript.

- **Part VII**   Magic with Type

  Helps you specify Web typography by using HTML and Cascading Style Sheets (CSS), vary type size by using CSS, create nonunderlined text links with CSS, vary type color on rollover, experiment with type alignment techniques, wrap type around images, align images and type against backgrounds, create lists with graphic bullets, and design columns of type by using table cells.

- **Part VIII**   Magic with Forms

  Explores form-alignment techniques with graphics and text, visual Submit button tricks, TEXTAREA wrapping techniques, cross-platform consistency tips, pull-down menu tricks, and form-verification techniques with JavaScript.

Following Along and Jumping Around

This book is designed in a nonlinear fashion—you are free to skip around at your leisure and read about the techniques that interest you the most. However, you are welcome (and encouraged) to read this book from cover to cover, section by section and follow along in a linear fashion if you are so inclined. This way, you won't miss any valuable information and can easily refer back to any section after you read it once.

A Word from the Author

I thank you for selecting *HTML Web Magic, Second Edition* from a shelf full of Web development titles.

This book demonstrates some of the hottest professional techniques for delivering information and graphics to a wired Internet audience. By reading each section and employing the techniques within, you will empower yourself with the most up-to-date Web design skills.

The book's companion site at `http://www.rpirouz.com/html` contains online examples as well as timely updates to the text.

Please feel free to contact me with any comments, questions, or general observations about this ever-changing technology.

Raymond Pirouz
`rpirouz@rpirouz.com`

Tell Us What You Think!

As the reader of this book, *you* are our most important critic and commentator. We value your opinion and want to know what we're doing right, what we could do better, what areas you'd like to see us publish in, and any other words of wisdom you're willing to pass our way.

As the Executive Editor for the Web Graphics and Design team at Macmillan Computer Publishing, I welcome your comments. You can fax, email, or write me directly to let me know what you did or didn't like about this book—as well as what we can do to make our books stronger.

Please note that I cannot help you with technical problems related to the topic of this book, and that due to the high volume of mail I receive, I might not be able to reply to every message.

When you write, please be sure to include this book's title and author as well as your name and phone or fax number. I will carefully review your comments and share them with the author and editors who worked on the book.

Fax: [317-817-7070]

E-mail: graphics@mcp.com

Mail: Executive Editor
          Web Graphics and Design

          Macmillan Computer Publishing
          201 West 103rd Street
          Indianapolis, IN 46290 USA

PART I

Introduction

As with the rest of the Web, HTML is a constantly evolving technology. At the time of this writing, HTML has evolved to a 4.0 specification as endorsed by the W3C (World Wide Web Consortium at `http://www.w3c.org`) and is in its most advanced state ever. The opportunities to experiment with the new technology are limitless and definitely thrilling.

Before you dive into all the exciting possibilities, however, begin with an overview of some fundamental Web design principles and tips to keep in mind while you read the rest of this book. Even if you decide to skip the basics overview and jump right in, don't forget to look over the HTML 4.0 Quick Reference Chart—a worthy companion for your upcoming HTML coding sessions.

Basic Web Design Tips

Basics of Web Design

Designing Web sites isn't all about zooming type, sizzling links, and advanced technology. As a Web developer in hopes of creating a successful Web site, you should consider the following:

1   Identify your site's key purpose. What is the one thing you want your site to do? What benefit or experience do you want your visitor to walk away with?

2   Recognize your bandwidth limitations. Do your pages take too long to load on a 28.8 modem? Make sure you optimize all images and keep file sizes small.

3   Who is your target audience? Who are you designing your site for? How will you deliver the information on your Web site so that your target audience will benefit from it? Make sure to design your Web site with end users (rather than yourself) in mind.

4   GIFs or JPEGs? Make sure you don't waste bandwidth by limiting JPEGS to full-color photographic images. Unless you display photos on your site, use optimized GIFs for all graphics if at all possible.

5   What monitor resolution will most of your visitors be using to access your Web site? Make sure your site is accessible by users with monitors limited to a 640×480 resolution.

6   Have you optimized your site for multiple platforms and multiple browsers? Make sure that you use the "browser-safe" palette for Mac/PC compliance as well as testing your site on at least Netscape and Internet Explorer browsers.

7   Make sure that your site's navigation is consistent and easy to use throughout the pages of your Web site.

8   Plan a strategy to get your audience to click deeper within your site.

9   If you specify fonts with the <FONT> tag or with CSS, make sure you specify fonts common to most platforms (in other words, Verdana, Arial, Helvetica, Courier New, Courier, Times New Roman, and Times).

10   Make sure to use your own images rather than "borrowing" from others. Copyright infringement is a serious offense.

11   Always keep two copies of your entire Web site. You should back up your entire site as often as possible in case of server crashes or hacks by cyber-terrorists.

12   Plan a strategy to ensure that your visitors return.

Basic HTML Coding Tips

This book assumes that you have a basic working knowledge of the HTML programming language. The following HTML coding tips and pointers should get you in the HTMLing mood:

1 Although HTML is NOT case-sensitive, it's a good idea to keep your code case consistent—either `<HTML>` or `<html>`. Although it doesn't really matter if you do this, it's helpful for leading your eye through the code and differentiating it from regular text within the code.

2 When saving your HTML files, you can either use an .html extension or an .htm extension (if your computer does not allow longer extensions). Make sure, however, to limit your filenames to lowercase letters if you use a UNIX-based server, as UNIX is case-sensitive when it comes to filenames. Also, do not use "spaces" within filenames, as this will throw off some systems. Instead, using the "underscore" character (_)ensures filename recognition among all systems.

3 It's a good idea to keep a tag list in a separate file on your computer. For example, keep a list of all the commonly used HTML tags such as `<IMG SRC="X" WIDTH="X" HEIGHT="X" BORDER=0 ALT="X">`. This way, when you need to place an image somewhere, you can simply copy the tag from your tag list and paste it into your HTML page.

4 You can save plenty of future editing time by adding comment tags (`<!-- comment here -->`) throughout your HTML document to section off and label your code.

5 *Always* include image dimensions within `<IMG>` tags. Failing to include this valuable data results in slight delays between the time it takes to load the page and display images.

6 Use ALT text within your `<IMG>` tags *only* when you have information to provide. Avoid empty ALTs (`ALT=""`), as they can annoy users with text browsers. For example, if you create a spacer GIF using a stretched out transparent GIF, specifying `ALT=""` within your `<IMG>` tag causes empty quotes to appear for someone entering your site with a text browser. If you use lots of these on your site, you will litter a nongraphic browser's page with a bunch of empty quote marks that irritate those with disabilities as well as those not wanting to see graphics.

7 Although sometimes optional, it's a good idea to close tags such as `<TD>`, `<TR>`, `<TABLE>`, `<HTML>`, and so on.

HTML 4.0 Quick Reference Chart

The following is a listing of the HTML 4.0-compliant tags/attributes commonly used by Web designers and their descriptions organized by tag type:

3

HTML Reference Chart

Main Tags	*Description*
`<HTML></HTML>`	Beginning and ending tags of an HTML document
`<HEAD></HEAD>`	Document head section identifiers
`<META>`	Meta-information (resides within `<HEAD></HEAD>` tags)
`<META HTTP-EQUIV="Refresh" CONTENT="X">`	Refreshes current page every X seconds
`<META HTTP-EQUIV="Refresh" CONTENT="X; URL=NEXTPAGE.HTML">`	Refreshes current page in X seconds and jumps to the URL
`<META NAME="Keywords" CONTENT="X">`	Communicates the site's keywords to search engines that recognize the `<META>` tag
`<META NAME="Description" CONTENT="X">`	Communicates the site's description to search engines that recognize the `<META>` tag
`<TITLE></TITLE>`	Identifies the HTML page title (resides within `<HEAD></HEAD>` tags)
`<BODY></BODY>`	Identifies the body, or main section, of the HTML document
`<BODY BACKGROUND="URL">`	Specifies a tiling background image
`<BODY BGCOLOR="#XXXXXX">`	Specifies the page's background color with a hexadecimal value (in other words, #FFFFFF or #000000)

Main Tags	*Description*
`<BODY TEXT="#XXXXXX">`	Specifies HTML text color within the page
`<BODY LINK="#XXXXXX">`	Specifies HTML or image border link color within the page
`<BODY VLINK="#XXXXXX">`	Specifies HTML or visited image border link color within the page
`<BODY ALINK="#XXXXXX">`	Specifies HTML or image border link color when the link is activated (or clicked on)
`<BODY MARGINWIDTH="0" MARGINHEIGHT="0">`	Sets the left and top margins of the page to 0 in Netscape 4.0+
`<BODY LEFTMARGIN="0" TOPMARGIN="0">`	Sets the left and top margins of the page to 0 in Internet Explorer
`<BODY ONLOAD="X()">`	Specifies the initiation of a Script event X() when the HTML page loads into the browser

Type Tags	*Description*
`<BASEFONT SIZE="X">`	Establishes a default font size from 1–7 (X, default is 3) throughout the HTML page
`<H></H>`	Heading from 1–6 (in other words, `<H1></H1>`, `<H2></H2>`, and so on)
`<B></B>`	Bold text
`<STRONG></STRONG>`	Strong text (similar to bold)
`<I></I>`	Italic text
`<U></U>`	Underlined text
`<STRIKE></STRIKE>`	Strikethrough text
`<SUB></SUB>`	Subscript text
`<SUP></SUP>`	Superscript text
`<TT></TT>`	Teletype text (fixed width)
`<SMALL></SMALL>`	Smaller text

5

continues

HTML Reference Chart (continued)

Type Tags	Description
`<BIG></BIG>`	Larger text
`<FONT SIZE="X">`	Specifies font size from 1–7
`<FONT FACE="FONTNAME">`	Specifies font name (in other words, Verdana, Helvetica, Arial)
`<FONT COLOR="#XXXXXX">`	Specifies font color with a hexadecimal value (in other words, #FFFFFF or #000000)

Cascading Style Sheets (CSS)	Description
`<STYLE TYPE="text/css"></STYLE>`	Beginning/closing tags for CSS, which must reside between the `<HEAD></HEAD>` tags
`P{color:#XXXXXX}`	Assigns a text color to a paragraph (P can be replaced with any other text formatting tag such as H, SPAN, and so on)
`P{background:#XXXXXX}`	Assigns a background color to a paragraph
`P{padding:length/%/auto}`	Sets the amount of padding (or space) between text and a paragraph border; up to 4 values can be specified in order of TOP, RIGHT, BOTTOM, and LEFT
`P{font-size:mm/cm/in/pt/pc/em/ex/px}`	Assigns font sizing within a paragraph (can be assigned with the following units of measure: millimeters/centimeters/inches/points/picas/ems/x-heights/pixels)
`P{font-family:font name}`	Specifies the paragraph's font

Cascading Style Sheets (CSS)	*Description*
`P{letter-spacing: mm/cm/in/pt/pc/em/ex/px }`	Specifies the letter-spacing of the paragraph (pt or px)
`P{text-align:left/right/center/justify}`	Aligns text within a paragraph
`P{text-indent: mm/cm/in/pt/pc/em/ex/px /%}`	Indents the first line within a paragraph
`.CLASS{font-size: mm/cm/in/pt/pc/em/ex/px }`	Assigns CSS properties to `CLASS`
`A:link{color:#XXXXXX}`	Assigns a color to `A:link` (similar procedure for `A:visited` and `A:active` links)
`A:link{font-size: mm/cm/in/pt/pc/em/ex/px }`	Specifies a font size for `A:link`
`A:link{font-family:font name}`	Specifies a font name for `A:link`
`A:link{text-decoration:none}`	Specifies nonunderlined `A:link`

Layout Tags	*Description*
`<BLOCKQUOTE></BLOCKQUOTE>`	Indents a block of text
` `	Inserts line break
`<BR CLEAR=LEFT/RIGHT/ALL>`	Inserts clearing line break
`<CENTER></CENTER>`	Centers objects
`<DIV>`	Divides a page into logical sections
`<DIV ALIGN=LEFT/CENTER/RIGHT>`	Aligns data within a `DIV` section
`<DIV CLASS=CLASSNAME>`	Assigns a `CLASS` to a `DIV` section
`<HR>`	Inserts a horizontal rule across the page or within a table data cell
`<HR ALIGN=LEFT/CENTER/RIGHT>`	Inserts an aligned horizontal rule
`<HR SIZE=X>`	Specifies the thickness of the horizontal rule in pixels (X)
`<HR WIDTH=X>`	Specifies the width of a horizontal rule in pixels (X)

7

continues

HTML Reference Chart (continued)

Layout Tags	Description
`<HR NOSHADE>`	Applies a solid black horizontal rule
`<NOBR>`	Prevents a line break
`<P>`	Creates new paragraphs
`<P ALIGN=LEFT/CENTER/RIGHT>`	Aligns paragraph text
`<PRE></PRE>`	Preformatted text (includes all spaces and returns)

Link Tags	Description
`<A HREF="URL"></A>`	Links text or image to a URL
`<A HREF="URL" TARGET="_BLANK"></A>`	Links text or image to a URL within a brand new browser window
`<A HREF="URL" TARGET="FRAMENAME"></A>`	Links text or image to a URL within a frame
`<A HREF="URL" TARGET="_SELF"></A>`	Within frames, links text or image to a URL within the frame in which the link was clicked
`<A HREF="URL" TARGET="_PARENT"></A>`	Within frames, links text or image to a URL within the FRAMESET parent of the document
`<A HREF="URL" TARGET="_TOP"></A>`	Within frames, eliminates FRAMESET parent and links text or image to a URL within the same browser window

Image Tags	Description
`<IMG SRC="URL">`	Displays image at URL location
`<IMG SRC="URL" ALIGN=TOP/MIDDLE/BOTTOM>`	Aligns image relative to text baseline

Image Tags	*Description*
`<IMG SRC="URL" ALIGN=LEFT/RIGHT>`	Aligns image relative to page, table, or frame
`<IMG SRC="URL" ALT="ALTTEXT">`	Provides alternate descriptive text for users with nongraphic browsers
`<IMG SRC="URL" USEMAP="#MAPNAME">`	Specifies an image map and points to map name
`<IMG SRC="URL" WIDTH="X" HEIGHT="X">`	Specifies image dimensions in pixels (X)
`<IMG SRC="URL" BORDER="X">`	Specifies whether or not to include a border (X) around an image (0 = no, 1 = yes)
`<IMG SRC="URL" HSPACE="X" VSPACE="X">`	Specifies horizontal and vertical spacing in pixels
`<IMG LOWSRC="URL" SRC="URL">`	Specifies an initial low-resolution loading of an image before the actual image is loaded
`<IMG NAME="X" SRC="URL">`	Names an image for use with JavaScript

Lists	*Description*
`<DL></DL>`	Begins/ends a definition title
`<DD></DD>`	Begins/ends a definition
`<DT></DT>`	Begins/ends a definition term
`<OL></OL>`	Begins/ends an ordered list
`<OL COMPACT></OL>`	Creates a compact ordered list
`<OL TYPE=A/a/I/i/1></OL>`	Creates an ordered list, specified by type (A for uppercase letters, a for lowercase letters, I for uppercase roman numerals, i for small roman numerals, and 1 for numbers—default)
`<LI></LI>`	Lists item (default bullet when used with `<UL>` and numbered list when used with `<OL>`)

9

continues

HTML Reference Chart (continued)

Lists	Description
`<LI TYPE=A/a/I/i/1></LI>`	Controls the format of a list item
`<UL></UL>`	Begins/ends an unordered list
`<UL COMPACT></UL>`	Creates a compact unordered list
`<UL TYPE=DISC/CIRCLE/SQUARE></UL>`	Specifies bullet style

Form Tags	Description
`<FORM ACTION="URL" METHOD=GET/POST></FORM>`	Begins/ends and defines the parameters of a form
`<INPUT TYPE="TEXT/PASSWORD/CHECKBOX/RADIO/SUBMIT/RESET/IMAGE">`	Specifies input field as text, password field, check box, radio button, submit button, reset button, or visual submit button
`<INPUT TYPE=HIDDEN>`	Specifies a hidden field
`<INPUT NAME="FIELDNAME">`	Names a form field
`<INPUT CHECKED>`	Specifies a selected check box or radio button
`<INPUT SIZE=X>`	Specifies field size in characters
`<OPTION>`	Creates menu options that can be selected on forms
`<OPTION SELECTED="SELECTED">`	Specifies a selected option from a menu form
`<OPTION VALUE="VALUE">`	Specifies the initial value of a menu option
`<SELECT></SELECT>`	Creates a menu in forms
`<SELECT NAME="NAME"></SELECT>`	Identifies the data collected by the menu

Form Tags	*Description*
`<SELECT MULTIPLE></SELECT>`	Specifies more than one option in the menu
`<SELECT SIZE="X"></SELECT>`	Specifies the number of items visible in the menu (X)
`<TEXTAREA ROWS=X COLS=Y></TEXTAREA>`	Creates an input box with the height dimension (X) in ROWS and the width dimension (Y) in COLS
`<TEXTAREA NAME="NAME"></TEXTAREA>`	Identifies the input box
`<TEXTAREA WRAP></TEXTAREA>`	Specifies automatic text wrap in TEXTAREA

Table Tags	*Description*
`<TABLE></TABLE>`	Begins/ends table
`<TABLE BORDER="X">`	Specifies whether table borders are on (X = 1) or off (X = 0)
`<TABLE CELLSPACING="X">`	Defines spacing between cells in pixels
`<TABLE CELLPADDING="X">`	Defines thickness of table cell borders in pixels
`<TABLE WIDTH="X">`	Specifies table width in pixels
`<TABLE WIDTH="%">`	Specifies table width in percentage (relative to the browser page width)
`<TR></TR>`	Defines table row
`<TR ALIGN=LEFT/CENTER/RIGHT" VALIGN="TOP/MIDDLE/BOTTOM">`	Specifies table row content horizontal and vertical alignment
`<TD></TD>`	Defines table data cell (appears within table rows)
`<TD ALIGN="LEFT/CENTER/RIGHT" VALIGN="TOP/MIDDLE/BOTTOM">`	Specifies table data cell content horizontal and vertical alignment
`<TD NOWRAP>`	Specifies no linebreaks within table data cell

continues

HTML Reference Chart   (continued)

Table Tags	Description
`<TD COLSPAN="X">`	Specifies number of columns (X) for a table data cell to span horizontally across
`<TD ROWSPAN="X">`	Specifies number of rows (X) for a table data cell to span vertically down
`<TD WIDTH="X">`	Specifies table data cell width in pixels
`<TD WIDTH="%">`	Specifies table data cell width in percentage (relative to the table size)
`<TH></TH>`	Defines table header
`<TH ALIGN="LEFT/CENTER/RIGHT" VALIGN="TOP/MIDDLE/BOTTOM">`	Specifies horizontal and vertical alignment within table header cell
`<TH NOWRAP>`	Specifies no linebreaks within table header cell
`<TH COLSPAN="X">`	Specifies number of columns (X) for a table header cell to span horizontally across
`<TH ROWSPAN="X">`	Specifies number of rows (X) for a table header cell to span vertically down
`<TH WIDTH="X">`	Specifies table header cell width in pixels
`<TH WIDTH="%">`	Specifies table header cell width in percentage (relative to the table size)
`<CAPTION ALIGN="TOP/BOTTOM"></CAPTION>`	Defines table caption

Frameset Tags	Description
`<FRAMESET></FRAMESET>`	Resides in the HTML page header and defines the frame elements
`<FRAMESET COLS="X,X">`	Defines frames in columns, defined by widths in pixels or percentages
`<FRAMESET ROWS="X,X">`	Defines frames in rows, defined by heights in pixels
`<FRAMESET BORDER="0/1/2/3/etc.">`	Specifies the thickness of frame borders: on (1, 2, 3, and so on) or off (0)
`<FRAMESET FRAMESPACING="1/0">`	Defines spacing between frames: on (1) or off (0)
`<FRAMESET FRAMEBORDER="1/0">`	Defines the visibility (1) or invisibility (0) of frame borders

Frame Tags	Description
`<FRAME SRC="URL">`	Specifies URL to be loaded into the frame
`<FRAME ALIGN="LEFT/CENTER/RIGHT">`	Defines alignment of items within the frame
`<FRAME FRAMEBORDER="1/0">`	Specifies whether to display (1) or hide (0) frame borders
`<FRAME BORDERCOLOR="#XXXXXX">`	Determines the border color (only if specified) for the frame
`<FRAME FRAMESPACING="0/1/2/3/etc.">`	Specifies space (if any) added between frames
`<FRAME NAME="NAME">`	Names the frame for future targeting
`<FRAME NORESIZE>`	Prevents viewers from resizing the frame
`<FRAME MARGINWIDTH="X"MARGINHEIGHT="X">`	Specifies the width and height of invisible margins within frames

13

continues

HTML Reference Chart   (continued)

Frame Tags	*Description*
`<FRAME SCROLLING="0/1/AUTO">`	Determines whether (1) or not (0) the frame will scroll—AUTO forces the browser to detect whether scrolling is necessary and add scrollbars accordingly

Multimedia Tags	*Description*
`<APPLET="URL" HEIGHT="X" WIDTH="X">` `<IMG SRC="ALTERNATE IMAGE.GIF" HEIGHT="X" WIDTH="X"></APPLET>`	Defines a Java applet and points to a URL, specifying width and height attributes. For Java disabled browsers, an alternate image is pointed to within the `<APPLET>` tags.
`<OBJECT CODETYPE="X" CLASSID= "URL" WIDTH="X" HEIGHT="X">` `<IMG SRC="ALTERNATE IMAGE.GIF" HEIGHT="X" WIDTH="X"> </OBJECT>`	HTML 4.0 standard for defining a multimedia object (sound, movie, and so on). As with the preceding description, an alternate GIF `<IMG>` tag may be used within `<OBJECT>` tags for browsers without specific plug-ins.
`<EMBED SRC="URL" WIDTH="X"HEIGHT="X">` `<NOEMBED>Your browser does not have the required plug-in!</NOEMBED></EMBED>`	Netscape 3.0+ friendly (but not HTML 4.0 standard) method for embedding sounds, movies, and plug-ins, including a `<NOEMBED>` alternative for those lacking the capability to display the sound, movie, or other plug-in.

A Word About JavaScript

Although this book concentrates on presenting some of the most effective HTML techniques for designing compelling Web sites, it's hard not to touch upon the awesome power of JavaScript.

Unlike Java, which is inaccessible to Web designers due to its complex programming and compiling requirements, JavaScript is fairly easy to copy/paste and resides within HTML. In fact, JavaScript can be thought of as an HTML booster, adding flexibility and enhancing the Web designer's ability to craft responsive pages and interfaces.

This is not a JavaScript book, but some of the techniques touch upon JavaScript code used to achieve specific ends.

With that in mind, you might want to check out these helpful online and hard-bound JavaScript resources:

- WebCoder.com (http://www.webcoder.com)
- BUILDER.COM Programming and Scripting (http://www.builder.com/Programming)
- WebReference.com (http://www.webreference.com/js/)
- Web Developer (http://www.webdeveloper.com/categories/javascript/)
- Webmonkey (http://www.hotwired.com/webmonkey/javascript/)
- *The Complete Idiot's Guide to JavaScript* (ISBN 0789711362)

As Web designers with easy access to the VIEW>SOURCE command, be sure to acknowledge the original programmers of the "borrowed" JavaScript code if they require it. (Generally there will be a © Copyright symbol and terms of use commented within the JavaScript. If no such requirements exist, the code is yours to modify and use.)

The JavaScript code I demonstrate in this book initially originated from the previous named resources (my favorite being WebCoder.com) and continually evolves, as does the technology.

For the most up-to-date JavaScript resources, be sure to visit this book's companion site at http://www.rpirouz.com/html. ●

15

PART II

Magic with First Impressions

No matter how many incredible HTML techniques your site employs, it will receive very little attention unless people know it exists.

The trick to making a positive first impression involves letting people know you're out there, getting them to your site, and making sure that their browsers can handle what you have prepared to dish out. By taking a proactive first step to *prepare* for your visitors, you're one step closer to a positive first impression.

Using the \<META> Tag to Get Listed

Use this technique to do the following:

- **Get listed with major search engines.** This is the first step in getting noticed by the Internet audience. You'd be surprised at the incredible number of people who actually *use* search engines to find information on the Web.

- **Provide a description of your site.** You need a solid description of your site—something that tells visitors why they should take the time to stop by.

- **Increase hits to your site.** The more people who know of your existence, the more likely you are to get visitors to your Web site.

Getting listed with the Internet's top seven search engines is not as difficult as you might think and can bring you plenty of unique visitors over time. All you need to do is equip your Web site's home page with the appropriate \<META> tag information, organize your list of search engines to register with, and wait for the masses to wipe their feet at your welcome mat.

\<META> keyword and description Attributes

Generally, \<META> tags reside between the \<HEAD>\</HEAD> tags and after the \<TITLE>\</TITLE> tags. The keyword attribute is used to list a number of key words separated by commas that are related to your Web site's content. The description attribute is used to list a one-sentence description of your Web site, explaining why someone would want to visit it.

There are two major types of search engines: spiders (sometimes referred to as robots, bots, and crawlers) and indexes (sometimes referred to as directories). The major difference between the two types of search engines is that indexes are manually updated, whereas spiders are more automated.

For example, the Yahoo! search engine located at http://www.yahoo.com is an index whose content is manually updated by REAL people. In order to get listed on the Yahoo! directory, you have to fill out Yahoo!'s online form and wait to get a response from a real person saying that your site has been added to its database. Often times, Yahoo! is very picky about the kind of sites it adds to its database, and often, it's backlogged due to numerous daily requests for listings. Spiders, however, add Web sites to their directories in the following manner: You go to a search engine such as HotBot (http://www.hotbot.com) or AltaVista (http://digital.altavista.com) and submit your URL by clicking on the site's "add URL" link. After this is done, the search engine sends out a spider to investigate the submitted URL. If the link is good, the spider collects any \<META> tag keywords and descriptions and adds the submission to the search engine's database.

When a user requests a topic search at a search engine, the search engine spider compares the search request with the millions of keywords it has on file and then brings up the most pertinent pages containing keywords similar to the submitted text. If the keywords you submit for your Web site happen to match the requested text, your page will show up as one of those matching pages. When your page shows up, its link will be followed by the one-sentence description you submitted along with your keywords. One drawback on search engines is that their databases are not *always* up to date. They generally rely on submitted URLs to keep their database fresh. If, for example, you change your URL from www.mysite.com to www.mysite2.com, you are responsible for resubmitting your new URL—the search engine spider will *not* automatically update your information as it changes.

Study the <META> Tag Anatomy

The following is the standard <META> tag keyword and description configuration within a standard HTML page:

```
<HTML>
<HEAD>
<TITLE>YOUR PAGE</TITLE>
<META NAME ="keywords" CONTENT="keyword 1, keyword2, keyword3, keyword 4,
keyword 5, keyword 6">
<META NAME="description" CONTENT="You can't afford to skip over this
page.">
</HEAD>
<BODY>
Your web site here.
</BODY>
</HTML>
```

You need to have this <META> tag information only in your Web site's home page (generally index.html). Search engines will look only at your home page. You might, however, include the tags within all the pages of your site. The only drawback is that if you want to change/modify/add a keyword or alter the description, you have to do it to ALL your files. Another way to submit your site to search engines is to create unique <META> tag information for each page within your site, focusing on the specific information covered therein. This way, you can submit multiple URLs of your Web site (one for each page for example, http://www.yoursite.com, http://www.yoursite.com/home1.html, http://www.yoursite.com/products.html, and so on.) to search engines as long as the information on each page is *truly* unique. (Otherwise you might get busted for spamming the index or "spamdexing.")

TIP Some search engines skip over <META> tags. **One way to make sure they pick up a sense of what your site is about is to duplicate your "keyword" and "description" text into a comment field below your <META> tags. This tip also applies to Web sites incorporating frames, as search engines often have a difficult time accessing data past the index.html pages containing framesets.**

19

Get Organized

It's a good idea for you to organize your plan of attack. This is more of a strategic technique than a graphic one, but trust me—you'll thank me for it when people you never knew start sending you email because they found your site through a search engine.

The seven big search engines you need to rush are as follows:

- Yahoo! (`http://www.yahoo.com`)
- Infoseek (`http://www.infoseek.com`)
- Lycos (`http://www.lycos.com`)
- HotBot (`http://www.hotbot.com`)
- WebCrawler (`http://www.webcrawler.com`)
- Excite (`http://www.excite.com`)
- AltaVista (`http://www.altavista.digital.com`)

Of these search engines, Yahoo! is the most time-consuming to submit to, as you must fill out a special form (which asks you to list keywords and provide a one-sentence decription of your site). The others simply ask you to submit your site's URL. They then automatically send a spider to fetch your <META> tag information and store it in their databases.

See a Listing in Action

When I designed the companion Web site for this book at `http://www.rpirouz.com/html`, I submitted the site to the Infoseek (`http://www.infoseek.com`) search engine. Here's a simplified version of the site's index.html file (with the original <META> tag information intact):

```
<HTML>
<HEAD>
<TITLE>HTML WEB MAGIC</TITLE>
<META NAME="keywords" CONTENT="HTML, HTML WEB MAGIC, HTML BOOK, RAY-
MOND PIROUZ, WEB DESIGN, WEB DEVELOPMENT, HTML TIPS, HTML TRICKS,
JAVASCRIPT ROLLOVERS, ROLLOVERS, TABLES, FRAMES, OPENING WINDOWS">
<META NAME="description" CONTENT="HTML Web Magic, by Raymond Pirouz
and published by New Riders, is filled with up-to-date HTML web
design tips and techniques.">
<!-- HTML Web Magic, by Raymond Pirouz and published by New Riders,
is filled with up-to-date HTML web design tips and techniques. HTML,
HTML WEB MAGIC, HTML BOOK, RAYMOND PIROUZ, WEB DESIGN, WEB DEVELOP-
MENT, HTML TIPS, HTML TRICKS, JAVASCRIPT ROLLOVERS, ROLLOVERS,
TABLES, FRAMES, OPENING WINDOWS -->
<SCRIPT LANGUAGE="JavaScript">
<!--//
//-->
```

```
</script>
</HEAD>
<BODY BGCOLOR="#ffffff" LINK="#CC0000" ALINK="#666666" VLINK="#999999"
TEXT="#000000">

<CENTER><H1>HTML Web Magic</H1></CENTER>

</BODY>
</HTML>
```

Notice that I included a commented copy of the <META> tag information just in case some spiders ignore the <META> data. After submitting the Web site to Infoseek, I was presented with the listing in the following figure.

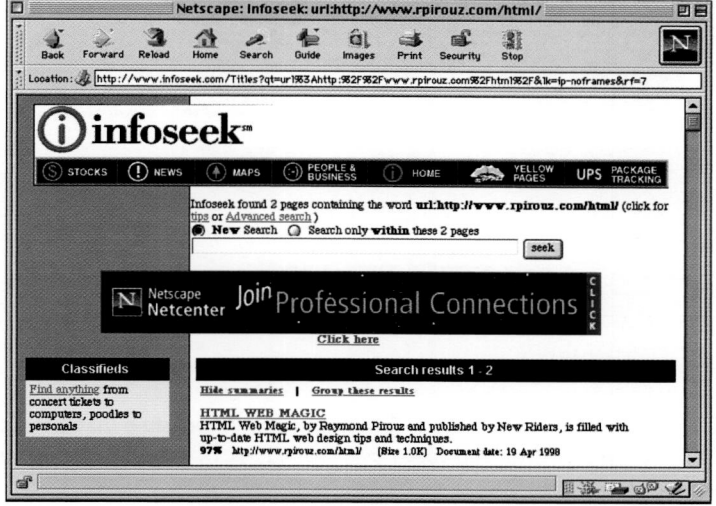

Infoseek result of the HTML WEB MAGIC Companion Site by URL.

Notice that the purple "HTML WEB MAGIC" link is taken directly from the submitted HTML page's <TITLE></TITLE> tag.

> **TIP** **Actually, it is quite essential for you to include a <TITLE> for your Web site, as it's a great opportunity to dish out important keywords. For example, a Web site selling carrots should most definitely have the word "carrot" within its <TITLE> somewhere. The title "Home-Grown Carrots for Sale" would be listed as a result by a search engine looking for the words home, home-grown, carrots and sale.**

Also, notice the one-sentence description, inviting users to visit the site "filled with up-to-date HTML Web design tips and techniques." Of course, you can write a one-paragraph description within the <META> description attribute, but as you can see in the previous figure, search engines will only list the first two lines, so you might as well keep your description sentence short and to the point.

Interestingly, upon searching for the keyword, "HTML WEB MAGIC," the following result was returned by the Infoseek search engine.

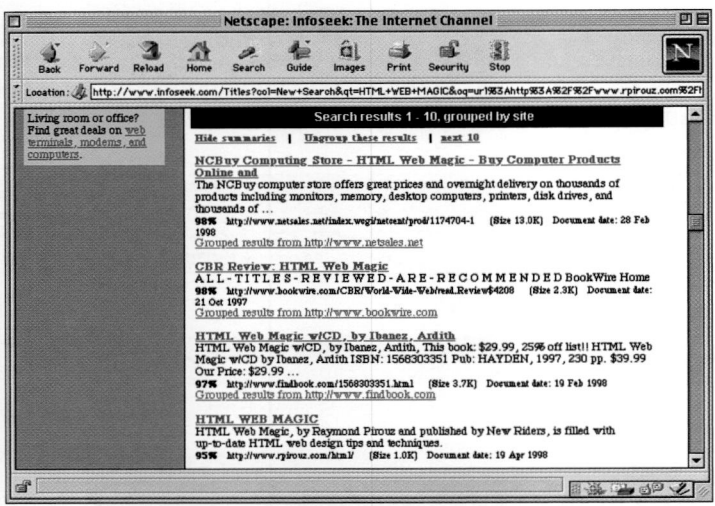

Infoseek result of the HTML WEB MAGIC Companion Site by name.

As you can see, the site was listed fourth out of 108 possible matches. To learn more about the powerful and often overlooked <META> tag, check out these online resources:

- WebDeveloper.com
  (http://www.webdeveloper.com/categories/html/html_metatags.html)

- <META> tag info page (http://www.stack.nl/~galactus/html/meta.html)

- <META> tag page (http://vancouver-webpages.com/META/)

- <META> tag generator (http://vancouver-webpages.com/VWbot/mk-metas.html) ●

Creating a Slide Show with META Refresh

Use this technique to:

- **Create rotating banner links.** Devote a single frame (within a framed site) to rotating graphics that engage the viewer.

- **Automatically cycle from page to page.** Let your viewers sit back and relax as a virtual art gallery of images is automatically presented to them.

- **Tell an animated story.** Reminiscent of traditional cel-based animation, you can create thematically linked Web pages and cycle through them to tell a story.

Creating a Loop

The slide show effect relies on using the META Refresh function to create a linked series of HTML pages that continuously loop from the first to last page and then back again to the first page.

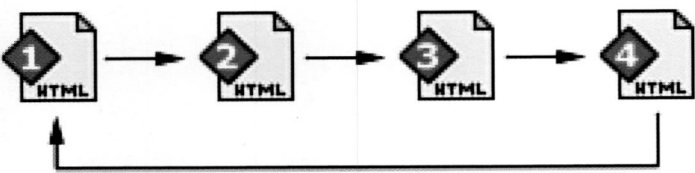

This figure illustrates a series of continually looping HTML pages powered by the META Refresh function.

To create a looping series of HTML pages, you need a minimum of two HTML pages (no maximum number). Say you have the following four HTML pages:

```
index1.html
index2.html
index3.html
index4.html
```

In each of these index.html files, you need to code the META Refresh function (remembering to keep the META tag within the <HEAD></HEAD> tags and after the <TITLE></TITLE> tags) as such:

```
<META HTTP-EQUIV="Refresh" CONTENT="numberofseconds;
URL=nexturl.html">
```

To create the loop, you must rename the nexturl.html text as such for each of the four files:

```
index1.html --> index2.html
index2.html --> index3.html
index3.html --> index4.html
index4.html --> index1.html
```

Notice that in the fourth HTML page (because it's the last in the series), the META Refresh function points back to index1.html to start the loop all over again.

See the Slide Show in Action

The following example demonstrates how R35 LLC employs the slide show technique to deliver rotating graphic banner ads in one of the three frames within its Web site:

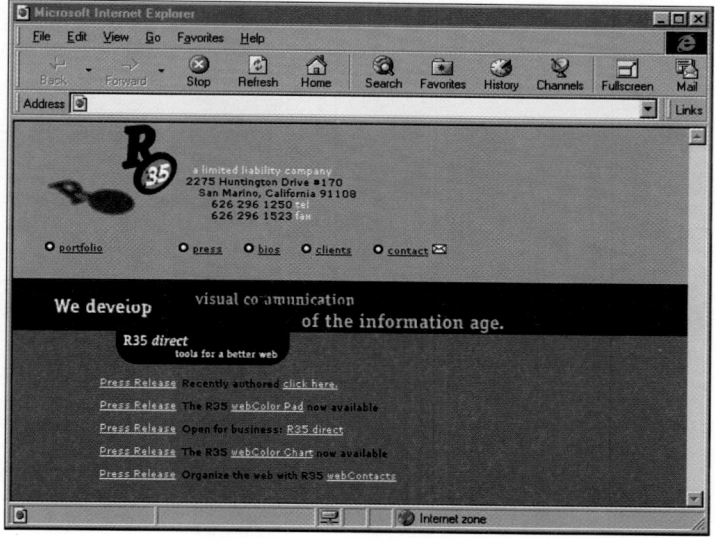

R35 LLC site with rotating middle graphic (filename=homead1.htm).

Here is the HTML for the rotating banner page shown here:

```
<HTML>
<HEAD>
<TITLE>R35</TITLE>
<META HTTP-EQUIV="refresh" CONTENT="15;URL=homead2.htm">
</HEAD>
<BODY MARGINWIDTH=0 MARGINHEIGHT=0 LEFTMARGIN=0 TOPMARGIN=0 BGCOL-
OR="#333300" LINK="#ffffff" VLINK="#ffffff" ALINK="#ffffff" TEXT="#000000">
<TABLE WIDTH=500 CELLPADDING=0 CELLSPACING=0 BORDER=0>
<TD WIDTH=500 ALIGN=CENTER>
<IMG WIDTH=428 HEIGHT=51 SRC="we.gif" ALT="We develop strategic visual com-
munication for consumers of the information age." BORDER=0>
```

25

```
</TD>
</TABLE>
</BODY>
</HTML>
```

As you can see in the this code, a META Refresh function is telling the page to wait 15 seconds before jumping to the next URL, in this case, homead2.htm.

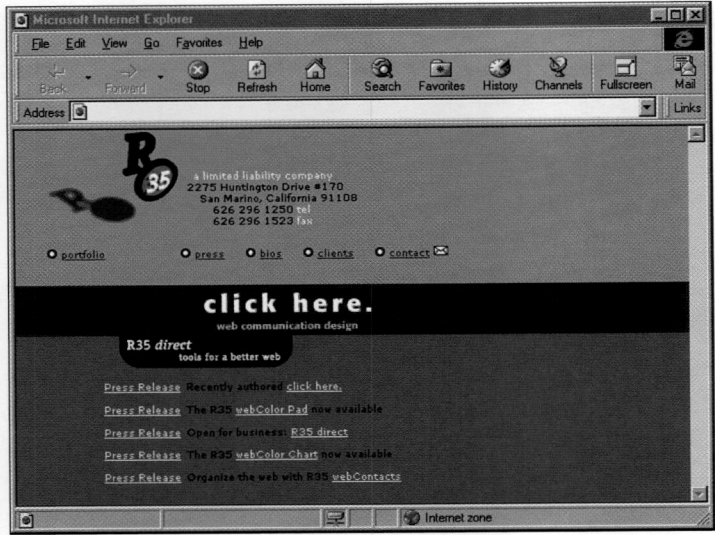

R35 LLC site with rotating middle graphic (filename=homead2.htm).

Here is the HTML for the rotating banner page shown here:

```
<HTML>
<HEAD>
<TITLE>R35</TITLE>
<META HTTP-EQUIV="refresh" CONTENT="15;URL=homead3.htm">
</HEAD>
<BODY MARGINWIDTH=0 MARGINHEIGHT=0 LEFTMARGIN=0 TOPMARGIN=0 BGCOL-
OR="#333300" LINK="#ffffff" VLINK="#ffffff" ALINK="#ffffff"
TEXT="#000000">
<TABLE WIDTH=500 CELLPADDING=0 CELLSPACING=0 BORDER=0>
<TD WIDTH=500 ALIGN=CENTER>
<A HREF="direct/index3.htm" onMouseOver="window.status='check it out
at R35 direct.'; return true;" target="_blank"><IMG WIDTH=225
HEIGHT=51 SRC="chere.gif" ALT="click here." BORDER=0></A>
</TD>
</TABLE>
</BODY>
</HTML>
```

This code is very similar to the HTML used for the first rotating banner page, with one exception—the graphic has changed to `chere.gif` and the META Refresh target destination after 15 seconds is now `homead3.htm`. As you can see, each page is brought up with a different graphic, which then leads the viewer to the next page in the series of ads. Notice also that each graphic is linked to a URL. If the user were to click on any one of these graphics, they would be taken to a product page (being advertised by these rotating banner pages).

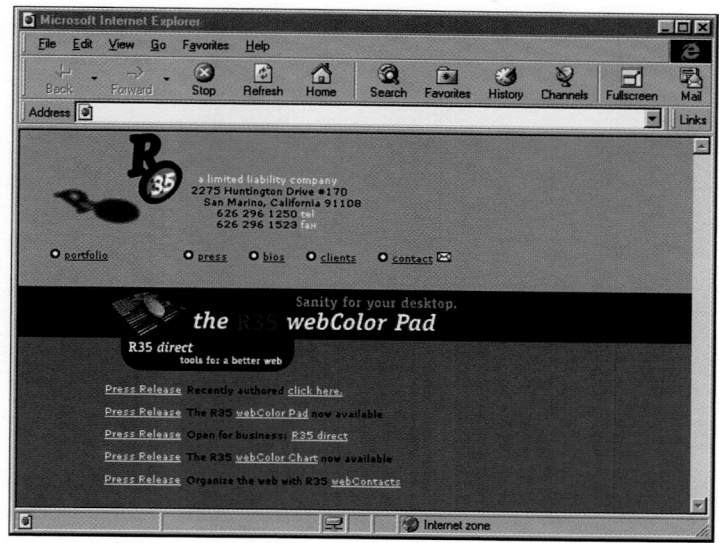

R35 LLC site with rotating middle graphic (filename=`homead3.htm`*).*

Here is the HTML for the rotating banner page shown here:

```
<HTML>
<HEAD>
<TITLE>R35</TITLE>
<META HTTP-EQUIV="refresh" CONTENT="15;URL=homead4.htm">
</HEAD>
<BODY MARGINWIDTH=0 MARGINHEIGHT=0 LEFTMARGIN=0 TOPMARGIN=0 BGCOL-
OR="#333300" LINK="#ffffff" VLINK="#ffffff" ALINK="#ffffff" TEXT="#000000">
<TABLE WIDTH=500 CELLPADDING=0 CELLSPACING=0 BORDER=0>
<TD WIDTH=500 ALIGN=CENTER>
<A HREF="direct/index.html" target="_blank"
onMouseOver="window.status='check out those ultimate digital design
tools.'; return true;"><IMG WIDTH=334 HEIGHT=51 SRC="webpadad.gif" ALT="The
R35 webColor Pad." BORDER=0></A>
</TD>
</TABLE>
</BODY>
</HTML>
```

As you can see here, the META Refresh function will send the viewer to
`homead4.htm`, which is the last ad in the series of rotating pages.

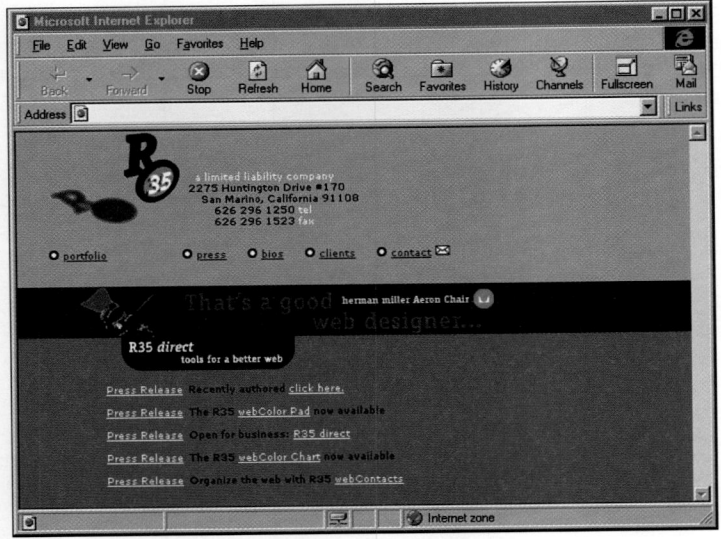

R35 LLC site with rotating middle graphic (filename=`homead4.htm`).

Here is the HTML for the final rotating banner page. Note how the META Refresh
function points back to the first file (`homead1.htm`) in the group. This creates the
"looping" effect, where the viewer is taken from page 1 to 2 to 3 to 4 and then
back to 1 again:

```
<HTML>
<HEAD>
<TITLE>R35</TITLE>
<META HTTP-EQUIV="refresh" CONTENT="15;URL=homead1.htm">
</HEAD>
<BODY MARGINWIDTH=0 MARGINHEIGHT=0 LEFTMARGIN=0 TOPMARGIN=0 BGCOL-
OR="#333300" LINK="#ffffff" VLINK="#ffffff" ALINK="#ffffff"
TEXT="#000000">
<TABLE WIDTH=500 CELLPADDING=0 CELLSPACING=0 BORDER=0>
<TD WIDTH=500 ALIGN=CENTER>
<A HREF="direct/index2.htm" target="_blank" onMouseOver="window.sta-
tus='check out those ultimate digital design tools.'; return
true;"><IMG WIDTH=400 HEIGHT=51 SRC="sit.gif" ALT="The Aeron Chair."
BORDER=0></A>
</TD>
</TABLE>
</BODY>
</HTML>
```

TIP When designing graphic ads with the slide show technique, make sure that your pages appear for at least 10 to 15 seconds if they contain words or animations or if you want them to stick around long enough to get clicked. However, be sure not to bore your audience—there's a fine line between pages that change too fast and ones that simply D-R-A-G on—it's up to you to experiment with the timing and determine what works best for your graphics and target audience.

Designing graphic ads can be an effective way to lead viewers deeper within your Web site. For a quick tour of other Web sites employing similar techniques, check out the following:

- HotWired (http://www.hotwired.com)
- Suck (http://www.suck.com)
- Macromedia (http://www.macromedia.com) ●

Designing a Splash Page with META Refresh

Use this technique to:

- **Create a front door to your site.** You can welcome visitors to your site with a simple graphic (representative of your site's content—either symbolic or literal) and automatically jump to your home page after a set period of time.

- **Provide users with a unique initial experience.** Most visitors are used to being overwhelmed with a lot of text and navigation buttons from which to choose when they enter a site. A splash page can be a breath of fresh air for many users.

- **Draw your audience in.** Splash pages can create a sense of excitement, mystery, and suspense, developing an interest and compelling a click.

Using the META Refresh Function

To achieve the splash page effect, use another attribute of the META tag: the Refresh function.

the-FunHouse.com splash page.

The preceding figure represents a fictional Web site on the Web called the-FunHouse.com. Take the following steps to create the splash page effect demonstrated here:

1 Create your splash page graphic.

the-FunHouse.com splash page.

Using your favorite image-editing program (I'm using Adobe Photoshop 5.0), create a splash page graphic that uses the Netscape 216 Web-safe colors so that you end up with an optimized, quick-loading file.

2 Observe the META Refresh anatomy.

Here's how to write the META Refresh function (remembering to keep the META tag within the <HEAD></HEAD> tags and after the <TITLE></TITLE> tags):

```
<META HTTP-EQUIV="Refresh" CONTENT="numberofseconds; URL=nexturl.html">
```

3 Code your splash page HTML file, integrating the META Refresh code within it:

```
<HTML>
<HEAD>
<TITLE>the-FunHouse.com</TITLE>
```

4 Insert your META Refresh function within your page's <HEAD></HEAD> tags and after the <TITLE> tag, setting the timer to 10 seconds before the page automatically changes location. Be sure to also set your target "jump-to" location (home2.html in this example):

```
<META HTTP-EQUIV="refresh" CONTENT="10;URL=home2.html">
</HEAD>
<BODY BGCOLOR="#FF6633">
<BR>
<BR>
<BR>
```

5 Center your page's content:

```
<CENTER>
```

6 Insert your splash page graphic. Always provide a link from the splash page graphic to the META Refresh jump-to location so that those who don't want to wait for the META Refresh can simply click to jump in right away (as demonstrated here):

31

```
<A HREF="home2.html"><IMG WIDTH=297 HEIGHT=56 SRC="funhouse.gif"
BORDER="0" alt="the-FunHouse.com"></A>
```

7 Finish centering your page's content and end the HTML:

```
</CENTER>
</BODY>
</HTML>
```

Note that the META Refresh is set to change pages 10 seconds after the page initially loads. At this Web site, if the user has not clicked on the splash page graphic within 10 seconds, he will automatically be taken to the `home2.html` link.

The bookdeal.com Web site is another example of an effective implementation of the splash page technique.

bookdeal.com splash page.

Visitors to this site see the preceding figure for 10 seconds, after which they are sent to bookdeal.com's home page.

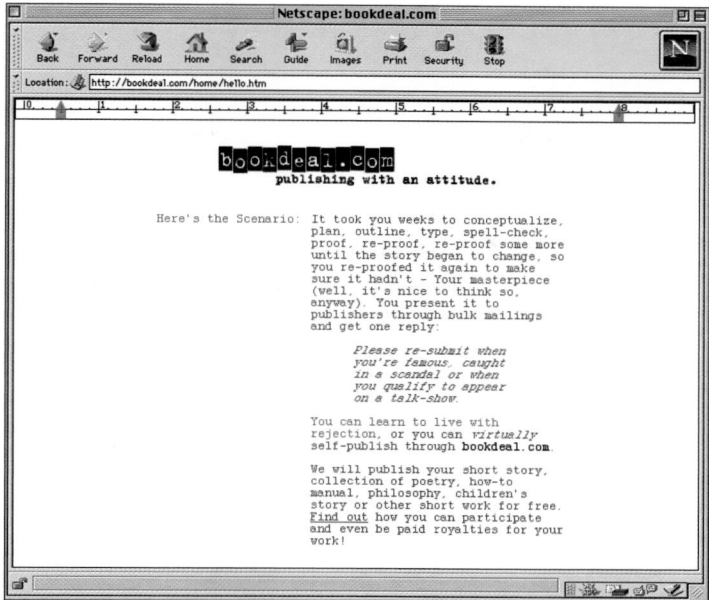

bookdeal.com home page.

 TIP It's a good idea to test your splash page to see if you allotted enough loading time before it jumps to the next location. Also, take care to note whether the average user has enough time to absorb the initial splash page graphic and take action on her own before being automatically sent elsewhere.

Designing a splash page can be an effective way to introduce a new visitor to your Web site. By providing a link from the splash page graphic to the jump-to page, you enable repeat visitors to quickly enter your Web site. If used creatively and in moderation, splash pages are fun to visit and visually engaging. Take a look at some other splash pages on the Net:

- WebCoder.com (http://www.webcoder.com)
- MetaDesign (http://www.metadesign.com)
- eye candy (http://www.eyecandy.org)
- Studio Archetype (http://www.studioarchetype.com) ●

Eliminate Browser Offset

Use this technique to:

- **Eliminate invisible borders.** Eliminating the invisible border evens the playing field and opens up a browser-consistent canvas upon which you can place images with precision.

- **Precisely align foreground images and text with backgrounds.** By eliminating browser offset, you can align text and images on top of a tiling background image, confident that its placement will remain consistent between browsers and platforms.

- **Attain absolute positioning without CSS.** The only way to attain absolute positioning is by using Cascading Style Sheets. However, not all browser versions are capable of displaying CSS pages, so eliminating the browser offset is still the best browser-safe alternative until CSS is more widely accepted.

The Invisible Border

Netscape and Internet Explorer create an invisible border that generally pushes images and text approximately 8 pixels down and 8 pixels across (these figures vary from browser to browser, with older browsers adding as much as 18 pixels down!) from the top-left corner of the page. If left uncorrected, this so-called "browser offset" can create a major inconsistency in the way images are presented and aligned with background images from one browser to the next.

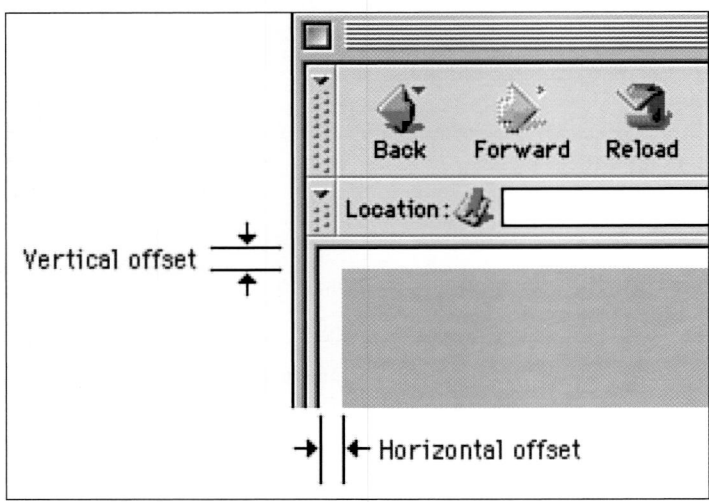

This illustration demonstrates a common browser offset value of 8 pixels down and 8 pixels in.

This illustration demonstrates an image placed upon a page with a green background, wherein the browser offset is creating a gap making the monkey's body look cut off instead of hanging down.

Specifying Invisible Margins

In 1997, Microsoft presented a way to eliminate the browser offset by offering the LEFT-MARGIN and TOPMARGIN properties, designed to allow Web developers to specify the exact invisible margin width and height within their BODY tags. (Setting the values to 0 eliminates the nuisance but only for Internet Explorer browsers.)

Unfortunately, Netscape did not follow suit until just recently with its 4.0 browser. Designers optimizing for Netscape 4.0 can use the MARGINWIDTH and MARGINHEIGHT properties (originally introduced for FRAMES) in their BODY tags to eliminate the browser offset (by setting their values to 0).

To eliminate browser offset in Microsoft IE 3.0+ and Netscape Navigator 4.0+, add the LEFTMARGIN, RIGHTMARGIN, MARGINHEIGHT, and MARGINWIDTH properties to your BODY tag:

```
<BODY LEFTMARGIN=0 RIGHTMARGIN=0 MARGINWIDTH=0 MARGINHEIGHT=0
BGCOLOR="#XXXXXX" LINK="#XXXXXX" TEXT="#XXXXXX">
```

35

With the browser offset eliminated, the monkey finally looks like he's hanging upside down instead of being cut off.

Tinkering with JavaScript

Because the MARGINWIDTH/MARGINHEIGHT/LEFTMARGIN/TOPMARGIN fix is good only for Netscape/IE 4.0 or better browsers, can you ensure some kind of consistency for viewers of older browsers? Yes—using JavaScript and a bunch of code. Be warned, however, that this technique takes lots of experimentation to master; you must have access to at least a Mac and a PC, with many of the older versions of both IE and Netscape for both platforms to make the technique work correctly.

Basically, the idea here is that because browser offset cannot be eliminated on all browser versions, you can test your page on all browsers and platforms to determine the number of pixels your images are off on each and every browser/platform combination. For example, you would test your page on:

- Mac   Netscape 2, 3, 4 and IE 2, 3, and 4
- PC Windows 95/98   Netscape 2, 3, 4 and IE 2, 3, and 4

If you wanted to be more thorough, you'd also test on:

- PC Windows NT   Netscape 2, 3, 4 and IE 2, 3, and 4
- UNIX   Netscape 2, 3, and 4

Some minor inconsistencies exist between the way browsers work on PC Windows 95 and PC Windows NT, so it's a good idea to test for both. As well, a small percentage of users are on UNIX machines, and it's a good idea to test for that platform as well (although not many designers have access to UNIX boxes).

As you can see, to do this right can be a daunting task, not to mention having to keep up with changes in the new browser versions. Nevertheless, some people do employ this technique (including myself), so here's how to do it:

1 Design your page as you normally would; this technique assumes that you are trying to line up foreground images with a background image.

2 Test your page on as many browsers and platforms as possible.

3 Measure the image placement inconsistencies (in pixels) based on each and every browser/platform configuration (in other words, PC Windows 95/Netscape 3.0 displays my graphic 10 pixels away from where I want it to line up with my background. Mac Netscape 3.0 displays my graphic 8 pixels away from where I want it to line up with my background).

4 Within your HTML, code the JavaScript to insert a spacer GIF (an invisible GIF used for white space) before your graphic to push it down X number of pixels so that it lines up with your background image.

5 Begin your JavaScript within your page's <HEAD></HEAD> tags. This code is excerpted from the Raymond Pirouz personal home page at http://www.rpirouz.com:

```
<SCRIPT LANGUAGE="JavaScript">
<!--//
```

6 Tell JavaScript that bName = browser's application name and bVer = browser's version number:

```
bName = navigator.appName;
bVer = parseInt(navigator.appVersion);
```

7 Using JavaScript's document.write function, which places HTML code within your page, tell JavaScript that if the browser is Netscape 4.0 for Macintosh, insert a 500-pixel wide, 17-pixel high spacer GIF (blank.gif) to help align the graphic with the background image. Your particular spacer GIF image size requirements will vary:

```
if (navigator.appVersion.charAt(navigator.appVersion.indexOf("(")+1) == "M"
&&
    bName == "Netscape" && bVer >= 4) { // Netscape 4 Mac
        document.write ("<IMG WIDTH=500 HEIGHT=17 SRC=blank.gif>")
        }
```

8 Tell JavaScript that if the browser is Netscape 3.0 for Macintosh, insert a 500-pixel wide, 17-pixel high spacer GIF (blank.gif) to help align the graphic with the background image. Your particular spacer GIF image size requirements will vary:

```
else if (navigator.appVersion.charAt(navigator.appVersion.indexOf("(")+1)
== "M" &&
    bName == "Netscape" && bVer == 3) { // Netscape 3 Mac
```

37

```
document.write ("<IMG WIDTH=500 HEIGHT=17 SRC=blank.gif>")
    }
```

9 Tell JavaScript that if the browser is IE 4.0 for Macintosh, insert a 500-pixel wide, 20-pixel high spacer GIF (`blank.gif`) to help align the graphic with the background image. Your particular spacer GIF image size requirements will vary:

```
else if (navigator.appVersion.charAt
(navigator.appVersion.indexOf("(")+1) == "M" &&
    bName == "Microsoft Internet Explorer" && bVer >= 4) {
// Explorer 4 Mac
        document.write ("<IMG WIDTH=500 HEIGHT=20
SRC=blank.gif><BR>")
    }
```

10 Tell JavaScript that if the browser is IE 3.0 for Macintosh, insert a 500-pixel wide, 20-pixel high spacer GIF (`blank.gif`) to help align the graphic with the background image. Your particular spacer GIF image size requirements will vary:

```
else if (navigator.appVersion.charAt
(navigator.appVersion.indexOf("(")+1) == "M" &&
    bName == "Microsoft Internet Explorer" && bVer == 3) {
// Explorer 3 Mac
        document.write ("<IMG WIDTH=500 HEIGHT=20
SRC=blank.gif><br>")
    }
```

11 Tell JavaScript that if the browser is Netscape 4.0 for PC, insert a 500-pixel wide, 20-pixel high spacer GIF (`blank.gif`) to help align the graphic with the background image. Your particular spacer GIF image size requirements will vary:

```
else if (navigator.appVersion.indexOf("Win") != -1 &&
    bName == "Netscape" && bVer >= 4) { // Netscape 4 PC
      document.write ("<IMG WIDTH=500 HEIGHT=20 SRC=blank.gif><br>")
    }
```

12 Tell JavaScript that if the browser is Netscape 3.0 for PC, insert a 500-pixel wide, 13-pixel high spacer GIF (`blank.gif`) to help align the graphic with the background image. Your particular spacer GIF image size requirements will vary:

```
else if (navigator.appVersion.indexOf("Win") != -1 &&
    bName == "Netscape" && bVer == 3) { // Netscape 3 PC
      document.write ("<IMG WIDTH=500 HEIGHT=13 SRC=blank.gif>")
    }
```

13 Tell JavaScript that if the browser is IE 4.0 for PC, insert a 500-pixel wide, 13-pixel high spacer GIF (`blank.gif`) to help align the graphic with the background image. Your particular spacer GIF image size requirements will vary:

```
else if (navigator.appVersion.indexOf("Win") != -1 &&
    bName == "Microsoft Internet Explorer" && bVer >= 4) {
// Internet Explorer 4 PC
        document.write ("<IMG WIDTH=500 HEIGHT=13 SRC=blank.gif><br>")
        }
```

14 Tell JavaScript that if the browser is anything older than IE 4 for PC, insert a 500-pixel wide, 12-pixel high spacer GIF (`blank.gif`) to help align the graphic with the background image. Your particular spacer GIF image size requirements will vary:

```
else if (navigator.appVersion.indexOf("Win") != -1 &&
    bName == "Microsoft Internet Explorer" && bVer < 4) {
// Internet Explorer 3 PC
        document.write ("<IMG WIDTH=500 HEIGHT=12 SRC=blank.gif><br>")
        }
```

15 End JavaScript:

```
//-->
</script>
```

The following figure displays how the Raymond Pirouz personal home page (http://www.rpirouz.com) appears on a Netscape 4.0 browser (Mac). Notice that "RP" logo graphic is lined up exactly on the line created by the white/black background image.

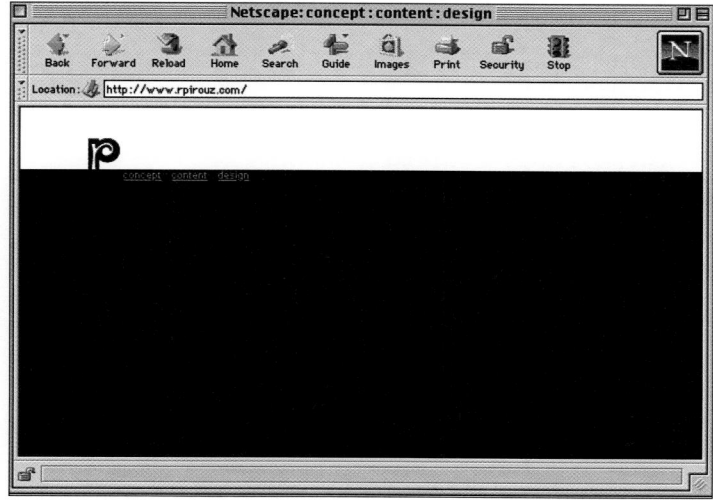

39

The Raymond Pirouz personal home page uses JavaScript to determine the user's browser type and place a transparent spacer GIF to help align foreground images to the background.

As you can see in the following figure, however, this technique is NOT foolproof. Each new browser version release requires that you tweak your code so that your image lines up correctly (as each browser will behave differently on each platform, and seldom are new browser versions exactly identical to their predecessors).

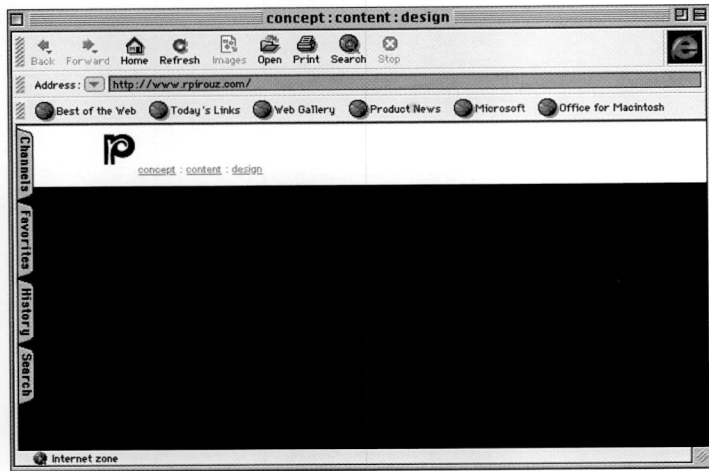

One obvious drawback to using this image: having to keep up with new browser releases with different configuration requirements.

The one major limitation to this technique is that you will always have to keep up with new browser releases and experiment with your JavaScript code to ensure that your images line up correctly on as many browsers/platforms as possible.

For another example of this technique, check out the Phillips Design Group Web site at http://www.pdgroup.com.

Browser Offset Resources

As you can see, "total" control is not yet possible, as Netscape Navigator 3.0, Microsoft Explorer 2.0, and older browsers do not recognize the browser offset elimination technique and JavaScript implementation is quirky at best. For more information on browser offset, check out the following sites:

- Creating Killer Web Sites Online (http://www.killersites.com/ 1-design/offsets.html)

- Yale Style Manual
  (http://www.med.yale.edu/caim/manual/pages/cross_platform.html) ●

Determining Your Visitor's Browser and Platform

Use this technique to do the following:

- **Provide a custom experience tailored to your user's browser.** By detecting which browser your visitor is using, you can customize the way your page displays based on certain features enabled by that particular browser.

- **Provide a custom experience tailored to your user's platform.** By detecting which platform your visitor is using, you can deliver content specifically tailored for that platform.

Although the latest browser versions (4.0 at the time of this writing) are a major improvement over their predecessors, many slight irregularities still remain, forcing us to take precautions when employing certain technologies.

Sending Browsers to Specific Pages

The Microsoft Web site (http://www.microsoft.com) employs JavaScript technology specific to its Internet Explorer line of browsers (specifically IE 4.0 and better). In order to ensure that browsers other than IE 4.0+ do not experience technical difficulties as a result of trying to understand proprietary JavaScript code, Microsoft Web developers have placed the following JavaScript within the <HEAD></HEAD> tags of the Microsoft home page:

```
<SCRIPT TYPE="text/javascript">
<!--
    if ((navigator.userAgent.indexOf("MSIE")!=-1) &&
navigator.appVersion.substring(0,1) > 3)    {
                    window.location.replace("/ie40.htm");
    }
//-->
</SCRIPT>
```

The preceding JavaScript tells the browser that if it is Internet Explorer version 4.0 or better, it should go to a page specifically designed for it at /ie40.htm. All other browsers, including all versions of Netscape and older versions of Internet Explorer (3.0 and below) will be presented as seen in the following figure.

As you can see in this figure, in the upper-right corner, a graphic says, "see what you're missing..." referring to the fact that you should download Internet Explorer 4.0. How does Microsoft know that you don't have IE 4.0? Because the preceding JavaScript "sniffed" you out as someone who did not come to the site with IE 4.0. In contrast, those with IE 4.0+ will see the second figure.

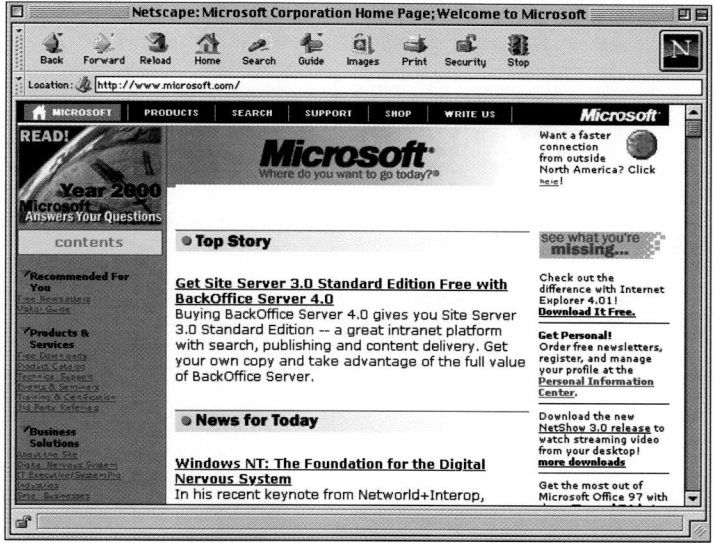

The Microsoft home page designed for older versions of Internet Explorer and all versions of Netscape Navigator, as well as other browsers.

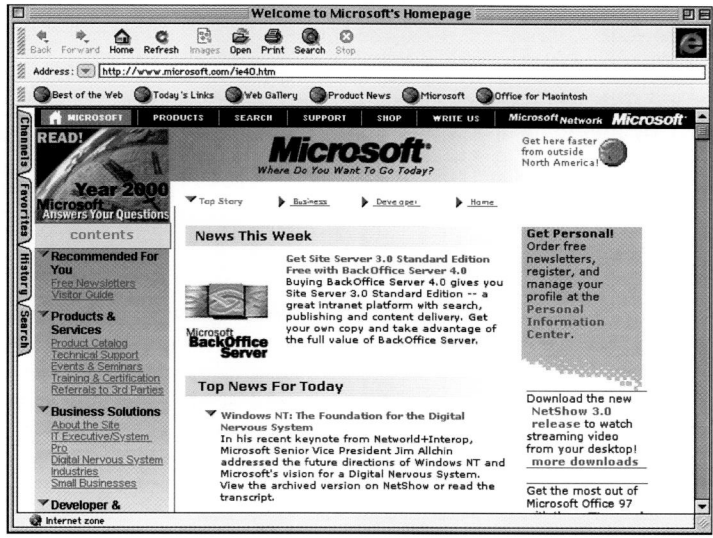

The Microsoft home page designed for users of the Internet Explorer 4.0+ browser series.

43

Notice that Microsoft's home page is noticeably different for users of older browsers as well as Netscape browsers than for users of IE 4.0+ browsers.

Just for fun, what if the user of an older browser or Netscape browser ventures into the /ie40.htm page designed specifically for the IE 4.0+ browser? The result is not pleasant and appears in the following figure.

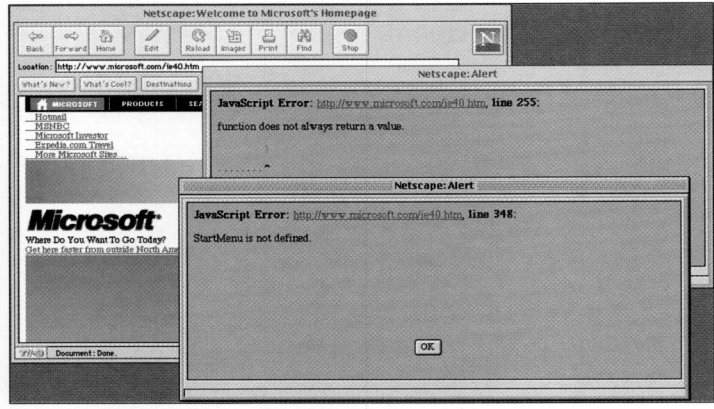

The Microsoft Internet Explorer 4.0+ specific home page as it would appear for anyone using a Netscape browser or an older version of IE (3.0 or older).

In this figure, notice that the IE 4.0 specific page is being accessed by a Netscape Navigator 3.0 GOLD browser. The numerous JavaScript errors signal that this site was NOT optimized for use with this browser version. Microsoft was wise in deploying the simple JavaScript technique previously presented in order to prevent such errors.

Discriminating Between Browsers

Sometimes it is necessary to discriminate between browsers. In other words, it is necessary to find out what browser is trying to access your site and serve information specific to the way that particular browser likes to see it. For example, when embedding a plug-in into your page (we will use Macromedia's Shockwave for this example), it's important to realize that Netscape and Explorer prefer different methods of working with these multimedia gems. Whereas Netscape prefers the <EMBED> tag, Microsoft Internet Explorer prefers the <OBJECT> tag with ActiveX control.

Take the following steps to ensure browser friendly embedding:

Determining Your Visitor's Browser and Platform

1 Begin the HTML as usual:

```
<HTML>
<HEAD>
<TITLE>SHOCKWAVE PAGE</TITLE>
</HEAD>
<BODY>
```

2 Get into JavaScript:

```
<SCRIPT LANGUAGE = "JavaScript">
<!--
```

3 Define your variables; in this case, you will determine what the browser's name is by defining the `browserName` variable and what the browser's version is by defining the `browserVersion` variable:

```
browserName = navigator.appName;
browserVersion = parseInt(navigator.appVersion);
```

4 Determine the browser by telling JavaScript that if the browser is Netscape and the version is greater than or equal to (>=) 3, your browser is called `"n3"`. Otherwise, if your browser is Microsoft Internet Explorer, your browser is called `"e3"`. Otherwise, the browser is called, `"n2"`:

```
if (browserName == "Netscape" && browserVersion >= 3) br = "n3";
else if (browserName == "Microsoft Internet Explorer") br = "e3";
else br = "n2";
```

5 Display the Shockwave file for Netscape 3+ by telling JavaScript that if the browser is called `"n3"`, do this:

```
if (br == "n3") {
document.write('<EMBED SRC="SHOCKWAVE.DCR" HEIGHT=320 WIDTH=240 PLUG-
INSPAGE=" http://www.macromedia.com/shockwave/">');
}
```

6 Display the Shockwave file for IE by telling JavaScript that if the browser is called `"e3"`, do this:

```
else if (br == "e3") {
document.write('<OBJECT CLASSID="clsid:166B1BCA-3F9C-11CF-8075-
444553540000"');
document.write('CODEBASE="http://active.macromedia.com/director/cabs/sw.cab
#version=5,0,1,61"');
document.write('WIDTH="240" HEIGHT="320" NAME="Shockwave" ID="movie">');
document.write('<PARAM NAME="SRC" VALUE="SHOCKWAVE.DCR">');
document.write('<PARAM NAME="BGCOLOR" VALUE="#000000">');
document.write('</OBJECT>');
}
```

7 Display the Shockwave file for Netscape 2 or other browsers by telling JavaScript that if the browser is called `"n2"`, do this:

```
else {
document.write('<EMBED SRC="SHOCKWAVE.DCR" HEIGHT=320 WIDTH=240 PLUG-
INSPAGE=" http://www.macromedia.com/shockwave/">');
}
```

8 End JavaScript:

```
// -->
</SCRIPT>
```

9 End your HTML:

```
</BODY>
</html>
```

10 Put it all together:

```
<HTML>
<HEAD>
<TITLE>SHOCKWAVE PAGE</TITLE>
</HEAD>
<BODY>
<SCRIPT LANGUAGE = "JavaScript">
<!--
browserName = navigator.appName;
browserVersion = parseInt(navigator.appVersion);
if (browserName == "Netscape" && browserVersion >= 3) br = "n3";
else if (browserName == "Microsoft Internet Explorer") br = "e3";
else br = "n2";
if (br == "n3") {
document.write('<EMBED SRC="SHOCKWAVE.DCR" HEIGHT=320 WIDTH=240 PLUG-
INSPAGE=" http://www.macromedia.com/shockwave/">');
}
else if (br == "e3") {
document.write('<OBJECT CLASSID="clsid:166B1BCA-3F9C-11CF-8075-
444553540000"');
document.write('CODEBASE="http://active.macromedia.com/director/cabs/s
w.cab#version=5,0,1,61"');
document.write('WIDTH="240" HEIGHT="320" NAME="Shockwave"
ID="movie">');
document.write('<PARAM NAME="SRC" VALUE="SHOCKWAVE.DCR">');
document.write('<PARAM NAME="BGCOLOR" VALUE="#000000">');
document.write('</OBJECT>');
}
else {
document.write('<EMBED SRC="SHOCKWAVE.DCR" HEIGHT=320 WIDTH=240 PLUG-
INSPAGE=" http://www.macromedia.com/shockwave/">');
```

46

```
}
// -->
</SCRIPT>
</BODY>
</HTML>
```

Determining the Platform

Using JavaScript, you can determine your user's platform and provide custom-tailored content. The following example determines a user's platform (either MAC 68k, MAC PPC, or WINDOWS 95) and provides the user with an appropriate link to download custom software.

1 Begin the HTML as usual:

```
<HTML>
<HEAD>
<TITLE>SOFTWARE FOR YOUR MAC or WIN'95</TITLE>
</HEAD>
<BODY>
```

2 Get into JavaScript:

```
<SCRIPT LANGUAGE = "JavaScript">
<!--
```

3 Determine the platform by telling JavaScript to look at the computer platform that is visiting the browser. There might be hundreds of different platforms to "sniff" out, but we're only looking for the most common ones (Windows 95, Macintosh PowerPC, and 68k Macintosh):

```
function platformWin95() {
    if (navigator.appVersion.indexOf("95") != -1) return true;
    else return false;
}
function platformPPC() {
    if (navigator.appVersion.indexOf("PPC") != -1) return true;
    else return false;
}
function platform68K() {
    if (navigator.appVersion.indexOf("68k") != -1) return true;
    else return false;
}
```

47

4 Serve the goods by telling JavaScript to write a specific piece of HTML code based on what platform is visiting the site:

```
if (platformWin95()) {
document.write('<A HREF ="WIN95.EXE">Download</A> our Windows 95 ver-
sion.');
```

```
}
else if(platformPPC()) {
document.write('<A HREF = "MAC.SIT">Download</A> our Macintosh Power
PC version.');
}
else if(platformPPC()) {
document.write('<A HREF = "MAC.SIT">Download</A> our 68040 Macintosh
version.');
}
```

5 End JavaScript:

```
// -->
</SCRIPT>
```

6 End your HTML:

```
</BODY>
</HTML>
```

7 Put it all together:

```
<HTML>
<HEAD>
<TITLE>SOFTWARE FOR YOUR MAC or WIN'95</TITLE>
</HEAD>
<BODY>
<SCRIPT LANGUAGE = "JavaScript">
<!--
function platformWin95() {
    if (navigator.appVersion.indexOf("95") != -1) return true;
    else return false;
}
function platformPPC() {
    if (navigator.appVersion.indexOf("PPC") != -1) return true;
    else return false;
}
function platform68K() {
    if (navigator.appVersion.indexOf("68k") != -1) return true;
    else return false;
}
if (platformWin95()) {
document.write('<A HREF ="WIN95.EXE">Download</A> our Windows 95 ver-
sion.');
}
else if(platformPPC()) {
document.write('<A HREF = "MAC.SIT">Download</A> our Macintosh Power
PC version.');
```

```
}
else if(platformPPC()) {
document.write('<A HREF = "MAC.SIT">Download</A> our 68040 Macintosh ver-
sion.');
}
// -->
</SCRIPT>
</BODY>
</HTML>
```

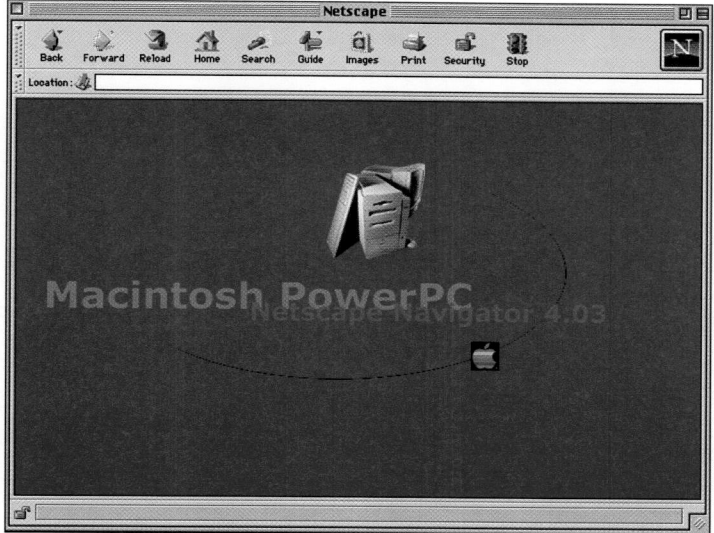

One example of taking browser/platform detection to the next level is illustrated here—an online store that detects browser/platform, creates a personal home page for each customer graphically displaying their current specs, and provides custom-tailored product reviews and special offers. ●

Detecting Specific Plug-ins

Use this technique to:

- **Avoid error messages.** Image is everything. Detecting possible conflicts and handling them will make you look like a pro.

- **Make sure your visitor is properly equipped.** If you are using advanced technology in your Web site that requires a plug-in (Shockwave/Flash) and can detect if your visitors are ill-equipped, you can take them to a warning page you design that enables them to download the software before entering your site.

It's much nicer to get a customized warning from a Web site than it is to get an ERROR MESSAGE or a broken link icon from the browser. This technique shows you how to create a message that tells users who don't have the proper technology exactly what they are missing, decreasing their frustration.

Writing the Code

The following technique determines if the viewer has the Shockwave plug-in. If the plug-in is not present, the script jumps to a "nonshocked" page where you can tell your visitor to get the plug-in, as illustrated in the following figure.

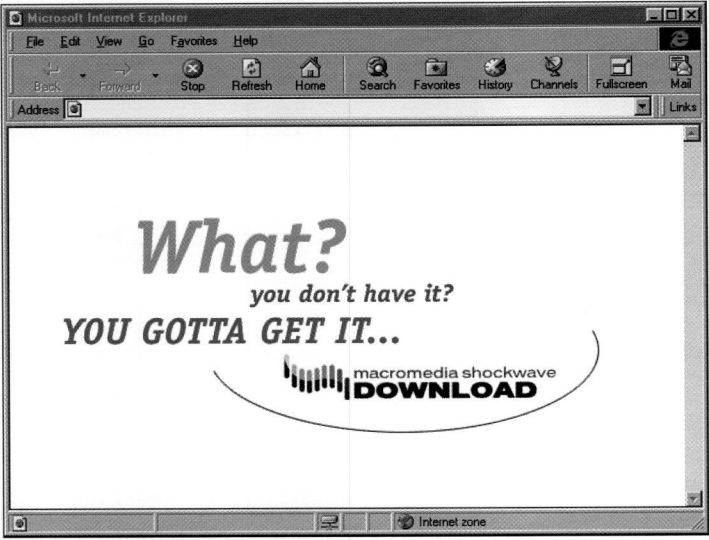

A "nonshocked" page, telling visitors to get the plug-in.

1 Begin the HTML as you normally would:

```
<HTML>
<HEAD>
<TITLE>LOOKING FOR SHOCKWAVE</TITLE>
```

2 Get into JavaScript:

```
<SCRIPT LANGUAGE="JavaScript">
<!--
```

3 Define your plug-in detection function (in this case, detectPlugin) by telling JavaScript that when looking for the "Shockwave for Director" plug-in to send those users without it to "nonshocked.html":

```
function detectPlugin(pluginName)
{
if (navigator.plugins[pluginName]) return true;
else return false;
}
if (!detectPlugin("Shockwave for Director"))
{
location.replace("nonshocked.html")
}
```

4 End the JavaScript and HTML:

```
// -->
</SCRIPT>
</HEAD>
<BODY>
SHOCKWAVE FILE GOES HERE
</BODY>
</HTML>
```

5 Put it all together:

```
<HTML>
<HEAD>
<TITLE>LOOKING FOR SHOCKWAVE</TITLE>
<SCRIPT LANGUAGE="JavaScript">
<!--
function detectPlugin(pluginName)
{
if (navigator.plugins[pluginName]) return true;
else return false;
}
if (!detectPlugin("Shockwave for Director"))
{
```

51

```
location.replace("nonshocked.html")
}
// -->
</SCRIPT>
</HEAD>
<BODY>
SHOCKWAVE FILE GOES HERE
</BODY>
</HTML>
```

For more information on working with Macromedia Shockwave files and plug-in detection techniques as the technology evolves, check out the Macromedia Shockwave Web site at http://www.macromedia.com/shockwave. ●

Design an Alternate Page for Older Browsers

Use this technique to:

- **Send non-JavaScript-capable browsers to a warning page.** If your Web site relies heavily on JavaScript, it's a good idea to let those with older browsers know it.

- **Give your viewer a chance to upgrade.** Just because some visitors might not have the newest browsers or the coolest plug-ins doesn't mean they shouldn't be allowed the opportunity to get them. You can design a page that is functional while reinforcing a positive first impression on your audience.

By using JavaScript, you can detect your visitor's browser version and platform, as well as find out if they have certain plug-ins your Web site requires.

Using the <NOSCRIPT> Tag

What if your visitor is using a browser that's so old it doesn't recognize JavaScript? The <NOSCRIPT> tag enables you to weed out the browsers that don't recognize the <SCRIPT> tag (which is used to initialize JavaScript) by giving them a special message or sending them to another page.

Here's how you can incorporate the <NOSCRIPT> tag into your home page to send those with older browsers to an alternate page by using META REFRESH:

1 Begin your HTML as you normally would:

```
<HTML>
<HEAD>
<TITLE>Your Home Page</TITLE>
```

2 Add your JavaScript code within your <HEAD></HEAD> tags:

```
<SCRIPT LANGUAGE="JavaScript">
<!--//

Your JavaScript Code Here

//-->
</SCRIPT>
```

3 Insert your <NOSCRIPT> tag:

```
<NOSCRIPT>
```

4 Tell your page what to do with users of non–JavaScript-ready browsers:

```
<META HTTP-EQUIV=REFRESH CONTENT="5;URL=ALTPAGE.HTML">
```

5 End your `<NOSCRIPT>` tag:

```
</NOSCRIPT>
```

6 End your `<HEAD>` tag:

```
</HEAD>
```

7 Continue coding your home page as you normally would.

At this point, if users surfing with non–JavaScript-compliant browsers arrive at your home page, they are directed to an alternate page (named ALTPAGE.HTML in step 4—you can name it anything you want).

The following figure is a simple example of an alternate page displayed to those using older browsers. With the 5.0 browser versions being released by the end of 1998, there's no excuse for people not to upgrade—no excuse at all seeing how browsers are distributed for FREE.

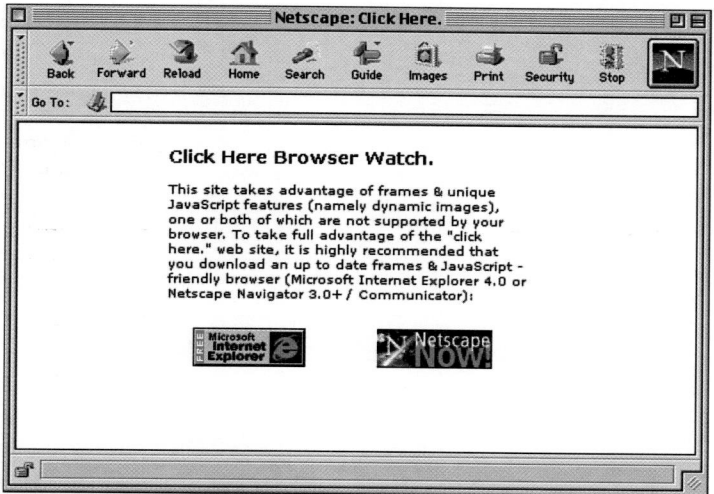

The "Click Here Browser Watch." page (`http://www.rpirouz.com/click`) recommends that viewers with older browsers upgrade for optimal performance.

Design Tips

When designing your alternate page, keep the following design tips in mind:

- Keep it simple and light on the graphics. If people with older browsers or non-graphic browsers are being sent there, it doesn't make sense to give it your all from a whiz-bang standpoint.

- If you'd like to provide graphics to enhance the page visually, try creating your own custom icons for the links to browser upgrades and the plug-ins your site requires.

- Tell the viewers why they have been sent to this page. Tell them what functionality their browser might be lacking, if their platform is not compatible with your site, or whatever the case might be. The more information you provide, the better.

For a very nice example of a browser detect/alternate page, visit IDEO at `http://www.ideo.com.` ●

Make Descriptive Links

Use this technique to do the following:

- **Provide your visitors with detailed information.** You can give your visitors more information about a link so that they have a better idea of what they'll get when they click.

- **Conserve precious screen real estate.** Keep the screen uncluttered, while providing direct textual feedback based on user request.

- **Enhance your navigation with creative copywriting.** You can make your links much more enticing by using creative "call to action" status bar messages.

The next best thing to JavaScript rollovers, descriptive links use the browser's status bar message area (lower region of the browser) to perform their function.

Integrating Descriptive Links

Descriptive links are extremely simple to integrate into your HTML. Simply add the following code to your <A HREF> tag:

```
onMouseOver="window.status='Your Message Here'; return true"
```

Adding this JavaScript onMouseOver event handler to your <A HREF> tag and specifying the window.status property forces a message to appear in the status bar located at the bottom of Web browsers. The phrase return true forces the message to appear within the status bar as long as the user's cursor is rolled over the link containing the onMouseOver event handler.

Here's how it looks within a sample tag:

```
<A HREF="test.html" onMouseOver="window.status='Your Message Here';
return true">CLICK ME</A>
```

Enhancing Your Site's Interactivity

As simple as links are to implement, they can enhance the overall interactivity of your Web site considerably. Take a look at an example of how the http://www.rpirouz.com Web site employs the technique.

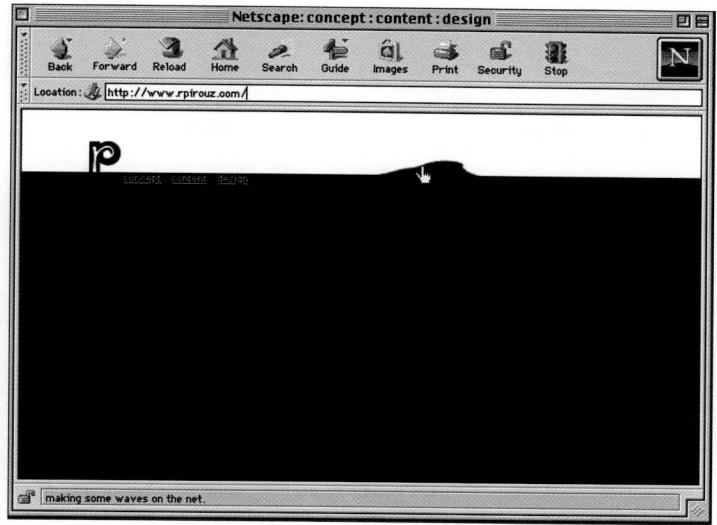

Using descriptive links.

The following code was used to create this effect:

```
<A HREF="waves.htm" onMouseOver="window.status='making some waves on the
net.'; return true"><IMG SRC="waves.gif" BORDER=0></A>
```

Notice that you can apply the `window.status` effect to images as well as HTML links. In fact, the GIF image in this figure is an animated GIF. You can create visually interesting animations that, when rolled over, offer a text description through the browser's status window at the bottom. Make sure to specify `BORDER=0` within your `<A HREF>` tag to eliminate any unnecessary borders around your image. In addition, don't forget to include the semicolon (;) between your status bar message and the `return true` statement within your JavaScript code, as it is required.

Now take a look at another example using this technique from the same site.

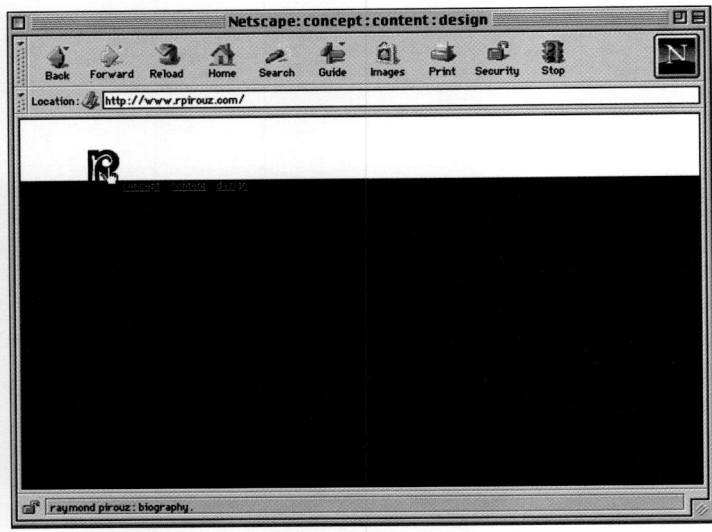

Descriptive links add interactivity.

The following code was used to create this effect:

```
<A HREF="contact.htm" onMouseOver="window.status='raymond pirouz:
biography.'; return true"><IMG SRC="mainlogo.gif" BORDER=0></A>
```

The status bar message not only enhances navigation but also enables you to experiment with more visual and iconic means of navigation, using the status bar message to reinforce your links.

Both of the preceding examples demonstrate how a sparsely layed out Web site can be enhanced with the subtle, yet added, interactivity of the descriptive link without cluttering the actual Web page with unnecessary descriptive text. Even pictographic and iconographic Web sites can benefit from the descriptive link while maintaining a clean, uncluttered image.

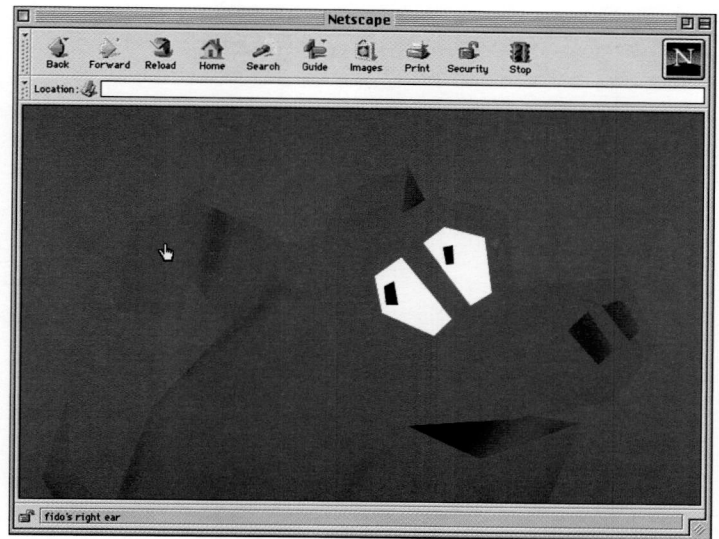

Fido's right ear as a descriptive link. ●

PART III

Magic with Images

The art of Web design involves combining code, text, and images to creatively communicate a message. Although images are a very important component of Web design, they can also be extremely demanding on the Net's infrastructure, often choking it down to a slow crawl.

Fortunately, when created, optimized, and utilized in moderation, images can add balance, motion, and interaction to a page without significantly hindering load time.

Create Colorful GIF Rules and Frames

Use this technique to:

- **Create visual boundaries between content.** Incorporating attractive visual dividers enhances your content while keeping your viewers focused on one section of content at a time.

- **Specify distinctive sections within your page.** Using colorful graphic rules and shapes over the standard HTML <HR> tag enhances your page and gives it a customized, distinctive look.

- **Think small, live large.** Small graphics take much less time to load and display than larger ones. Take small GIF files and create large graphic rules and shapes by using the image HEIGHT and WIDTH attributes.

Creating GIF Rules

If you think that the <HR> tag is too limiting, join the club. You can take an optimized GIF and stretch it, join it up with a rounded-corner GIF, and create the appearance of a 10K graphic with two 2K images. Amazing? Sure. Before going into what can be done visually, take a close look at the HTML you'll need to create GIF rules and shapes:

```
<IMG SRC="IMAGE.GIF" WIDTH="X" HEIGHT="X" BORDER="0">
```

The <IMG> tag calls and controls images and is the only piece of HTML code you need when laying out colorful GIFs. The WIDTH and HEIGHT attributes are generally used to tell HTML the true width and height of an image (the original size it was designed at in pixels), but you can also exaggerate these values to force HTML to scale your images. You would use the BORDER attribute only if the GIF is going to be a link and you'd rather not have a border around your image.

Now that you have the HTML code, you'll need an image editing tool such as Adobe Photoshop (http://www.adobe.com/prodindex/photoshop) to create custom GIFs that you'll be stretching and converting into rules, borders, and graphic frames.

 When designing your GIFs in an image editing program, be sure to use the 216 Web-safe colors so that your optimized images don't dither in Web browsers. You can download a browser-safe CLUT (Color Look Up Table) from Lynda Weinman's Web site (http://www.lynda.com/files/CLUTS).

I Design a 5 × 5 pixel, solid colored image within your image editor. Try to duplicate what you see in the following figure by first calling your image and specifying its WIDTH and HEIGHT attributes as five pixels in order to see what your original image will look like when compared to the one you will be stretching:

```
<IMG SRC="SOLID.GIF" WIDTH=5 HEIGHT=5>
```

A solid, 5 × 5 pixel GIF (enlarged on left). Next to it, the same GIF is stretched out to 300 pixels.

2 Add some breaks (<BR>) in between your code to start the next image a bit farther down the page:

```
<BR>
<BR>
```

3 Call your original 5 × 5 pixel image again, but this time specify a WIDTH of 300 and keep your HEIGHT at five pixels:

```
<IMG SRC="SOLID.GIF" WIDTH=300 HEIGHT=5>
```

Basically, the preceding code displays your little 5 × 5 pixel GIF, below which it stretches the same image out to 300 pixels. Can you see how using a small GIF can easily replace the predictable <HR> tag? What about variations on this idea? Take a look at the following figure:

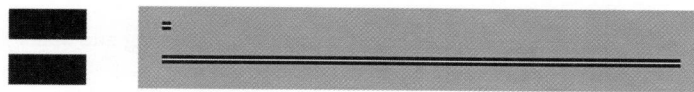

A 5 × 5 pixel GIF with a white line through it (enlarged on the left). Next to it, the same GIF is stretched out to 300 pixels.

You can decorate your GIFs as you see fit, using colors that match your site's color scheme; you are no longer limited to the default gray available through the <HR> tag. You can also stretch your GIFs vertically by modifying the image HEIGHT attribute, displayed as follows:

A 5 × 5 pixel GIF with a white line through it (enlarged on the left). Across from it, the same GIF is stretched vertically down to 300 pixels.

You can duplicate what you see in the preceding figure by following these steps:

1 Design a 5 × 5 pixel GIF image with a colored (or white) line running through its center.

2 Call your image within HTML by using the `<IMG>` tag and specify its `WIDTH` and `HEIGHT` parameters as its default size (5 × 5):

```
<IMG SRC="SOLID3.GIF" WIDTH=5 HEIGHT=5>
```

3 Add two non-breaking spaces (` `) so that HTML renders two spaces after your first image:

```
 
 
```

4 Call your original 5 × 5 pixel image again, but this time specify a `HEIGHT` of 300 and keep your `WIDTH` at five pixels:

```
<IMG SRC="SOLID3.GIF" WIDTH=5 HEIGHT=300>
```

Putting It Together in the Browser

You can create a unique set of horizontal and vertical rules very much like what you see in the following figure by following these steps:

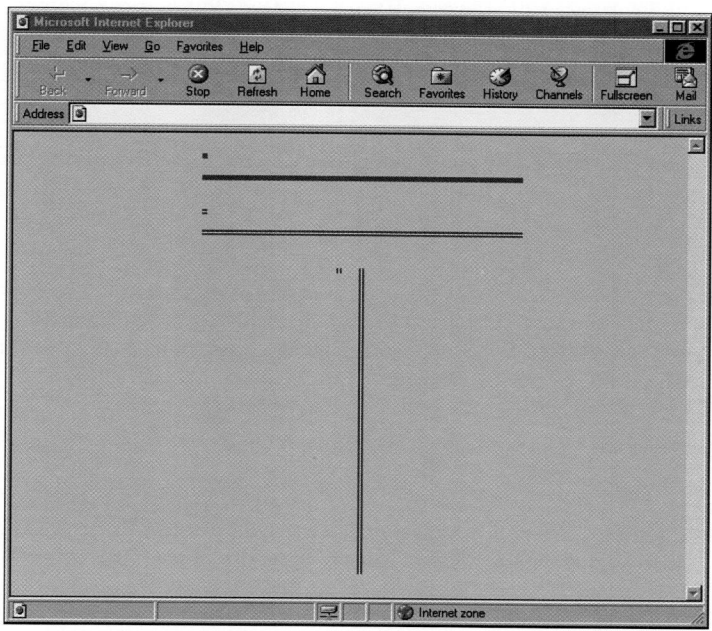

5 × 5 pixel GIFs and their accompanying stretched rule versions.

1 Begin your HTML as you normally would:

```
<HTML>
<HEAD>
<TITLE>Convert Small GIFs to Rules</TITLE>
```

2 Establish a background color:

```
<BODY BGCOLOR="#999966">
```

3 Center your page's contents by placing the `<CENTER>` tag before any other content:

```
<CENTER>
```

4 Establish a 300-pixel-wide table with a `CELLPADDING` of five pixels (`CELLPADDING` measures the distance between the cell border and its contents):

```
<TABLE WIDTH=300 BORDER=0 CELLPADDING=5 CELLSPACING=0>
```

5 Begin your table row:

```
<TR>
```

6 Within a table data cell that is 300 pixels wide, place your solid image GIF, under which you create a stretched version of the 5 × 5 pixel original by changing its WIDTH attribute:

```
<TD WIDTH=300 ALIGN=LEFT><IMG SRC="SOLID.GIF" WIDTH=5
HEIGHT=5><BR><BR><IMG SRC="SOLID.GIF" WIDTH=300 HEIGHT=5></TD>
```

7 End your table row and begin a new one to house the rest of your graphics and rules:

```
</TR>
<TR>
```

8 Repeat the same effect as above, but this time change the color or design of your original 5 × 5 pixel image to see how the change in design shows up on the stretched graphic:

```
<TD WIDTH=300 ALIGN=LEFT><IMG SRC="SOLID2.GIF" WIDTH=5
HEIGHT=5><BR><BR><IMG SRC="SOLID2.GIF" WIDTH=300 HEIGHT=5></TD>
</TR>
```

9 Introduce a new 5 × 5 pixel image that you place at its original size and then stretch it 300 pixels vertically using the HEIGHT attribute:

```
<TD WIDTH=300 ALIGN=CENTER><IMG SRC="SOLID3.GIF" WIDTH=5
HEIGHT=5>  <IMG SRC="SOLID3.GIF" WIDTH=5 HEIGHT=300></TD>
```

10 End your table row, <TABLE> tag, <CENTER> tag, </BODY>, and </HTML> tags to define the end of the page:

```
</TR>
</TABLE>
</CENTER>
</BODY>
</HTML>
```

Designing a Frame

Frames using optimized GIF images can be easily created by using simple HTML.

1 To begin, you must design your frame parts within an image editing application, such as Adobe Photoshop.

All four custom-designed GIF pieces that make up the frame.

2 After you have your graphics ready and saved as individual GIF files, position them so that they fit together by using a table, as demonstrated in the following browser window:

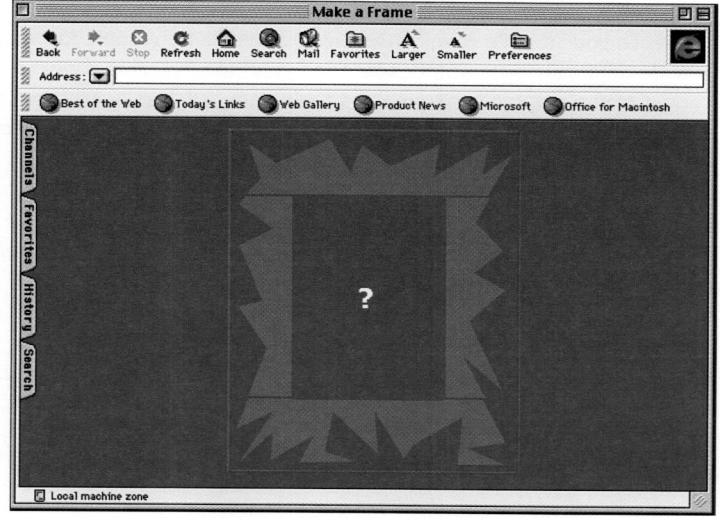

Putting the pieces together and deciding upon some text for the center.

69

Notice that in the preceding figure, the table border is set to 2, so you can see how you'll have to put the images together. Notice also that the table is a three-column layout, with the top and bottom rows spanning all three columns. With this kind of layout, you can use the center empty cell to place HTML type or another image. Our example uses HTML type and is finalized in the code that follows.

3 Begin your HTML as you normally would:

```
<HTML>
<HEAD>
<TITLE>Make a Frame</TITLE>
<BODY BGCOLOR="#3300CC" TEXT="#ffffff">
```

4 Center your page's contents:

```
<CENTER>
```

5 Establish a 250-pixel-wide table, calling for no border width, no CELLPADDING, or CELLSPACING so there is no space between the table's data:

```
<TABLE WIDTH=250 BORDER=0 CELLPADDING=0 CELLSPACING=0>
<TR>
```

6 Create your top table row, spanning three columns (COLSPAN=3). This is where the top of the frame will go as the top.gif image:

```
<TD WIDTH=250 COLSPAN=3><IMG SRC="top.gif" WIDTH=250 HEIGHT=55></TD>
</TR>
<TR>
```

7 Create your middle row, consisting of a left frame graphic for your first table data cell, some empty space for your second table data cell, and the right frame graphic for your third table data cell. This is why we set the above table data cell to span three columns—so that it fits perfectly atop these three table data cells:

```
<TD WIDTH=52 ALIGN=LEFT><IMG SRC="left.gif" WIDTH=52 HEIGHT=181></TD>
<TD WIDTH=132 ALIGN=CENTER><FONT
FACE=VERDANA><H1>your<br>photo<br>(or text)<br>here</H1></FONT></TD>
<TD WIDTH=66 ALIGN=RIGHT><IMG SRC="right.gif" WIDTH=66
HEIGHT=181></TD>
</TR>
<TR>
```

8 Finally, create the bottom table data cell containing your bottom frame graphic, again spanning all three columns (COLSPAN=3):

```
<TD WIDTH=250 COLSPAN=3><IMG SRC="bottom.gif" WIDTH=250 HEIGHT=64></TD>
</TR>
```

9 End all your tags and </HTML>:

```
</TABLE>
</CENTER>
</BODY>
</HTML>
```

The preceding code produces what you see in the following figure:

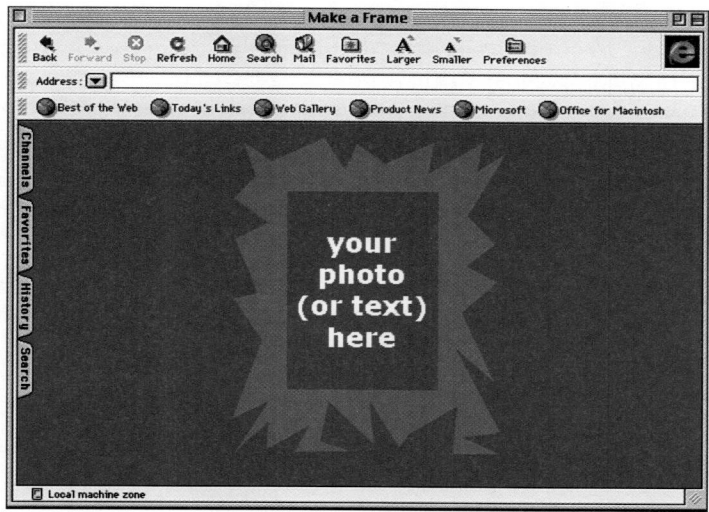

A frame created from optimized GIF images and connected together with HTML.

You are no longer limited by bandwith—only by your own imagination. For an online source of inspiration, check out the following webreview.com article, "The Art of Single Pixel Images" (http://webreview.com/wr/pub/98/01/02/feature/index.html). ●

Create White Space

Use this technique to:

- **Organize content.** Use white space to section off content, push things around, and organize columns and rows of data.

- **Lead your viewer's eye.** Use white space to make specific areas of your site stand out, thereby attracting your viewer's eye and possibly their clicker.

Using Spacer GIFs

Until Cascading Style Sheets (CSS) become a true standard, the creation of white space on Web pages will be accomplished through the use of "spacer GIFs." These lifesavers are basically transparent, 1 × 1 pixel GIFs that Web designers can stretch (by using the <IMG> WIDTH and HEIGHT attributes) to create invisible chunks of space—or white space. As you have probably guessed by now, white space doesn't have to be white—the term simply connotes a lack of substance (like invisible padding).

So what's the big deal about invisible padding? In design, structure is usually created by white space, or invisible grids that determine layouts and help organize information.

In HTML, you can create white space by simply calling a 1 × 1 pixel transparent GIF (that you can create in your image editing program) and stretching it by using your <IMG> tag:

```
<IMG SRC="spacer.gif" WIDTH=X HEIGHT=X>
```

Creating White Space with VSPACE and HSPACE

You can also use the VSPACE and HSPACE attributes to create white space. Note, however, that it's more tricky to deal with the HSPACE/VSPACE attributes because they work differently than the WIDTH/HEIGHT attributes. For example, if you want to create a 50×50 pixel space. Using the WIDTH and HEIGHT attributes only, you would specify the following in your HTML:

```
<IMG SRC="spacer.gif" WIDTH=50 HEIGHT=50>
```

If you wanted to use the VSPACE and HSPACE attributes, you would code your <IMG> tag like so:

```
<IMG SRC="spacer.gif" WIDTH=2 HEIGHT=2 VSPACE=24 HSPACE=24>
```

Why the odd numbering system? VSPACE and HSPACE work by adding space above, below (VSPACE), and to the left/right (HSPACE) of your image. Therefore, if you want 50 pixels, HSPACE and VSPACE should be 25—but wait! Don't forget the single-pixel

GIFs. With those kinds of dimensions, you would have a 51-pixel area instead of a perfect 50 pixels. To solve this, you must allot two pixels to the single-pixel GIF and reduce that from 50, which leaves you with 48 pixels to be filled by the HSPACE / VSPACE attributes.

48/2 = 24

Twenty-four pixels to the left and 24 pixels to the right of a two-pixel image equals 50 pixels.

Why Use HSPACE/VSPACE?

Why go through all the trouble if you can simply make the single-pixel GIF a 50 × 50 pixel image? Most browsers have a limited amount of RAM allocated to their image cache. After a while, spacer GIFs start to eat away at this memory and can cause some browsers to display thin, translucent lines where stretched single-pixel GIFs were supposed to appear. For this reason, some designers prefer to use the HSPACE/VSPACE alternative.

Ultimately it's up to you to determine the most convenient method of employing the spacer GIF technique.

Using Transparent Spacer GIFs

The following figure is a good example of why you should employ transparent spacer GIFs to move items around on a page for absolute positioning of objects.

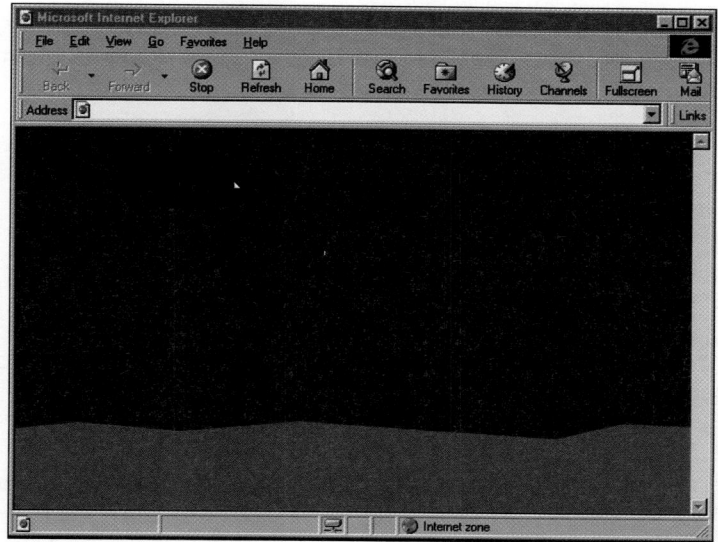

A porcupine awaits getting grounded and wants his dart to look like it's going somewhere.

73

The following image consists of a background GIF (called by the <BODY> tag as BACKGROUND="background.gif"), the porcupine.gif and the dart.gif.

We also need a spacer.gif to help us position these images within a table so we can achieve the effect in the following figure.

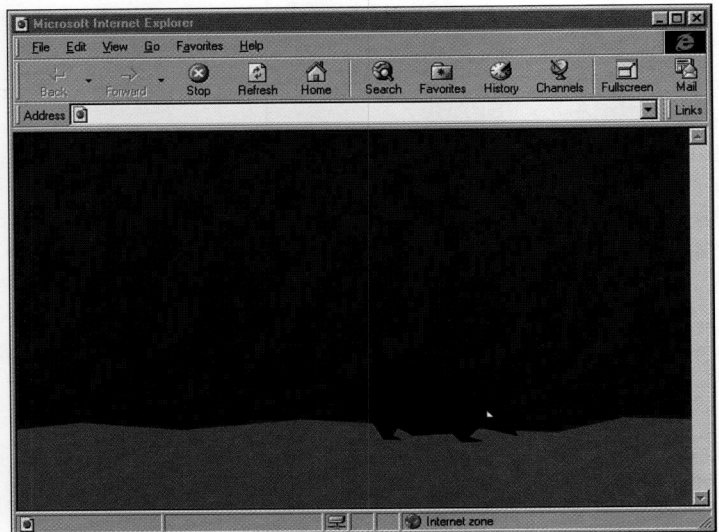

The porcupine is grounded and his dart looks like it's going somewhere fast.

Examine the following HTML and check out the figure that follows the steps to get a visual idea of how the spacer GIFs lay out:

1 Establish your HTML as you normally would:

```
<HTML>
<HEAD>
<TITLE>PORCUPINE</TITLE>
</HEAD>
<BODY BACKGROUND="background.gif">
```

2 Create a 475-pixel-wide table:

```
<TABLE WIDTH=475 BORDER=0 CELLPADDING=0 CELLSPACING=0>
<TR>
```

3 Create a table data cell and insert a spacer GIF within it, setting its WIDTH to 475 pixels and its HEIGHT to 98 pixels in order to push the rest of the graphics down the page:

```
<TD WIDTH=475 COLSPAN=2><IMG SRC="spacer.gif" WIDTH=475 HEIGHT=98></TD>
</TR>
<TR>
```

4 Insert your first image within the first table data cell of the second row:

```
<TD WIDTH=63 ROWSPAN=2 VALIGN=TOP><IMG SRC="dart.gif" WIDTH=63
HEIGHT=114></TD>
```

5 Fill the second table data cell with white space by using a spacer GIF by setting its
WIDTH and HEIGHT attributes:

```
<TD WIDTH=412><IMG SRC="spacer.gif" WIDTH=412 HEIGHT=114></TD>
</TR>
<TR>
```

6 Place your second image within the last table data cell and close all your tags,
ending the HTML:

```
<TD WIDTH=412 ALIGN=RIGHT><IMG SRC="porcupine.gif" WIDTH=182
HEIGHT=97></TD>
</TR>
</TABLE>
</BODY>
</HTML>
```

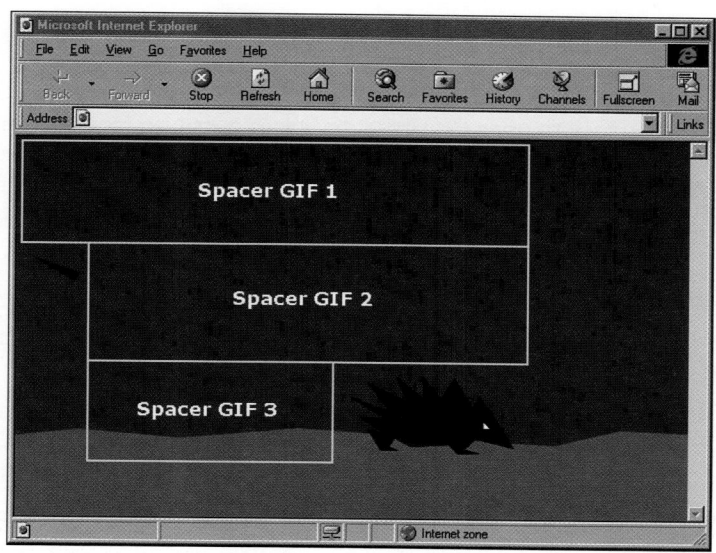

Here's how the spacer GIFs lay out to help push the objects into their places.

For more information on spacer GIFs, check out the *Creating Killer Web Sites* site
(http://www.killersites.com/1-design/single_pixel.html). ●

75

Make Images Appear Magically

Use this technique to:

- **Provide immediate gratification.** By using the <IMG LOWSRC> tag, you can make a low-resolution version of your image appear instantly, while the high-resolution one loads in the background. This satisfies viewers eager to see your page.

- **Create a sense of surprise.** You can use two completely different images in this technique (a closed curtain as the first image and an open curtain with a display as the second) to add a sense of drama or tension to the page.

- **Make your images appear over time.** Using the <IMG LOWSRC> tag can provide something for your viewers to look at while they wait for the bigger picture.

One of the biggest complaints you'll hear (or utter to yourself) about the Web is that it takes images *forever* to load. The LOWSRC attribute within the <IMG> tag solves the problem of having to wait for an image, given three factors:

1 Your LOWSRC image must be very small in filesize (2–4K or smaller is preferred for immediate results—bitmapped or 1-bit images work the best).

2 Your image must be saved as either a GIF or JPEG file.

3 Your images (both LOWSRC and your final image) must be the same pixel dimensions in size.

The only drawback to using the LOWSRC technique is its Netscape-only implementation—sorry, Internet Explorer. However, because Internet Explorer browsers simply ignore the LOWSRC attribute within your <IMG> tags, no one gets hurt if you use it. If anything, your Netscape users reap the rewards of instant image gratification.

Creating the LOWSRC Effect

Given that you meet the above criteria, follow these steps to create the LOWSRC effect:

1 Using your favorite image editing program (Adobe Photoshop or Macromedia Fireworks, for example) create a bitmap image (or a very small, optimized GIF), which you will be calling by using the LOWSRC attribute

within the <IMG> tag. Remember this image has to appear instantly while the main image is loading, so bitmapped (1-bit) images generally work best here.

2 Create the final full-color image that you will call (as you normally would) within the same <IMG> tag containing the LOWSRC attribute. This image can be a GIF or JPEG but not a progressive GIF or JPEG. Progressive images appear instantly (although in a low-res state) and define themselves over time as they load. Using progressive images interferes with the LOWSRC technique and renders it useless.

3 Code your LOWSRC <IMG> tag within your HTML document like so:

```
<IMG LOWSRC="bitmap.gif" SRC="highres.gif" WIDTH=250 HEIGHT=300 Alt="A
flower for you.">
```

Notice that both images share the same WIDTH and HEIGHT attributes within the <IMG> tag, so be sure they are equal in dimension when you design them. A good rule of thumb is to design both images within Photoshop by using its powerful layers feature to ensure consistent visuals and accurate dimensions.

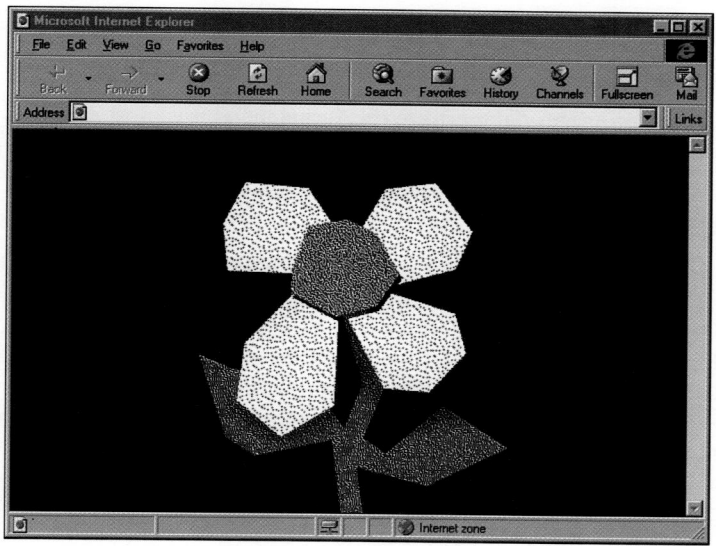

This is a 1-bit version of the high-res flower image.

77

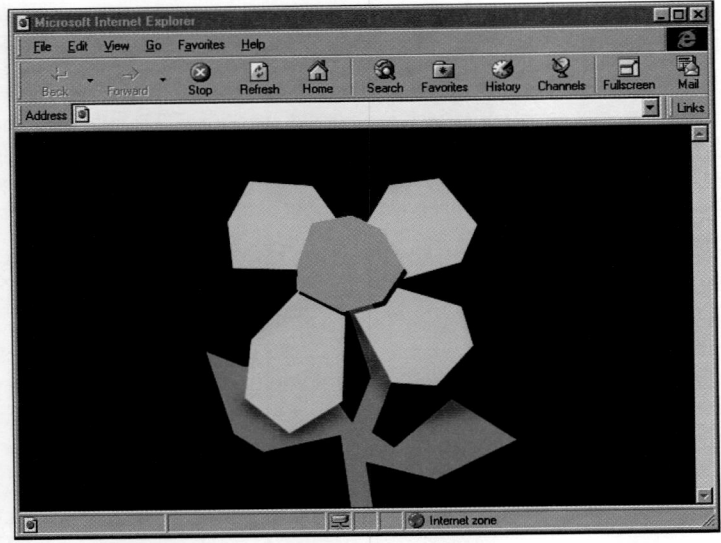

This is the high-res flower image—notice the difference between this and the 1-bit version.

The preceding images demonstrate this technique as it is most commonly used. Another way to use this effect is to create a mini-animation for a splash page.

Creating a Mini-Animation for a Splash Page

A splash page is an introductory page to your Web site that is not your home page. Think of it as a "title" page to your Web site. It might have your site's title and nothing else on it, or it might have a cute cartoon, illustration, animation, or typographic effect. Basically, a splash page is used to evoke some kind of feeling for your viewers before they enter your site. Whether it be surprise, fear, awe, or inspiration, splash pages can be a great way to make a first impression. In the following example, visitors initially see the sewer lid, but as the second image loads—surprise! The sewer lid is replaced, creating the illusion of an animated GIF without your having to create one.

Notice that in the following figures, a 1-bit image is not used for the LOWSRC. Although it is not *required* that you use a 1-bit image for the LOWSRC, if you're going to use a color image, make sure that it's an optimized, quick-loading file 2–5K in size.

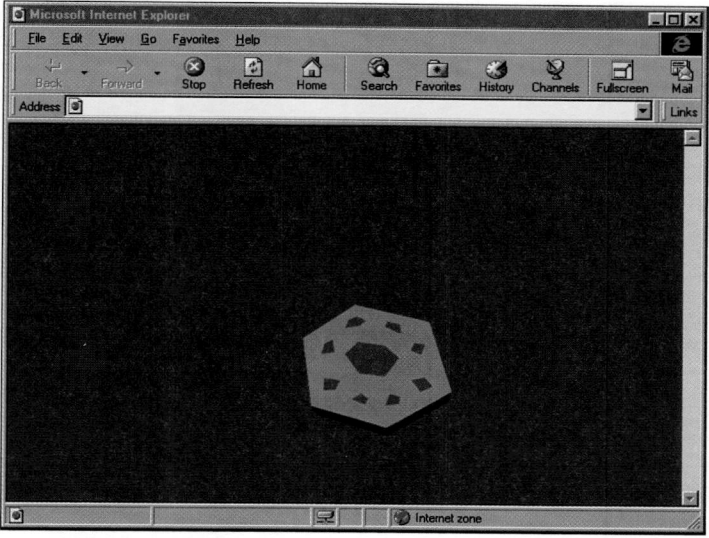

It's just a sewer lid.

But wait—there's more!

To create your own mini-animation by using the LOWSRC technique, follow these steps:

1. Get creative with an animation idea. For instance, what about a sewer door that opens to reveal a worker?

2. Create a 1-bit or optimized color image (2–5K in size), so that it loads quickly as the LOWSRC image. This image should be the first frame in your animation. Consider it a mini-story with a beginning and an end—this is the beginning image.

3. Create an ending image, making sure that it shares identical width and height dimensions with your LOWSRC image. As you can see in the sewer lid example, both images share the same dimensions but do not necessarily occupy the canvas in the same fashion. The difference between the first and second image is what creates the *illusion* of the animation.

4. Place the <IMG> tag by using the LOWSRC attribute within an HTML page (usually your home page) that contains nothing but this image, usually centered with the <CENTER> tag.

5. Attach a link to your <IMG> tag so that those wishing to bypass the page can quickly go deeper within your site. For example:

```
<A HREF="nextpage.html"><IMG LOWSRC="x.GIF" SRC="Y.GIF" HEIGHT=X
WIDTH=X></A>
```

You can also experiment by using the LOWSRC technique combined with the META REFRESH technique to create an animated slide show that requires no animated GIFs (see "Creating a Slide Show with Meta Refresh"). ●

Animate a Portion of a Large Image

Use this technique to:

- **Keep file sizes to a minimum.** Animating a portion of a large image helps reduce download time, while still delivering a unique visual.

- **Give life to larger images.** You can take a portrait and make the eyes move back and forth, or draw a dog with a wagging tail.

- **Attract the viewer's eye.** A hint of motion in an otherwise still image will definitely get your viewer's attention.

Sectioning the Image

Animated GIFs can be a wonderful asset to a Web site. At the same time, however, animated GIFs can get pretty hefty in filesize, especially if created from large images. Without scrapping the idea of animations altogether, there is a way to create a sense of motion while delivering one *seemingly* large image. Of course, *seemingly* suggests that there is a trick involved. Take a look at the following image.

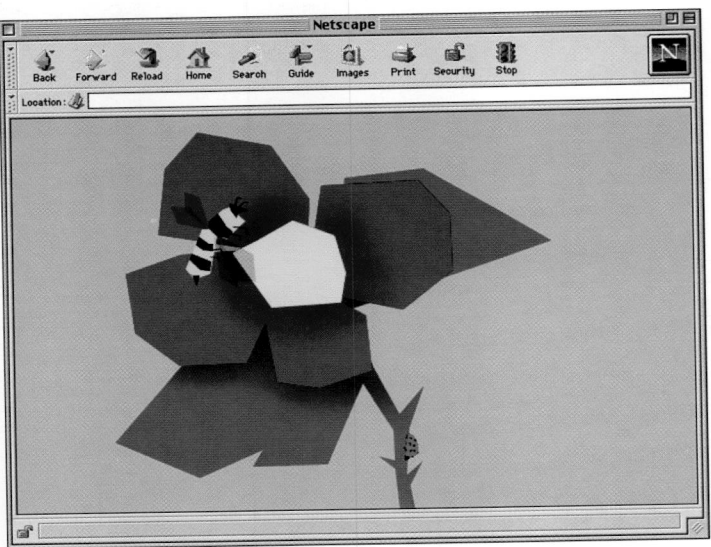

Bumblebee, flower, and ladybug.

The preceding image represents a large image, a part of which can be animated to create an interesting overall visual. Examine the divisions made to the same image as follows:

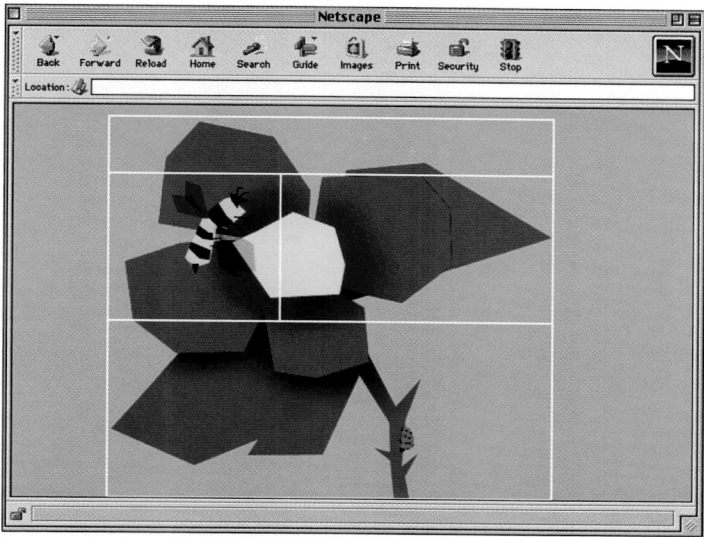

Large image divided up into four major sections.

If we section off the image with our image editing program (or Macromedia's Fireworks at http://www.macromedia.com/software/fireworks), we will have four smaller GIF images instead of one large image. This way an animated GIF can be created of, say, the bumblebee hovering over the flower:

Bumblebee cell-animation 1.

Bumblebee cell-animation 2.

Bumblebee cell-animation 3.

Bumblebee cell-animation 4.

Bumblebee cell-animation 5.

When the images are placed together by using an HTML table, the page is displayed as if it were one large image with the bumblebee hovering over a section of the flower. For more information on working with tables, see the section within this book called "Magic with Tables."

The following Web sites employ this technique beautifully—check them out:

- Don Barnett (http://www.donbarnett.com/)

- Prophet Communications' Spectacle (http://www.spectacle.com)

- Discovery Online (http://www.discovery.com) ●

Serve PNG Format Graphics

Use this technique to:

- **Deliver quick-loading 24-bit images.** Impress your visitors with full-color images that load as quickly as optimized GIFs.

- **Ensure a cross-platform friendly image.** Display the image properly on Macs and PCs without worrying about gamma issues.

- **Create the illusion of a faster-loading image.** Your viewers will immediately begin to appreciate your images thanks to PNG's two-dimensional interlacing feature.

The Benefits of PNG Graphics

Offering a lossless compression scheme, PNG (Portable Network Graphic) is the 24-bit, small-filesize alternative to the GIF file format (which is limited to 8-bit) and is *designed specifically* for the Web. A step better than JPEG, PNG does not use a lossy compression scheme, meaning that it does not discard image data. If it's so great, why aren't we using it? Well, many of the older browsers don't support PNG. The 4.0 browsers (20% of the market as of this writing) support the format, however, and it will gain industry-wide acceptance over the next year, poising PNG for dominance as the standard image-delivery format standard.

To demonstrate why PNG is better than GIF or JPEG, take a look at the following GIF image:

Optimized 5-bit GIF image.

In the preceding figure, notice that although the GIF compression format did a decent job with the image, there is banding going on near the chair (banding occurs when you actually see a severe gradation from light to dark or from one color to the next).

Creating PNG Files

To create your own PNG files, all you need is Adobe Photoshop 4.0, 5.0, or any other PNG-friendly image processor. Follow these steps and you'll be PNGing away:

1. Create a full-color RGB image. You can also scan a photograph or use stock full-color photography in RGB mode.

2. Keep your image in RGB mode; you do not need to change your image to indexed color as you do with GIF files.

3. In Photoshop, select Save from the File menu; you are prompted to select a file format in which to save your image. Select PNG from the pull-down menu and save your file with the .png extension.

4. Call your .png file into your HTML document using the <IMG> tag.

That's all there is to it. As long as your visitors' browsers are capable of displaying PNG files (4.0+ browsers), you can display your images quickly and beautifully. Now take a look at what a PNG image looks like within a browser window:

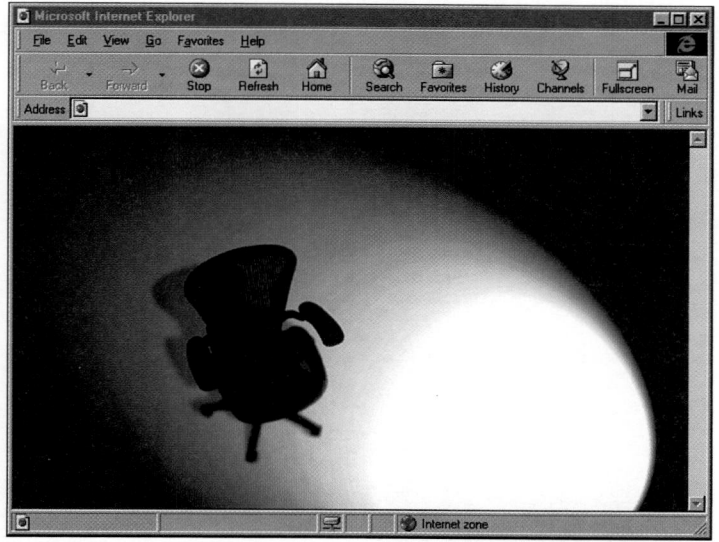

PNG (pronounced PING) image looks great compared to its GIF alternative.

For more information about PNG, check out the online resource, PNG Specification (http://www.boutell.com/boutell/png). ●

Create Image Maps

Use this technique to:

- **Achieve faster page loads.** Load one optimized image for your site navigation instead of having to load several images (or button graphics).

- **Consolidate your site's navigation.** Save lots of coding time by placing just one image on the page instead of many (at different sizes and different locations).

Image maps provide the easiest way to add graphic links to your Web site without having to design and position individual graphics. All you have to do is create a GIF image that you can then import into an image-map editor such as the following:

- Mapper for Macintosh (`ftp://ftp.calles.pp.se/pub`)

- Mapedit for Windows 98 and Windows NT
  (`http://www.boutell.com/mapedit`)

Working with Image Mappers

Most image mappers basically work the same way. You begin by importing in your image. (PICT or GIF images usually work fine for this.) The image mapper has a tool palette from which you can select the kind of tool with which to create your maps. In the following figure, I am presented with a square, circle, polygon, and pencil.

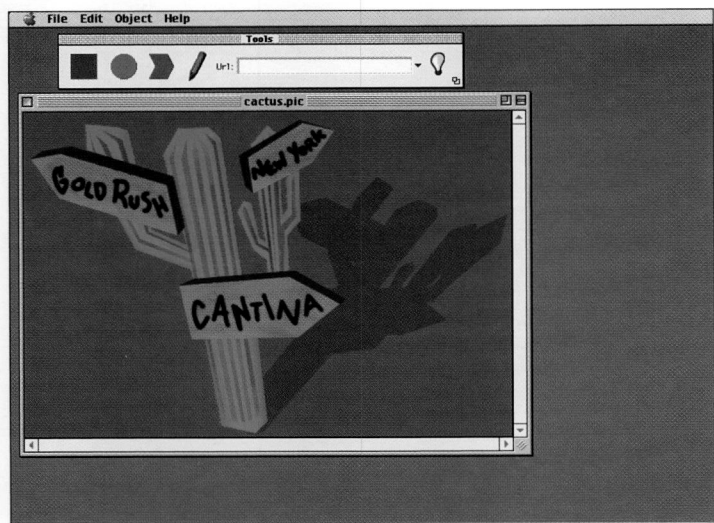

Image to be mapped opened in Mapper for Macintosh.

Polygon usually works the best for odd shapes, so in the following figure, a map is placed over the "cantina" link and the URL is placed in the target box within the image mapper palette.

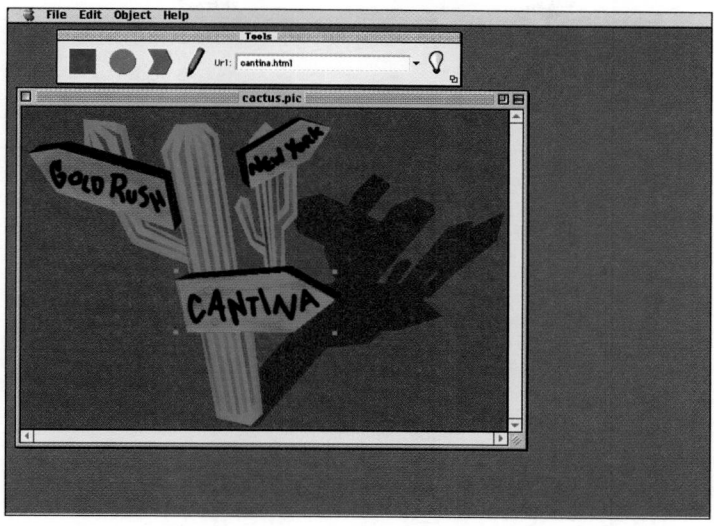

Map placed over the "cantina" link.

When incorporating polygons into your image maps, note that they are not recognized by older browsers. To ensure complete compatibility with older browsers when using image maps, limit yourself to using rectangles.

Extracting the HTML Source Code

Both Mapper for Macintosh and Mapedit for the PC enable you to extract the HTML source for the image map by telling the programs to save the HTML (usually located below the FILE heading), as displayed in the following.

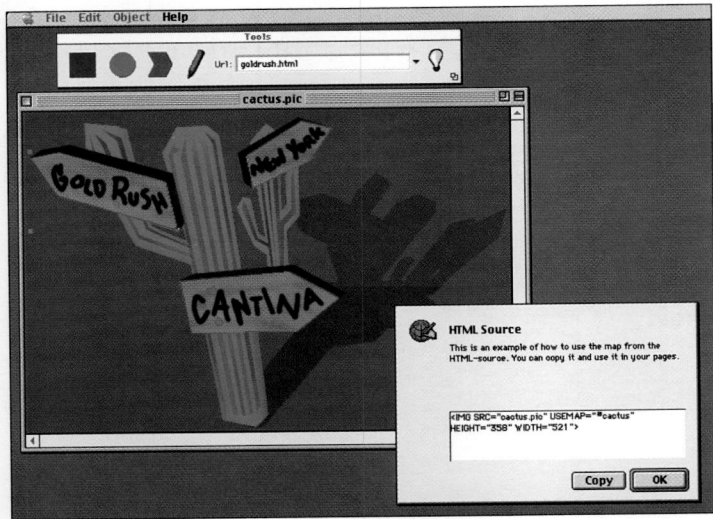

HTML source for the map file is made available.

Creating the Source for an Image Map

The image mapper creates the source for the image map, which can then be plugged into the HTML to create the CACTUS IMAGE MAP:

1 Begin your HTML:

```
<HTML>
<HEAD>
<TITLE>CACTUS IMAGE MAP</TITLE>
</HEAD>
<BODY>
```

2 Insert your image map GIF, making sure to use the USEMAP attribute to call the image map code you import from your image mapper software:

```
<IMG SRC="cactus.gif" BORDER=0 WIDTH=516 HEIGHT=355 USEMAP="#CACTUS">
```

3 Insert your image map code, having given it a name (in this case, "CACTUS"):

```
<MAP NAME="CACTUS">
```

4 Each area that is mapped on your image is represented within a single <AREA> tag, in which you can use JavaScript as you regularly would in an <A HREF> tag:

```
<AREA
SHAPE="polygon"
COORDS="164,133,36,93,8,51,38,45,152,79,164,133"
```

```
HREF="goldrush.html"
onMouseOver="imgOn('img1');window.status='go west, young man';return true">

<AREA
SHAPE="polygon"
COORDS="246,87,239,51,298,13,331,21,308,56,246,87"
HREF="newyork.html"
onMouseOver=";window.status='back to the city';return true">

<AREA
SHAPE="polygon"
COORDS="167,191,178,249,291,248,336,211,283,181,167,191"
HREF="cantina.html"
onMouseOver=";window.status='check out the cantina';return true">
```

5 Be sure to close the <MAP>, <BODY>, and <HTML> tags:

```
</MAP>
</BODY>
</HTML>
```

In this code, notice that a JavaScript `onMouseOver` command is placed within the image map so that when the viewer rolls over a link, descriptive text pops into the status bar. When viewers roll over a link, they will see a pointing finger and the status bar message made possible by JavaScript.

Rolling over a link displays a status bar message.   ●

91

Design JavaScript Rollovers

Use this technique to do the following:

- **Provide immediate feedback.** Let your users know that the link is HOT and that they placed their mouse pointer on a graphic (or hyperlink text) that takes them somewhere.

- **Enhance your site's navigation.** Navigation links benefit from rollovers because rollovers compel clicks—and if you want to get viewers deep into your site, what better way to help them along?

- **Bring your site to life.** Liven up your typical hypertext link or still image and make something happen when the user's cursor hovers over it.

Creating an intuitive navigational interface that remains consistent throughout the site is a good start, but adding JavaScript rollover capability to your site takes it to the next level of interactivity. Incorporating JavaScript rollover code is not as difficult or confusing as you might suspect. In fact, littering the Net are dozens of sites offering free code (the best being webcoder.com, builder.com, webreference.com, and webmonkey.com).

TIP **This technique is compatible with Netscape Navigator version 2.0 or higher and Microsoft Internet Explorer version 4.0 or higher. Older browsers ignore the rollover effect.**

The R35 Web site, shown in the following figure, incorporates JavaScript rollover images into its navigational structure.

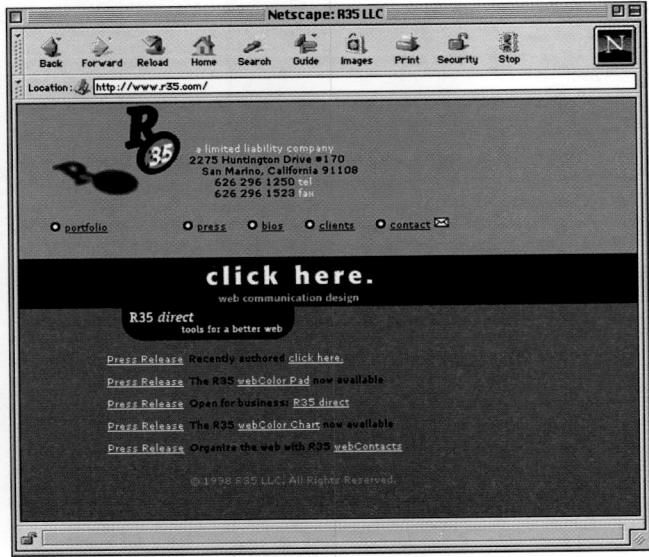

The R35 Web site uses JavaScript rollovers.

Designing the Rollover Images

When designing your rollover images, make sure that their "off" and "on" states share the same width and height dimensions. The best way to accomplish this is to design both states of the image at the same time:

1 In Photoshop, set up your rollover image canvas and design both "on" and "off" states by using Photoshop's layers, as shown in the following figure.

2 Begin by establishing your background layer and designing the element that both rollover images will share. In the R35 Web site example, both "on" and "off" states of the rollover image share the same black circle button element which is placed in the background layer.

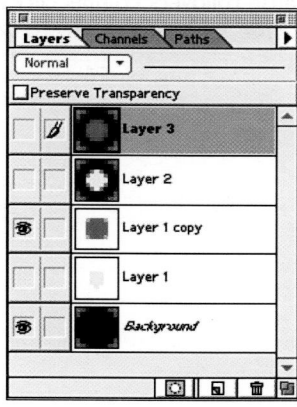

3 Create new foreground layers (Layer→New→Layer) and place the "on" and "off" state changes within these layers.

4 Merge each state layer (Layer 1 and Layer 1 copy in the preceding figure) with the Background to create the rollover images (Layer 2 and Layer 3 in the preceding figure).

The R35 Web site rollover image layout in Photoshop.

5 Save each of the two layers as a separate GIF. In the figure on the right, the rollover image "on" state is saved as button1.gif whereas its "off" state is saved as button0.gif. Note that both images come from the same Photoshop canvas, thus sharing the same image dimensions.

Take a look at the following figure and you can see that the pointer is rolled over the portfolio link and the circle GIF to the left of the link is red, indicating that the link can be activated.

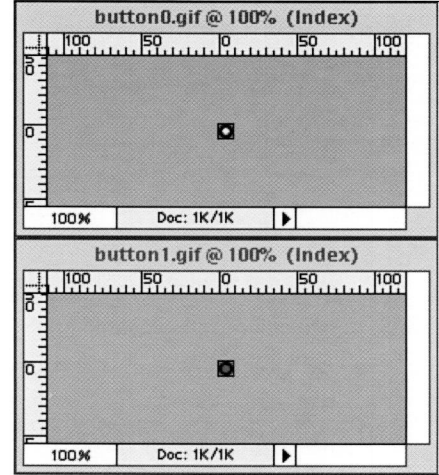

93

The R35 Web site rollover "on" and "off" state elements.

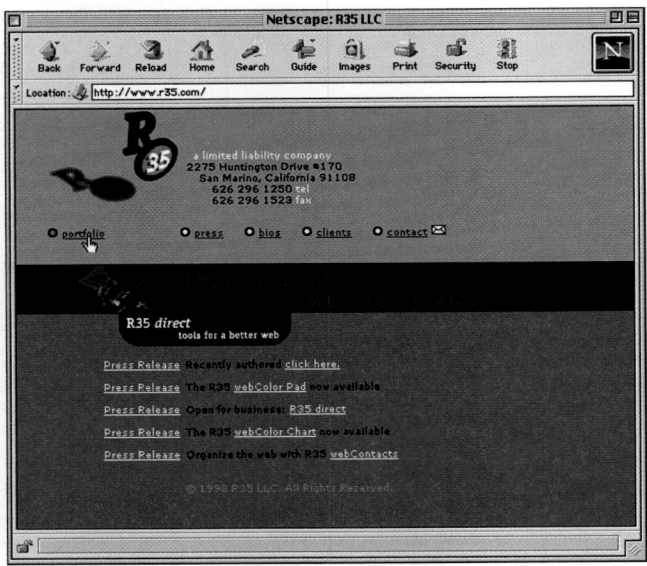

The R35 Web site with JavaScript rollover activated.

Creating the Rollover Effect

To create JavaScript rollovers, carefully examine the following steps (code originated at www.webcoder.com and has been modified for the purposes of this lesson).

JavaScript Declarations

1 Begin your HTML as you normally would with the following code:

```
<HTML>
<HEAD>
<TITLE>JavaScript Rollover</TITLE>
<SCRIPT LANGUAGE="JavaScript">
<!--//
```

This is nothing new. We established that this is an HTML page and that we're about to do some JavaScript.

2 Tell JavaScript to check if the browser understands document.images (JavaScript for control over images within the document):

```
if (document.images) {
```

This line says, "If the browser supports image swapping, go ahead and do something." If the viewer's browser does not support image swapping (that which makes rollovers happen), it ignores the code and does not display the rollovers (in other words, Internet Explorer 3.0).

3 Preload your images for the "on" state so that there is no lag time when the user rolls over the hot spots:

```
img1on = new Image();
img1on.src = "rollover1_on.gif";
```

Here, you tell JavaScript to preload a certain image (`rollover1_on.gif`) into the browser's cache so that it can display the image instantly when called. For every image that you want rolled over, you must have another pair of the preceding lines, except change the properties to `img2on`, `img3on`, `img4on`, and so on.

4 Preload your images for the "off" state:

```
img1off = new Image();
img1off.src = "rollover1_off.gif";
}
```

Here you tell JavaScript to preload another image, this time for the "off" state of the image. For every image that you want rolled over, you must have another pair of the preceding lines, except change the properties to `img2off`, `img3off`, `img4off`, and so on. Each rollover image has two "states" (like states of being): an "on" state and an "off" state. By default, the "off" state of the rollover appears until the user rolls the mouse over the link, at which point it turns "on." Simple enough? Let's continue.

5 Define the "on" state function:

```
function imgOn(imgName) {
    if (document.images) {
        document[imgName].src = eval(imgName + "on.src");
    }
}
```

Here, you tell JavaScript that when a certain function is called (in this case `imgOn`), JavaScript shows the "on" state of the image.

6 Define the "off" state function:

```
function imgOff(imgName) {
    if (document.images) {
        document[imgName].src = eval(imgName + "off.src");
    }
}
```

In this step, you tell JavaScript that when a certain function is called (in this case `imgOff`), JavaScript shows the "off" state of the image.

7 Incorporate the rollover functionality within your <A HREF> tags:

```
//-->
</SCRIPT>
</HEAD>
<BODY BGCOLOR="#ffffff" TEXT="000000">
```

95

Putting the JavaScript to Use

I You're done with the JavaScript declarations. Now we actually put the JavaScript code to use:

```
<A HREF="somewhere.html"
onMouseOver="imgOn('img1');window.status='something'; return true"
onMouseOut="imgOff('img1')"><IMG NAME="img1" WIDTH=X HEIGHT=X
SRC="rollover1_off.gif" BORDER=0></a>
```

Here, you say link to `"somewhere.html"` location; when the mouse rolls over the link (`onMouseOver`), show the image "on" state whose name is `"img1"`. Also, you tell JavaScript to place a custom message in the status bar (`window.status='something'`). Then go on to tell JavaScript that when the user rolls off the link (`onMouseOut`), show the image "off" state whose name is `"img1"`.

That's all fine and well, but what's this `"img1"`? This is the actual image you want to change—in the case of this example, it's the link itself. So when someone rolls over the image link in this example, it changes to the "on" state. Therefore, you have to design two versions of the same graphic for an "on" state and an "off" state.

2 End your HTML as you normally would with this code:

```
</BODY>
</HTML>
```

Test the code on your own and see what you come up with.

Putting It All Together

Here's the code again in its entirety; notice that I added two extra preload pairs of code (`img2` and `img3` "on" and "off" states) to show you how you can expand the code as you add more links to the page.

```
<HTML>
<HEAD>
<TITLE>JavaScript Rollover</TITLE>
<SCRIPT LANGUAGE="JavaScript">
<!--//
        if (document.images) {
            img1on = new Image();
            img1on.src = "rollover1_on.gif";

            img2on = new Image();
            img2on.src = "rollover2_on.gif";

            img3on = new Image();
            img3on.src = "rollover3_on.gif";
```

```
            img1off = new Image();
            img1off.src = "rollover1_off.gif";

            img2off = new Image();
            img2off.src = "rollover2_off.gif";

            img3off = new Image();
            img3off.src = "rollover3_off.gif";
      }
function imgOn(imgName) {
      if (document.images) {
            document[imgName].src = eval(imgName + "on.src");
      }
}
function imgOff(imgName) {
      if (document.images) {
            document[imgName].src = eval(imgName + "off.src");
      }
}
//-->
</SCRIPT>
</HEAD>
<BODY BGCOLOR="#ffffff" TEXT="000000">
<A HREF="somewhere.htm" onMouseOver="imgOn('img1');window.status='some-
thing'; return true" onMouseOut="imgOff('img1')"><IMG NAME="img1" WIDTH=X
HEIGHT=X SRC="rollover1_off.gif" BORDER=0></a>
</BODY>
</HTML>
```

JavaScript rollovers are quite effective at getting users to interact with your site. After you
master the art of dealing with some relatively painless code, you can reap the rewards of
having rollovers on your Web site.   ●

Design Image Map Rollovers

Use this technique to:

- **Simplify image management.** Instead of having multiple scripts for multiple images, you only have to deal with one image map script.

- **Avoid laying out multiple table cells.** Deal with one image and its placement, instead of having to lay out numerous, different images for visitors to roll over.

If you have not yet read "Design JavaScript Rollovers," which is the section that precedes this one, it's a good idea to take a look before you try this technique. Designing image map rollovers is actually not that complicated. Here's what you'll need:

1   Your original image map.

2   A duplicate copy of your image map for every rollover you need to display.

For example, if you have three rollovers, you'll need your image map GIF as well as three duplicates of your image map, each with a certain link highlighted (or however you decide to visually communicate your rollovers).

Image map rollover with an activated link.

When you roll over an image map, JavaScript basically replaces the entire image map with the one you specify for the link you're rolling over. As you can see in the preceding figure, JavaScript is displaying the version of my image map GIF in which I painted the "Gold Rush" link in yellow because my mouse cursor is over this particular link.

Creating the Single Image Map Rollover

To achieve this effect, follow these steps:

1 Begin your HTML as you normally would:

```
<HTML>
<HEAD>
<TITLE>IMAGE MAP ROLLOVER</TITLE>
```

2 Establish your JavaScript code:

```
<SCRIPT LANGUAGE="JavaScript">
<!--//
```

3 Make sure the browser supports image-swapping:

```
if (document.images) {
```

4 Pre-load your "on" and "off" states for your image map:

```
    img1on = new Image();
    img1on.src = "cactuson.gif";
    img1off = new Image();
    img1off.src = "cactusoff.gif";
}
```

TIP **This technique works for an image map with one rollover link and operates perfectly in Netscape Navigator and Internet Explorer 4.0 browsers or better. To find out how to create an image map with multiple rollovers, skip to the section titled "Creating the Multiple Image Map Rollover."**

99

5 Define your "on" state function:

```
function imgOn(imgName) {
        if (document.images) {
            document[imgName].src = eval(imgName + "on.src");
        }
}
```

6 Define your "off" state function:

```
function imgOff(imgName) {
        if (document.images) {
```

```
                    document[imgName].src = eval(imgName + "off.src");
            }
    }
}
//-->
</SCRIPT>
</HEAD>
<BODY>
```

7 Call your image and reference the map through the USEMAP variable within your <IMG> tag:

```
<IMG NAME="img1" SRC="cactusoff.gif" BORDER=0 WIDTH=516 HEIGHT=355
USEMAP="#CACTUS">
```

8 Define the parameters of your image map, incorporating the rollover functionality within the <MAP> tag as you would within an <A HREF> tag:

```
<MAP NAME="CACTUS">
<AREA
SHAPE="polygon"
COORDS="164,133,36,93,8,51,38,45,152,79,164,133"
HREF="goldrush.html"
onMouseOver="imgOn('img1');window.status='go west, young man';return
true"
onMouseOut="imgOff('img1')">
</MAP>
```

9 End your HTML as you normally would:

```
</BODY>
</HTML>
```

In this example, notice that the rollover technique is configured and coded the same way as it is within a normal JavaScript rollover situation. The only thing that's changed is the fact that the onMouseOver and onMouseOut commands now appear within the <MAP> tag.

Creating the Multiple Image Map Rollover

So you've got multiple "hot spots" on your image that you want changed when users roll over them? No problem—as long as they're coming in with 4.0 or better browsers, that is. At the time of this writing, we're slowly transitioning from 3.0 to 4.0 browsers, with 5.0 versions looming ahead. By the time you read this and begin to implement these techniques, the 5.0 browsers should be available soon and 4.0 browsers will be the standard versions to optimize for.

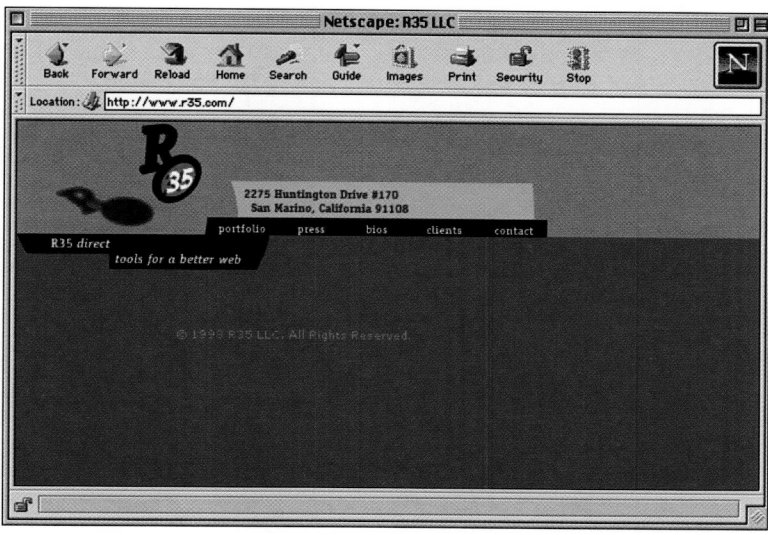

The R35 Web site using a multiple rollover image map.

The most recent evolution of the R35 Web site (located at `http://www.r35.com`) utilizes a multiple rollover image map to help users navigate through the Web site.

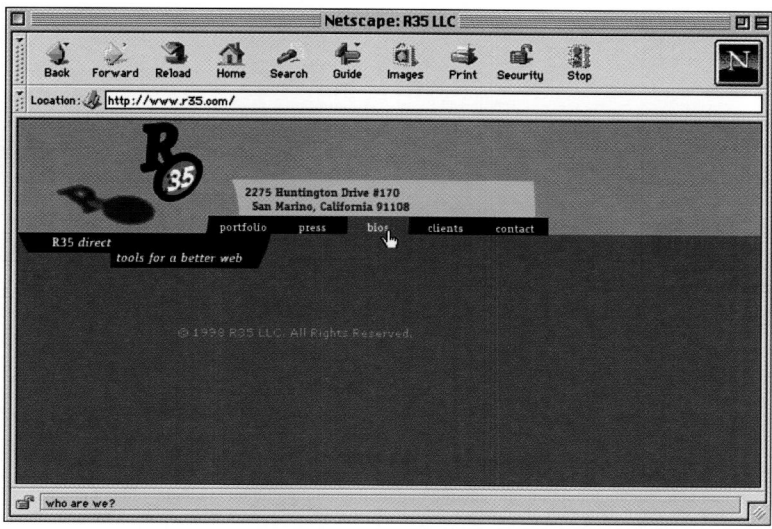

The R35 Web site with the "bios" link highlighted.

As you can see in the preceding figure, the links turn red as users roll over them. How is this accomplished? Well, there are five possible links: portfolio, press, bios, clients, and contact. For each of these links, a red highlight is required to create the rollover effect, not to mention the original image map, which has none of the links highlighted. This gives us a total of six GIF images that need to be created to accomplish this effect.

Writing the Code

To achieve this effect, complete these steps:

I Create your master GIF image (the one that has none of the highlights showing, which will be placed on your page and act as the image map).

The R35 Web site navigation master GIF image.

2 Create all your rollover image maps, highlighting each and every rollover area one-by-one for each of your "hot spots." In the following figure, portfolio is highlighted. Do the same for all rollovers.

The R35 Web site navigation with "portfolio" highlighted.

3 Begin your HTML as you normally would:

```
<HTML>

<HEAD>

<TITLE>R35</TITLE>

<META NAME="keywords" CONTENT="R35, direct, r35 direct, web design
tools, aeron chair, herman miller, webColor Pad, mousepad, mouse pad,
raymond pirouz, pirouz, raymond, click here, design, graphic design,
interactive, interactive CD-ROM, CD-ROM, interface design, advertis-
ing, banner, banner ads, image consulting, visual communication,
image, consulting, marketing, website, advertising agency, bookdeal,
mass communication">
```

```
<META NAME="description" CONTENT="R35 LLC develops strategic visual commu-
nication for consumers of the information age. R35 direct, a mail order
outlet targeted to serve web designers and developers, can be reached toll
free at 888 529 0903. R35 serves as parent company to BOOKDEAL.COM and
MASSCOMMUNICATION.COM, pioneers in the field of interactive publishing and
education. R35 senior partner, Raymond Pirouz, recently authored "click
here." [ISBN 1562057928] under New Riders. R35 senior partner, Dante
Truitt, is an expert in international business development.">
```

4 Establish your JavaScript code:

```
<SCRIPT LANGUAGE="JavaScript">
<!--//
```

5 Make sure the browser supports image swapping:

```
if (document.images) {
```

6 Preload the "on" and "off" states for your image map:

```
Off = new Array();
Off[0] = new Image();
Off[0].src = "nav_off.gif";

On = new Array();
On[1] = new Image();
On[1].src = "nav_1.gif";
On[2] = new Image();
On[2].src = "nav_2.gif";
On[3] = new Image();
On[3].src = "nav_3.gif";
On[4] = new Image();
On[4].src = "nav_4.gif";
On[5] = new Image();
On[5].src = "nav_5.gif";
}
```

7 Define the rollOver function:

```
if (document.images) {
    function rollOver(imgNum) {
        document.map.src = On[imgNum].src;
        }
}
```

8 Define the rollOut function:

```
if (document.images) {
    function rollOut(imgNum) {
        document.map.src = Off[imgNum].src;
        }
}
```

9 End defining JavaScript and continue with your HTML:

```
//-->

</SCRIPT>

</HEAD>

<BODY MARGINWIDTH=0 MARGINHEIGHT=0 LEFTMARGIN=0 TOPMARGIN=0
BGCOLOR="#cc9966" LINK="#333300" VLINK="#333300" ALINK="#333300"
TEXT="#000000">
```

10 You can place your image map in a table:

```
<table width=439 border=0 cellpadding=0 cellspacing=0>

<tr>

<td width=30 valign=top><IMG WIDTH=2 HSPACE=14 HEIGHT=2
SRC="blank.gif"></td>

<td width=125 valign=top><IMG width=125 height=92 SRC="logo.gif"
alt="r35" border=0></td>
```

11 Give a NAME to the image map (in this case, "map") and use the USEMAP attribute to call the image map defined later in this HTML code:

```
<td width=284 align=left valign=top><IMG WIDTH=284 HEIGHT=50
SRC="blank.gif"><BR><IMG NAME="map" WIDTH=284 HEIGHT=60
SRC="nav_off.gif" BORDER=0 USEMAP="#R35"></td>

</tr>

</table>
```

12 Define your image map and call your JavaScript rollover into action:

```
<MAP NAME="R35">
<AREA
      SHAPE="rect"
      COORDS="228,33,283,49"
      HREF="target URL here"
      onMouseOver="rollOver('5');window.status='a message here.';
return true"
      onMouseOut="rollOut('0')">


<AREA
      SHAPE="rect"
      COORDS="172,33,226,49"
```

```
      HREF="target URL here"
      onMouseOver="rollOver('4');window.status='a message here.'; return
true"
      onMouseOut="rollOut('0');">


<AREA
      SHAPE="rect"
      COORDS="118,33,169,49"
      HREF="target URL here"
      onMouseOver="rollOver('3');window.status='a message here.'; return
true"
      onMouseOut="rollOut('0');">



<AREA
      SHAPE="rect"
      COORDS="65,33,112,49"
      HREF="target URL here"
      onMouseOver="rollOver('2');window.status='a message here.'; return
true"
      onMouseOut="rollOut('0');">

<AREA
      SHAPE="rect"
      COORDS="5,33,61,49"
      HREF="target URL here"
      onMouseOver="rollOver('1');window.status='a message here.'; return
true"
      onMouseOut="rollOut('0');">

</MAP>
```

105

13 End your HTML:

```
</BODY>

</HTML>
```

As you can see, creating a multiple image map rollover uses slightly different code than a single image map rollover. Regardless of which technique you choose to employ, the image map rollover is a powerful and convenient technique to use for creating beautiful and interactive Web sites. ●

Create Rollover Animations

Use this technique to add an extra level of excitement to your rollovers. What if you create a hat graphic and when people roll over, a little rabbit animates out of it? Dazzle your visitors with this entertaining rollover technique.

Creating a rollover animation is nothing more than creating an animated GIF as your rollover "on" state (see "Design JavaScript Rollovers"). When the viewer rolls over your "off" state image, the rollover "on" state appears, and as long as the viewer has his cursor over the link, the animation plays (and loops if you set it to within your animated GIF builder).

 Please note that this technique is compatible with Netscape Navigator version 2.0 or higher and Microsoft Internet Explorer version 4.0 or higher. Older browsers ignore the rollover effect.

Take a look at the following image.

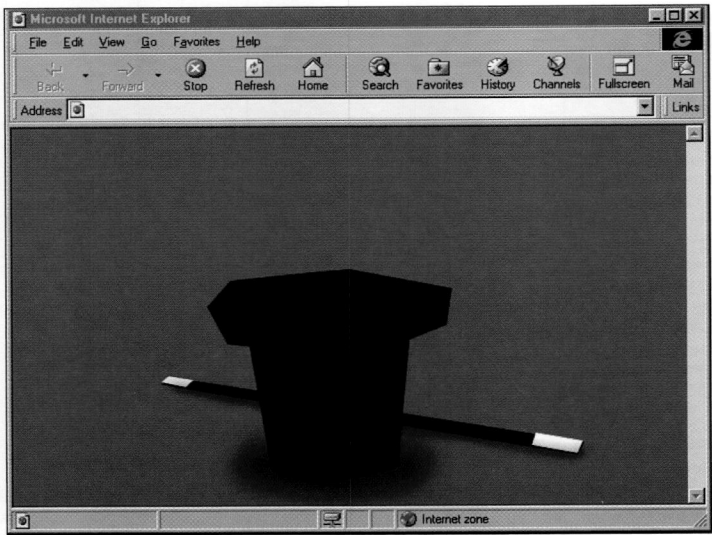

The magician's hat.

For the purposes of this example, say that the hat is a rollover button and that it is currently in its "off" state. Now if we roll over the graphic; here's what happens if we designed an animated GIF and placed it within the JavaScript code as the "on" state for this hat rollover.

Animated GIF frame 1.

Magically, out of the hat, a pair of rabbit's ears pop out. Now at this point, if we were to roll away from the hat, the "off" state (the empty hat) would reappear. If we decide to keep our mouse on the hat, the next frame appears.

The rabbit's out of the hat.

At this point, the animation stops (or loops back and forth if we structured it that way within the GIF builder program). In order to force your animation to loop, make sure you specify "looping on" in your favorite GIF animator. You can specify the animation to loop infinitely or for a specific number of times (in other words, 2, 3, or 4 loops).

The only limitation with this technique is that you should not create an animated GIF for the "off" state, because when you roll over an animation, it causes a bug in most browsers that renders the image unusable and the animation stops. It's safest to keep the animation in the "on" state at all times.

This technique can be accomplished by following these steps:

1 Begin your HTML as you normally do with this code:

```
<HTML>
<HEAD>
<TITLE>JavaScript Rollover</TITLE>
<SCRIPT LANGUAGE="JavaScript">
<!--//
```

2 Tell JavaScript to check if the browser understands `document.images` (JavaScript for control over images within the document):

```
if (document.images) {
```

3 Preload your animated GIF image for the "on" state so that there is no lag time when the user rolls over the hot spots:

```
img1on = new Image();
img1on.src = "animation_on.gif";
```

4 Preload your images for the "off" state:

```
    img1off = new Image();
    img1off.src = "hat_off.gif";
}
```

5 Define the "on" state function:

```
function imgOn(imgName) {
        if (document.images) {
            document[imgName].src = eval(imgName + "on.src");
        }
}
```

6 Define the "off" state function:

```
function imgOff(imgName) {
        if (document.images) {
            document[imgName].src = eval(imgName + "off.src");
        }
}
```

7 Incorporate the rollover functionality within your <A HREF> tag:

```
//-->
</SCRIPT>
</HEAD>
<BODY>
<A HREF="somewhere.html" onMouseOver="imgOn('img1');window.status='some-
thing'; return true" onMouseOut="imgOff('img1')"><IMG NAME="img1" WIDTH=X
HEIGHT=X SRC="hat_off.gif" BORDER=0></a>
```

8 End your HTML:

```
</BODY>
</HTML>
```

After coding the preceding steps into your HTML, you will see the animation if you roll over the triggering image. Make sure that both your "off" state triggering image as well as your "on" state animated GIF have the same height and width image dimensions for a perfectly smooth rollover effect. ●

Develop Multiple Rollovers

Use this technique to:

- **Highlight multiple graphics by rolling over one.** Kill two birds with one stone—or better yet, display two graphics when your visitor rolls over one for added effect.

What if you rolled over an image that caused not just one, but two images to change? Take a look at the following two images:

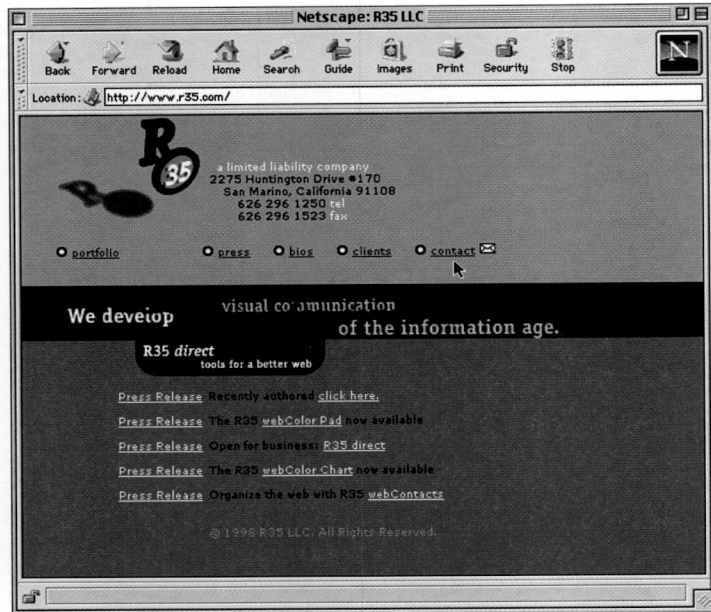

R35 multiple rollover example.

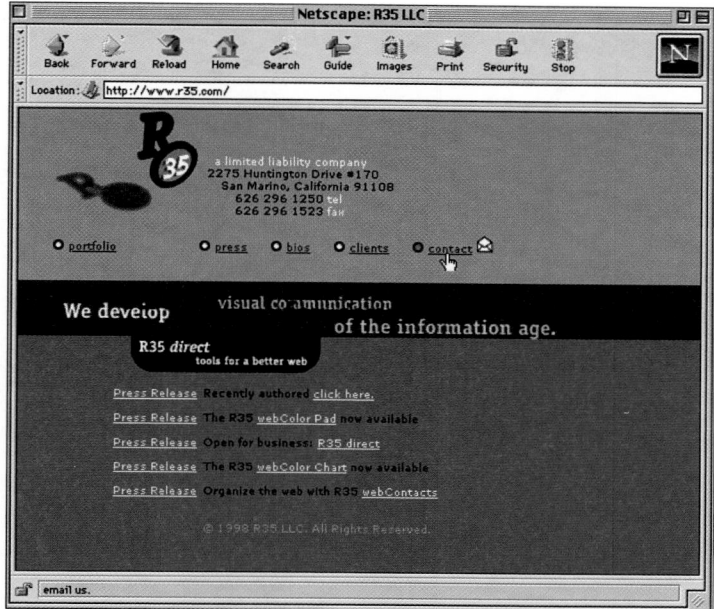

R35 multiple rollover executed.

Notice that upon rolling over the "contact" link, not only does the white circle turn red, but the envelope opens to signal the capability to send email.

Writing the Code

Let's get into how this is done, based on our previous discussion of JavaScript rollover code in "Design JavaScript Rollovers":

1 Begin your HTML:

```
<HTML>
<HEAD>
<TITLE>JavaScript Rollover</TITLE>
<SCRIPT LANGUAGE="JavaScript">
<!--//
```

2 Tell JavaScript to check if the browser understands document.images (JavaScript for control over images within the document):

```
if (document.images) {
```

111

3 Preload your images for the "on" state so there is no lag time when the user rolls over the hot spots:

```
img1on = new Image();
img1on.src = "rollover1_on.gif";
```

4 Preload the second rollover image that is to appear (in italics). Notice that we added a new "on" state and another new "off" state (in italics further down) for the 2nd rollover.

```
img2onx = new Image();
img2onx.src = "2xroll_on.gif";
```

5 Preload your images for the "off" state:

```
    img1off = new Image();
    img1off.src = "rollover1_off.gif";

    img2off = new Image();
    img2off.src = "2xroll_off.gif";
}
```

6 Define the "on" state function:

```
function imgOn(imgName) {
        if (document.images) {
            document[imgName].src = eval(imgName + "on.src");
        }
}
```

7 Define the "off" state function:

```
function imgOff(imgName) {
        if (document.images) {
            document[imgName].src = eval(imgName + "off.src");
        }
}
```

8 Add a third function `imgOnx(imgName)` used to ignite the second rollover:

```
function imgOnx(imgName) {
        if (document.images) {
            document[imgName].src = eval(imgName + "onx.src");
        }
}
//-->
</SCRIPT>
</HEAD>
<BODY BGCOLOR="#ffffff" TEXT="000000">
```

9 Within your <A HREF> tag, when calling the rollover using the onMouseOver handler, add the third function created to ignite the simultaneous rollover to the original rollover code (be sure to separate them with the ";"). Below, imgOn('img1') turns the first rollover on, and *imgOnx('img2')* causes the second image to turn on simultaneously with the first:

```
<A HREF="somewhere.htm" onMouseOver="imgOn('img1');
imgOnx('img2');window.status='something'; return true"
onMouseOut="imgOff('img1')"><IMG NAME="img1" WIDTH=X HEIGHT=X
SRC="rollover1_off.gif" BORDER=0></a>
<BR><BR>
```

10 Add the second image that will be simultaneously ignited using the imgOnx rollover function (note that it is called, img2):

```
<IMG NAME="img2" WIDTH=X HEIGHT=X SRC="2xroll_off.gif" BORDER=0>
```

11 End your HTML:

```
</BODY>
</HTML>
```

Experiment with this technique by adding more imgOn rollover functions and causing four or more images to simultaneously ignite as a result of rolling over one image. ●

PART IV

Magic with Tables

Tables have helped to liberate Web designers from the limitations of simple HTML layout and contributed to the organization and structuralization of many Web sites.

Tables provide designers with the ability to absolutely position images and text, adding a bit of flexibility and sanity to the sometimes insanely frustrating art of Web layout and design.

Define White Space

Use this technique to:

- **Establish your site's layout structure.** You can use tables to define your Web site's skeleton or foundation—establishing your page's boundaries.

- **Organize images and data.** Tables can help you organize the placement of images, data, and white space so that they remain rigid and display consistently within the structure you define.

- **Lead the viewer's eye through the site.** You can combine tables with spacer GIFs to create white space that will help your viewers see what YOU want them to see first.

Use tables to initially establish a Web site's foundation and skeletal structure. Before the advent of tables, there was no way to rigidly control the way information and graphics were housed and positioned relative to other objects on the page. When designing the page's structure, you can use tables to define blocks of white space that will be used to house information, graphics, and empty columns.

Create Your Site Skeleton

To create your Web site by using tables and white space, begin with your site skeleton as displayed in the following figure.

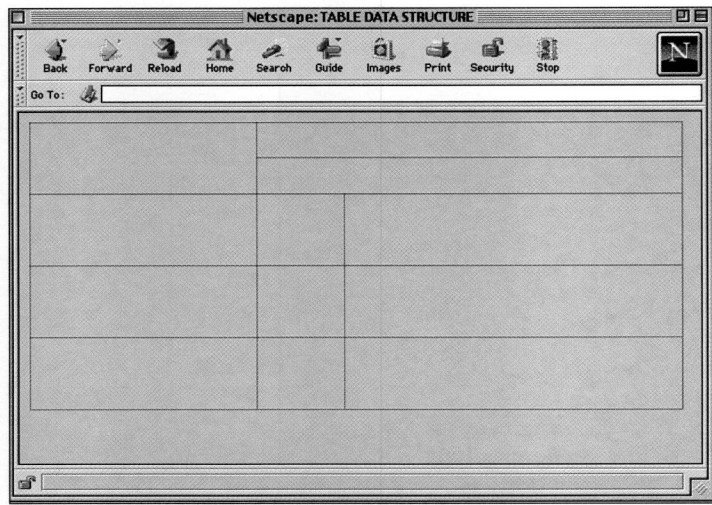

The skeletal structure of a 3-column, 4-row table.

Create the initial structure displayed in the preceding figure with the following steps:

1 Begin your HTML:

```
<HTML>
<HEAD>
<TITLE>TABLE DATA STRUCTURE</TITLE>
</HEAD>
<BODY BGCOLOR="#FFCC33" TEXT="#0000FF">
```

2 Create a 575-pixel wide table, setting the border to visible (1) so that you can see your results:

```
<TABLE WIDTH=575 CELLPADDING=0 CELLSPACING=0 BORDER=1>
```

3 Create three table data rows, experimenting with the COLSPAN and ROWSPAN attributes:

```
<TR>
```

4 Make sure to insert a nonbreaking space ( ) within your table data cells so they don't collapse on Netscape browsers:

```
<TD WIDTH=200 HEIGHT=65 ALIGN=CENTER ROWSPAN=2> </TD>
<TD WIDTH=375 HEIGHT=32 COLSPAN=2 ALIGN=CENTER> </TD>
</TR>
<TR>
<TD WIDTH=375 HEIGHT=33 COLSPAN=2 ALIGN=CENTER> </TD>
</TR>
<TR>
<TD WIDTH=200 HEIGHT=65 ALIGN=CENTER> </TD>
<TD WIDTH=75 ALIGN=CENTER> </TD>
<TD WIDTH=300 ALIGN=CENTER> </TD>
</TR>
<TD WIDTH=200 HEIGHT=65 ALIGN=CENTER> </TD>
<TD WIDTH=75 ALIGN=CENTER> </TD>
<TD WIDTH=300 ALIGN=CENTER> </TD>
</TR>
<TD WIDTH=200 HEIGHT=65 ALIGN=CENTER> </TD>
<TD WIDTH=75 ALIGN=CENTER> </TD>
<TD WIDTH=300 ALIGN=CENTER> </TD>
</TR>
```

5 End your <TABLE>, <BODY>, and <HTML> tags:

```
</TABLE>
</BODY>
</HTML>
```

117

Notice that the nonbreaking space ( ) is specified within the table data cells. In Netscape, all data fields must contain *something*, otherwise they will not display background colors or images and might "collapse." A data cell can be considered collapsed when it is either not visible or renders smaller than originally specified (in pixels).

Labeling Your White Space

Next, it's a good idea to label your white space by replacing the nonbreaking spaces with actual placeholder words (as in the following figure) so that you begin to see where the pieces of your Web site (navigation, content, images) fit within your skeleton. This step helps you determine if the number of columns and rows is adequate to house your page content.

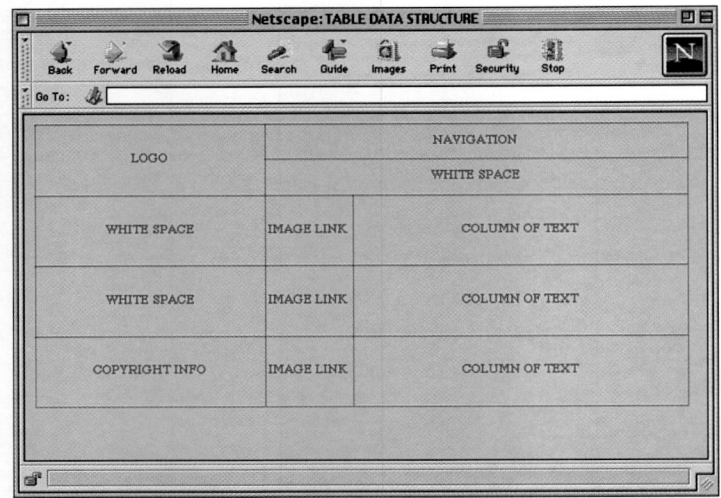

White space defined.

Placing Your Elements Within the Structure

Next, place your images, navigation, and text within the structure to bring your page to life. Using the preceding HTML code, simply fill in the gaps with your page's content like so:

Original HTML shell:

```
<TD WIDTH=200 HEIGHT=65 ALIGN=CENTER ROWSPAN=2> </TD>
```

Labeled HTML:

```
<TD WIDTH=200 HEIGHT=65 ALIGN=CENTER ROWSPAN=2>LOGO</TD>
```

Final HTML:

```
<TD WIDTH=200 HEIGHT=65 ALIGN=CENTER ROWSPAN=2><IMG WIDTH=200
HEIGHT=65 SRC="LOGO.GIF" ALT="noodlehaus"></TD>
```

Continue filling in the rest of your table data cells with content until you arrive at a page like this.

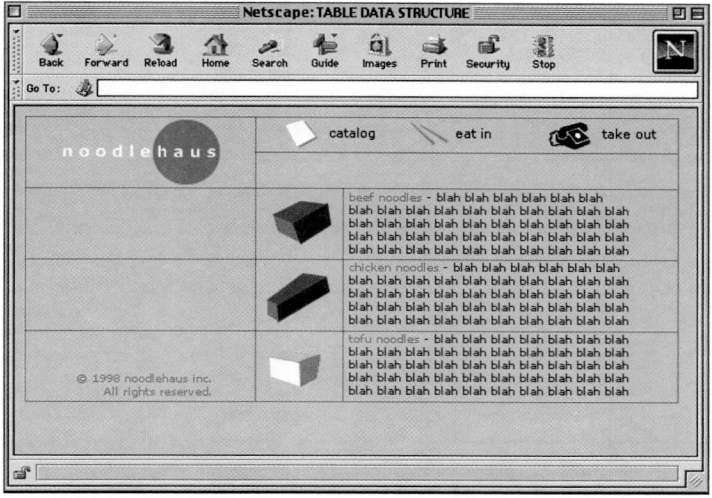

Putting the pieces together with borders on.

Finally, turn off table borders (BORDER=0) for that final finishing touch, giving transparent structure to the page.

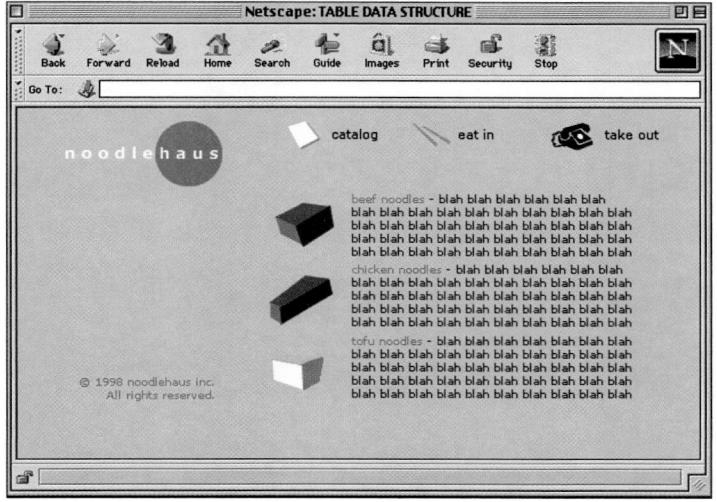

Turning table borders off for the launch.

As you can see here, white space combined with tables presents the page in an organized manner that leads the viewer's eye from the logo in the upper left, straight across the links to the right, and down the column of text and corresponding images. ●

Color Table Data Cells

Use this technique to:

- **Add quick-loading color without graphics.** Coloring table data cells is easy and painless, and it doesn't take any extra time to load and display.

- **Draw your viewer's eye to a specific section.** Color is a very powerful tool for drawing attention. Used strategically within table data cells, color can draw your viewer's attention to a section of type or other important data.

- **Speed page-load when combined with a transparent background GIF.** Cut down on the filesize of large images by giving them a transparent background and displaying them within a colored table data cell.

Coloring table data cells is the quickest way to add small to large quantities of solid color to your page without making your user wait for a graphic. Netscape Navigator 4.0+ and Microsoft Explorer 3.0+ support this function, so it's pretty standard and will be a no-brainer by the time 5.0+ browsers are released.

Attract Your Viewer

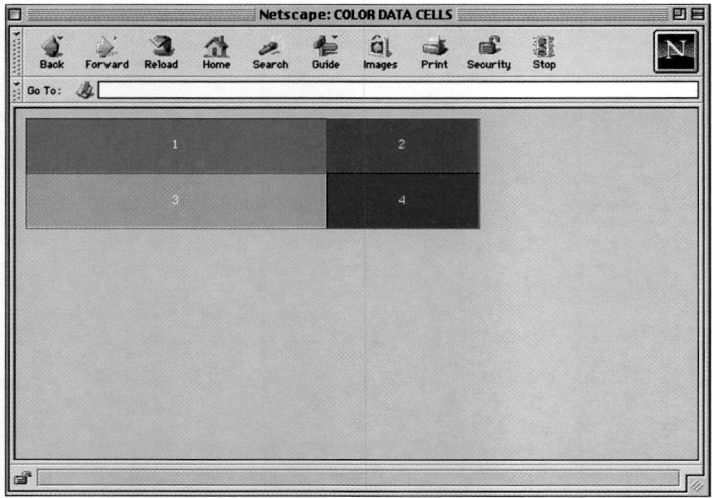

Coloring four table data cells.

Try duplicating the preceding figure image by typing in the following HTML and testing it on your browser:

1 Start your HTML:

```
<HTML>
<HEAD>
<TITLE>COLOR DATA CELLS</TITLE>
</HEAD>
<BODY BGCOLOR="#FFCC33" TEXT="#FFFFFF">
```

2 Create a 400-pixel wide table, setting the border to visible (1) so that you can see your results more clearly:

```
<TABLE WIDTH=400 CELLPADDING=0 CELLSPACING=0 BORDER=1>
<TR>
```

3 Add color to your table data cells by using the BGCOLOR attribute (make sure to specify browser-safe colors); experiment with different color combinations:

```
<TD WIDTH=200 BGCOLOR="#CC0033" HEIGHT=50 ALIGN=CENTER>1</TD>
<TD WIDTH=100 BGCOLOR="#990099F" HEIGHT=50 ALIGN=CENTER>2</TD>
</TR>
<TR>
<TD WIDTH=200 BGCOLOR="#FF9933" HEIGHT=50 ALIGN=CENTER>3</TD>
<TD WIDTH=100 BGCOLOR="#000066" HEIGHT=50 ALIGN=CENTER>4</TD>
</TR>
```

4 End your <TABLE>, <BODY>, and <HTML> tags:

```
</TABLE>
</BODY>
</HTML>
```

Notice how quickly the page displays. You can color table data cells to achieve many ends—the first of which can be to get your visitor's attention. Here's some code that accomplishes this task, as illustrated in the following figure:

```
<HTML>
<HEAD>
<TITLE>COLOR DATA CELLS</TITLE>
</HEAD>
<BODY BGCOLOR="#000000" TEXT="#FFFFFF">
<TABLE WIDTH=400 CELLPADDING=0 CELLSPACING=0 BORDER=0>
<TR>
```

```
<TD WIDTH=95></TD>

<TD WIDTH=5></TD>

<TD WIDTH=200><H1>Check this out</H1>Getting your audience's atten-
tion is as easy as coloring a table data cell. No matter how much
text you have in your page, you can easily draw your user's eye to a
specific section by using the power of color. Getting your audience's
attention is as easy as coloring a table data cell. No matter how
much text you have in your page, you can easily draw your user's eye
to a specific section by using the power of color. Getting your
audience's attention is as easy as coloring a table data cell. No
matter how much text you have in your page, you can easily draw your
user's eye to a specific section by using the power of color.
Getting your audience's attention is as easy as coloring a table
data cell. No matter how much text you have in your page, you can
easily draw your user's eye to a specific section by using the power
of color.</TD>

</TR>

<TR>

<TD BGCOLOR="#FFCC33" ALIGN=RIGHT WIDTH=95><FONT COLOR="#000000">Hey,
take a look at this.<BR>I knew you would. :-)</FONT></TD>

<TD WIDTH=5></TD>

<TD WIDTH=200>Getting your audience's attention is as easy as color-
ing a table data cell. No matter how much text you have in your
page, you can easily draw your user's eye to a specific section by
using the power of color.</TD>

</TR>

</TABLE>

</BODY>

</HTML>
```

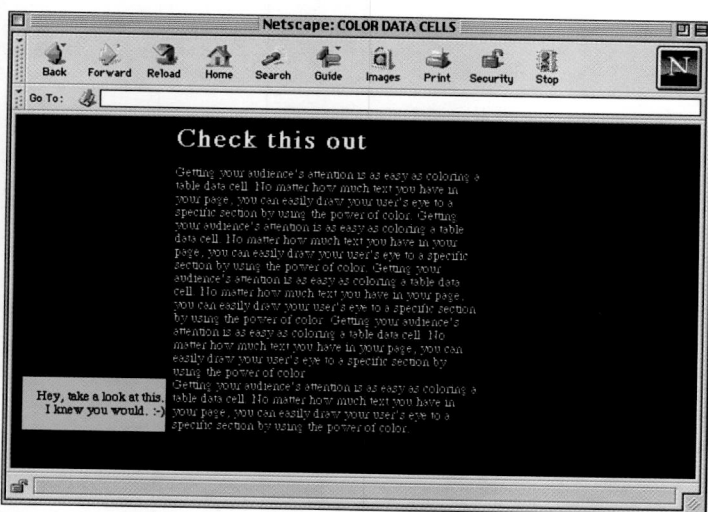

Color table data cells to attract your viewer's attention.

As you can see, color demands attention. When used sparingly and strategically, coloring data cells can quickly get your viewer's attention and get you the clicks you need.

Speed Up Image Loading

When designing GIF images with solid backgrounds, you can shave some bytes off your final image by saving your file as a transparent GIF and specifying your image's background as transparent.

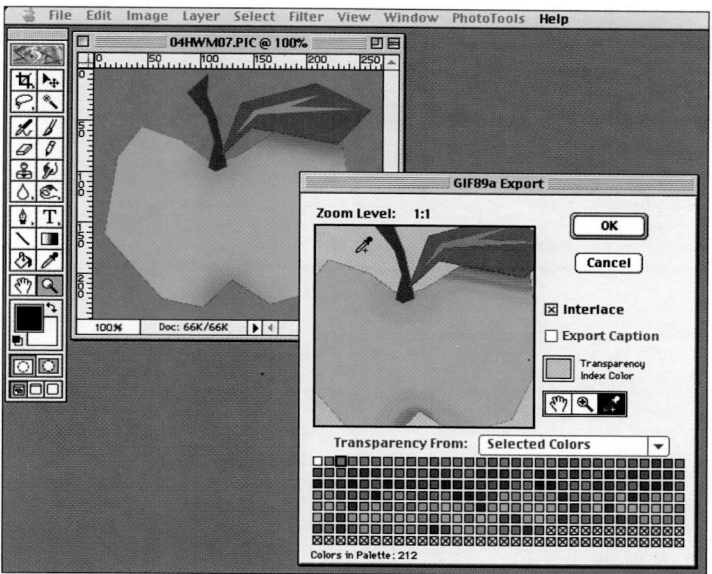

Specifying the image background as transparent in Photoshop.

Next, place the image within a colored data cell (specify your original image's background color for your table data cell background).

123

As you can see in the following figure, the image seamlessly sits within the table data cell and loads more quickly than if it had been saved with a solid background.

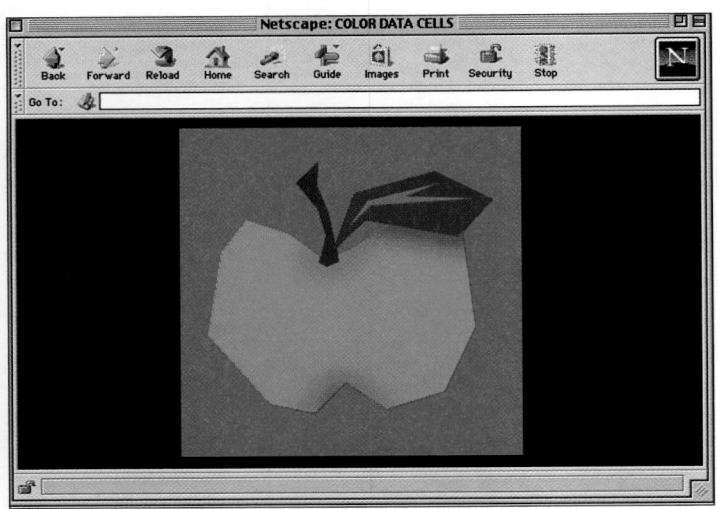

The table data cell color matches the image's original background color perfectly.

Please keep in mind that the filesize savings is much more substantial with large images that use solid backgrounds than with tiny GIF images. For example, you can now make the background in the preceding image as large as you like without affecting the size of the GIF image or hindering load-time.

Here's the code used to achieve the preceding example:

```
<HTML>
<HEAD>
<TITLE>COLOR DATA CELLS</TITLE>
</HEAD>
<BODY BGCOLOR="#000000" TEXT="#FFFFFF">
<CENTER>
<TABLE WIDTH=300 CELLPADDING=0 CELLSPACING=0 BORDER=0>
<TR>
<TD WIDTH=300 HEIGHT=300 VALIGN=CENTER ALIGN=CENTER
BGCOLOR="#CC3300"><IMG WIDTH=272 HEIGHT=246 SRC=apple.gif></TD>
</TR>
</TABLE>
</CENTER>
</BODY>
</HTML>
```

Please note that the same Web-safe color (CC3300) was used in the original GIF image as well as the HTML code to ensure consistency. ●

Layer Typography and Images

Use this technique to:

- **Create layering without CSS.** Finally! Layer type over graphics (or type over GIF type) without having to use Cascading Style Sheets.

- **Speed page-load when combined with an animated GIF.** Cut down on those large GIF animation filesizes by animating only a portion of your GIF image and positioning it on top of the larger original.

In HTML, true layering is possible only with Cascading Style Sheets (CSS). However, using the <TD> tag's BACKGROUND property, a GIF image can be specified as a background image on top of which type or other images can be placed, creating a "fake" layering effect. The BACKGROUND property within the <TD> tag is recognized by Microsoft IE 3.0+ and Netscape Navigator 4.0+.

Create Layered Typography

To generate a layered type look, begin with a GIF image that you intend on using as a data cell background.

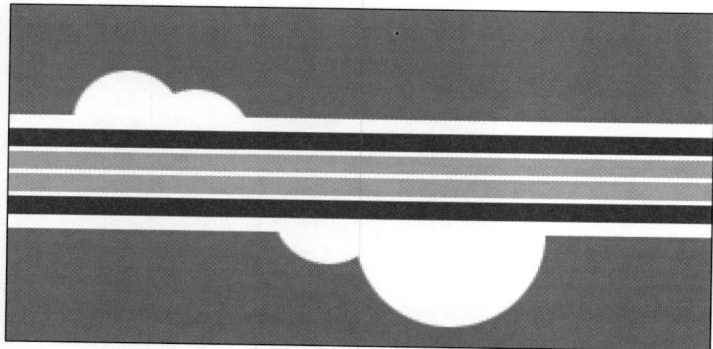

Background image for layering exercise.

The following code establishes the table and data cell:

```
<HTML>
<HEAD>
<TITLE>LAYERING WITH TABLE CELLS</TITLE>
</HEAD>
<BODY BGCOLOR="#000000" TEXT="#000000">
<BR>
<CENTER>
```

```
<TABLE WIDTH=300 CELLPADDING=0 CELLSPACING=0 BORDER=0>
<TR>
<TD WIDTH=300 HEIGHT=150 BACKGROUND="clouds.gif"></TD>
</TR>
</TABLE>
</CENTER>
</BODY>
</HTML>
```

Notice in the following figure that the HTML code does *not* provide the expected result.

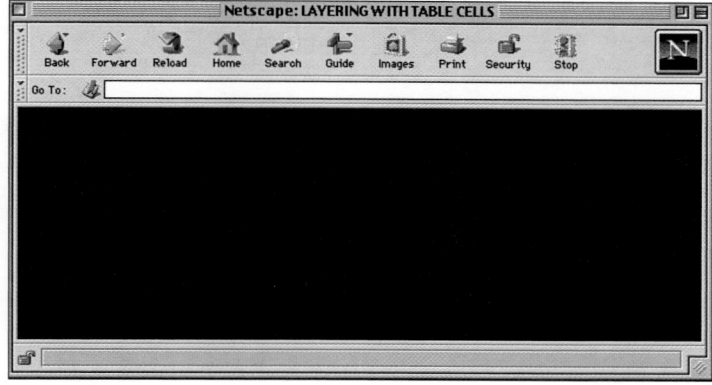

Browser window with no background image due to missing <TD> cell contents.

What can the problem be? Netscape requires some form of data within a <TD> tag in order for it to display background colors or background images. (This is not true for IE.) In this case, the table data cell has "collapsed" and is not visible in the browser. Make the following revision to the preceding code:

```
<TD WIDTH=300 HEIGHT=150 BACKGROUND="clouds.gif"> </TD>
```

By adding a nonbreaking space ( ) to the table data cell, you can force Netscape browsers to fully render your table data cell—avoiding collapse.

An image similar to the following will appear.

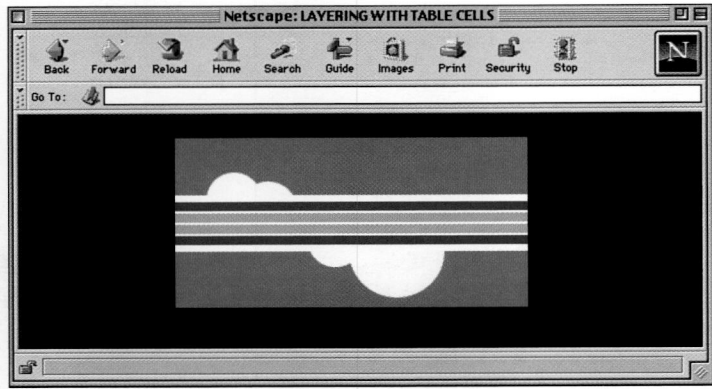

Table data cell background image.

Adding a Layer of Type

The preceding image is ready for a layer of type. To insert your type, simply do so in the same manner that you are used to: Specify your <FONT> attributes and use the <PRE> tag:

```
<PRE><FONT FACE="VERDANA, ARIAL, HELVETICA" SIZE=3
COLOR="#FFFFFF">Some type goes here.</FONT></PRE>
```

The preceding test demonstrates that layering is in fact taking place. Try the following code for yourself to obtain results similar to the following figure:

```
<HTML>
<HEAD>
<TITLE>LAYERING WITH TABLE CELLS</TITLE>
</HEAD>
<BODY BGCOLOR="#000000" TEXT="#000000">
<BR>
<CENTER>
<TABLE WIDTH=300 CELLPADDING=0 CELLSPACING=0 BORDER=0>
<TR>
<TD WIDTH=300 VALIGN=TOP ALIGN=LEFT HEIGHT=150
BACKGROUND="clouds.gif"><FONT FACE="VERDANA" SIZE=2
COLOR="#FFFFFF"><PRE>
<H1>                  Typography</H1>

      in the clouds...what a thrill...</TD>
</TR>
</TABLE>
</CENTER>
</BODY>
</HTML>
```

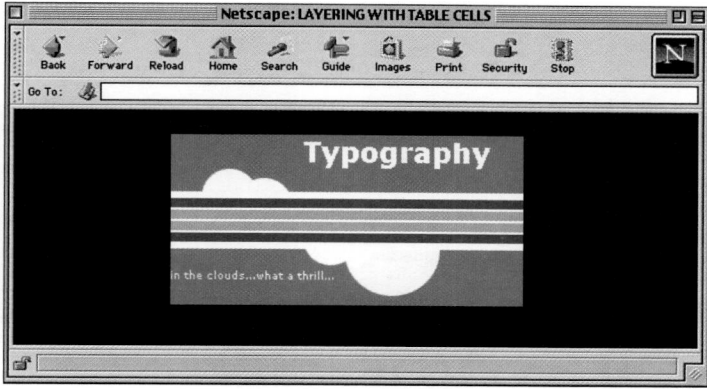

Typographic layering atop an image.

Notice that in the following figure, the cursor is used to highlight the text. The <PRE> tag is used to lay out the type in a preformatter fashion based on the number of spaces and hard returns placed within the HTML.

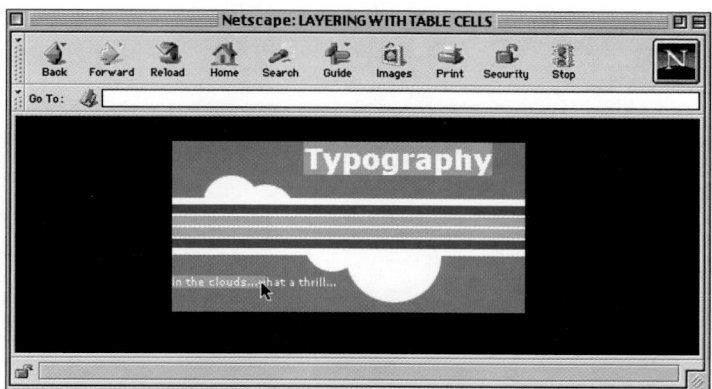

Dragging the cursor across the data cell highlights the type.

You can achieve sophisticated type/image combinations as demonstrated in the following figure with this simple-to-implement technique.

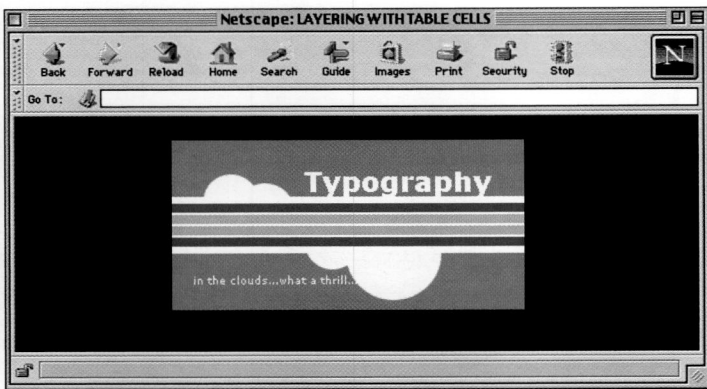

Different variation on layout.

Creating Type-on-Type Layering

The only way to achieve type-on-type layering is to create a GIF image of a word and call it into a <TD> cell as a background image:

```
<TD WIDTH=300 VALIGN=TOP ALIGN=LEFT HEIGHT=150 BACKGROUND="type.gif">
```

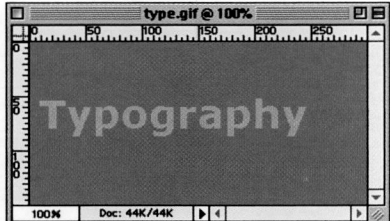

The word "Typography" is saved as a GIF image and specified as a background image within a <TD> cell.

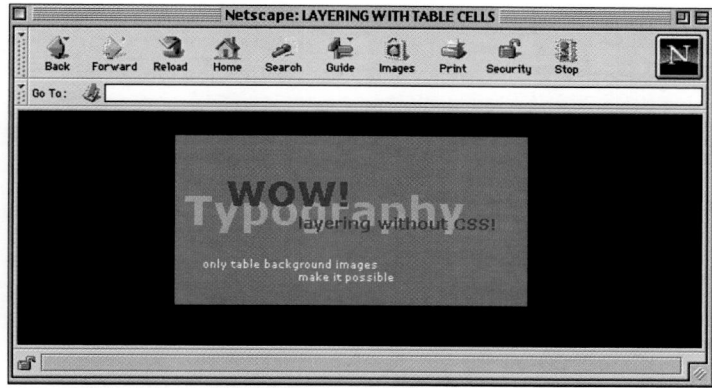

Type on type, achieving "fake" typography layering by using tables.

The following HTML is used to achieve the effect demonstrated in the preceding figure:

```
<HTML>
<HEAD>
<TITLE>LAYERING WITH TABLE CELLS</TITLE>
</HEAD>
<BODY BGCOLOR="#000000" TEXT="#000000">
<BR>
<CENTER>
<TABLE WIDTH=300 CELLPADDING=0 CELLSPACING=0 BORDER=0>
<TR>
<TD WIDTH=300 VALIGN=TOP ALIGN=LEFT HEIGHT=150 BACKGROUND="type.gif"><FONT
FACE="VERDANA" SIZE=2 COLOR="#FFFFFF"><PRE>
<FONT SIZE=7 COLOR="#003399">    <STRONG>WOW!</STRONG></FONT>
<H3>                      <FONT COLOR="#3300FF"> layering without
CSS!</FONT></H3>
        only table background images
                                make it possible</TD>
</TR>
</TABLE>
</CENTER>
</BODY>
</HTML>
```

131

Cropping Animated GIFs

This technique is very effective for animating a small portion of a larger image and optimizing the animation for quick load-times.

An owl with moving eyes.

Begin with your GIF image. Select an area that you want to animate. For this example, you animate the owl's eyes, making its eyeballs scan from left to right. In order to minimize the size of the final animated GIF, select the portion that will be the animation, as demonstrated in the following figure.

The owl's eyes have been selected for animation.

Once you make your selection, invert the selection and delete the rest of the image, coloring the empty space with a shade not found in the image's immediate palette. (For this image, orange was chosen.)

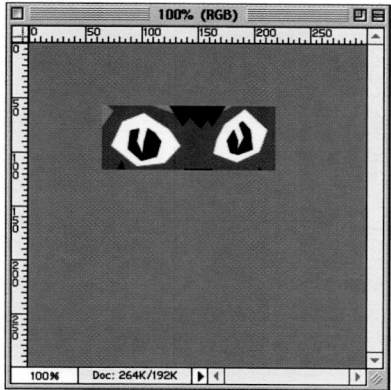

The owl's body has been replaced by a background color that will be knocked out as a transparency.

Next, create your animated GIF, setting the orange color to transparent. This creates a small animated GIF that can be placed within a <TD> cell whose background image you specify as a nonanimated full-image GIF of the owl. The foreground animated eyes sit perfectly on top of the background image, making it appear as though the entire image is the animation. You can accomplish this simply by using the following code when specifying your images:

```
<TD WIDTH=X VALIGN=TOP ALIGN=LEFT HEIGHT=X BACKGROUND="OWL.GIF"><IMG
WIDTH=X HEIGHT=X SRC="EYES.GIF"></TD>
```

In this code, "OWL.GIF" is the background image and "EYES.GIF" is the animated eyes. (Note that both images must have the same overall dimensions for this technique to work properly.) The alternative to using this technique is to slice your image up into sections and place each section of the image within tables to achieve the same effect. To learn how to do this, see the section entitled "Animate a Portion of a Large Image." ●

133

Design Invisible Linking Cells

Use this technique to:

- **Combine multiple images within a table to create the illusion of one solid image.** Gain more control over the placement of objects, text, and images when you "slice up" your large images and place them within borderless tables.

- **Design "fake" image maps.** Create "fake" image maps from sliced-up graphics placed within frames and linked to different sections of your site.

Sometimes image maps are not the most convenient way to lay out a site's navigation. When image map images take too long to load as a large 150K graphic or when they irritate users of nongraphic browsers, you can slice up your images and place them within invisible tables. Adding <A HREF> tags to your individually sliced-up images creates a "fake" image map.

Creating Image Maps

Here's how to create your own image map.

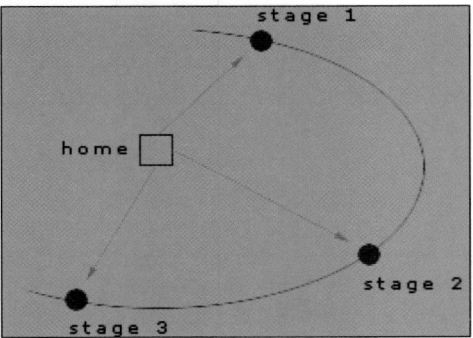

The navigation GIF that will be sliced up.

1 Begin with your GIF navigation, which you will section off for slicing in Adobe Photoshop or Macromedia Fireworks.

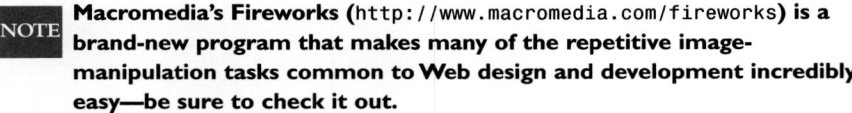

NOTE **Macromedia's Fireworks** (http://www.macromedia.com/fireworks) **is a brand-new program that makes many of the repetitive image-manipulation tasks common to Web design and development incredibly easy—be sure to check it out.**

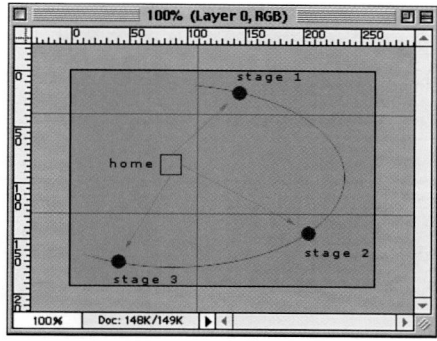

Adobe Photoshop's guides used to select and section off six new images from the original.

2 Section your image into the regions that you will save as separate GIF files, importing them into a table setup as follows. Your particular image heights, widths, and column numbers will vary:

```
<HTML>
<HEAD>
<TITLE>FAKE IMAGE MAPS</TITLE>
</HEAD>
<BODY BGCOLOR="#CCFF33" TEXT="#000000">
<BR>
<CENTER>
```

3 Create a table to house your images, initially setting the border to visible (1) so that you can see what's going on when testing it on your browser:

```
<TABLE WIDTH=262 CELLPADDING=0 CELLSPACING=0 BORDER=1>
```

4 Section your images into table data rows and columns:

```
<TR>
<TD WIDTH=109><IMG SRC="topa.gif" WIDTH=109 HEIGHT=38></TD>
<TD WIDTH=153><IMG SRC="topb.gif" WIDTH=153 HEIGHT=38></TD>
</TR>
<TR>
<TD WIDTH=109><IMG SRC="mida.gif" WIDTH=109 HEIGHT=89></TD>
<TD WIDTH=153><IMG SRC="midb.gif" WIDTH=153 HEIGHT=89></TD>
</TR>
<TR>
<TD WIDTH=109><IMG SRC="bota.gif" WIDTH=109 HEIGHT=65></TD>
<TD WIDTH=153><IMG SRC="botb.gif" WIDTH=153 HEIGHT=65></TD>
</TR>
</TABLE>
</CENTER>
</BODY>
</HTML>
```

The following figure shows what the images look like when placed within a table with borders turned on.

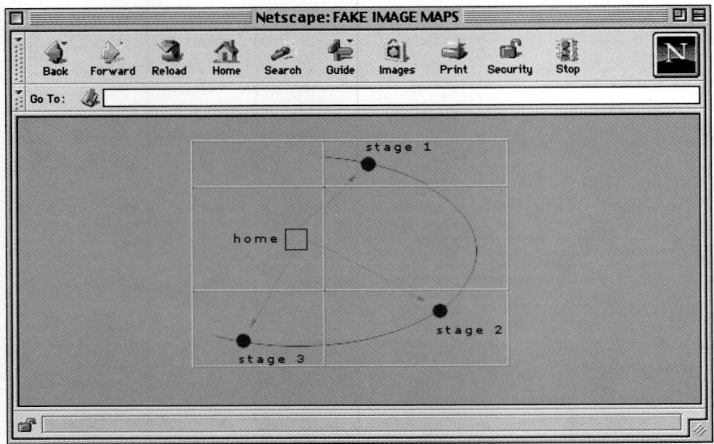

The images have been imported into the table data cells.

5 The next step is to assign <A HREF> tags to the images that will be linked to specific sections within the site. The following HTML shows the result of turning table borders off and adding an <A HREF> tag:

```
<HTML>
<HEAD>
<TITLE>FAKE IMAGE MAPS</TITLE>
</HEAD>
<BODY BGCOLOR="#CCFF33" TEXT="#000000">
<BR>
<CENTER>
```

6 Table borders are turned off (or invisible) by setting them to 0:

```
<TABLE WIDTH=262 CELLPADDING=0 CELLSPACING=0 BORDER=0>
<TR>
<TD WIDTH=109><IMG SRC="topa.gif" WIDTH=109 HEIGHT=38></TD>
```

7 Links are added to images by using <A HREF> tags:

```
<TD WIDTH=153><A HREF="stage1.html" onMouseOver="window.status='go to
stage 1.';return true"><IMG SRC="topb.gif" WIDTH=153
HEIGHT=38></a></TD>
</TR>
<TR>
<TD WIDTH=109><IMG SRC="mida.gif" WIDTH=109 HEIGHT=89></TD>
<TD WIDTH=153><IMG SRC="midb.gif" WIDTH=153 HEIGHT=89></TD>
</TR>
```

```
<TR>
<TD WIDTH=109><IMG SRC="bota.gif" WIDTH=109 HEIGHT=65></TD>
<TD WIDTH=153><IMG SRC="botb.gif" WIDTH=153 HEIGHT=65></TD>
</TR>
</TABLE>
</CENTER>
</BODY>
</HTML>
```

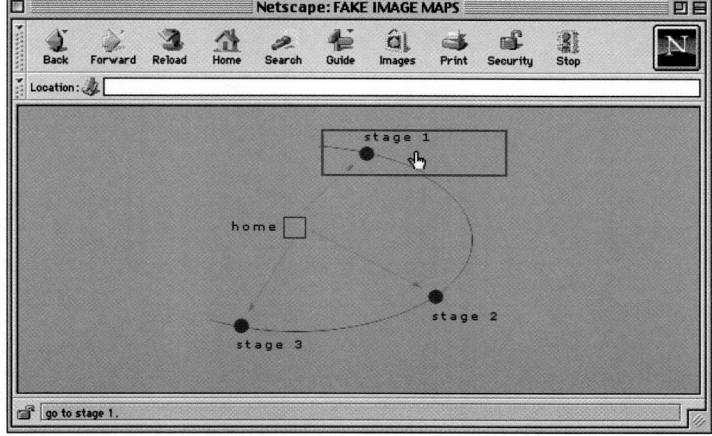

Testing the link.

As you can see in the preceding figure, forgetting to set the BORDER=0 attribute within the <A HREF> tag of the <IMG> link tags renders those ugly link borders around the images, giving away our little secret. Get rid of those borders by setting them to 0.

Here's the following HTML along with the final rendition of the page:

```
<HTML>
<HEAD>
<TITLE>FAKE IMAGE MAPS</TITLE>
</HEAD>
<BODY BGCOLOR="#CCFF33" TEXT="#000000">
<BR>
<CENTER>
<TABLE WIDTH=262 CELLPADDING=0 CELLSPACING=0 BORDER=0>
<TR>
<TD WIDTH=109><IMG SRC="topa.gif" WIDTH=109 HEIGHT=38></TD>
<TD WIDTH=153><A HREF="stage1.html" onMouseOver="window.status='go to stage
1.';return true"><IMG SRC="topb.gif" WIDTH=153 HEIGHT=38 BORDER=0></a></TD>
</TR>
<TR>
```

```
<TD WIDTH=109><A HREF="home.html" onMouseOver="window.status='go to
home.';return true"><IMG SRC="mida.gif" WIDTH=109 HEIGHT=89 BOR-
DER=0></A></TD>
<TD WIDTH=153><IMG SRC="midb.gif" WIDTH=153 HEIGHT=89></TD>
</TR>
<TR>
<TD WIDTH=109><A HREF="stage3.html" onMouseOver="window.status='go to
stage 3.';return true"><IMG SRC="bota.gif" WIDTH=109 HEIGHT=65 BOR-
DER=0></A></TD>
<TD WIDTH=153><A HREF="stage2.html" onMouseOver="window.status='go to
stage 2.';return true"><IMG SRC="botb.gif" WIDTH=153 HEIGHT=65 BOR-
DER=0></A></TD>
</TR>
</TABLE>
</CENTER>
</BODY>
</HTML>
```

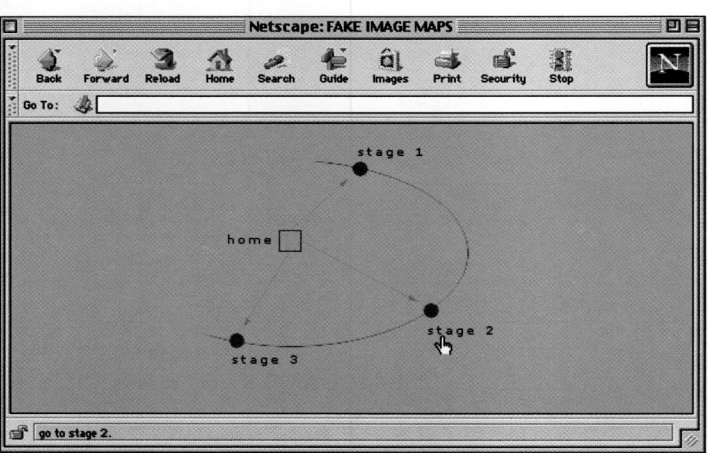

Borders set to 0—this is our final fake image map.

This technique is much more prevalent in Web design today simply because it
offers the flexibility of tables—enabling the designer to integrate the navigation
into other environments, mixing and matching HTML text within the table if so
desired. ●

Align Images and Text

Use this technique to:

- **Enhance the page's overall layout.** Use the structural attributes of tables to enhance your page and create more attractive layouts.

- **Lead the viewer's eye through the page.** By aligning images and text within structured table data cells and rows, you can create an attractive, organized means of information delivery.

- **Experiment with layout variations.** Tables offer the flexibility of a structural "shell" that can be used to test different layouts.

Tables are not only excellent structural tools, but they also function as perfect alignment tools that help designers elegantly lay out text, images, and other data.

Creating a Table

To properly align your text, begin with creating a table, and creating columns for the text and images, while keeping in mind a series of "gutters" to separate columns so that their contents don't run too close to one another.

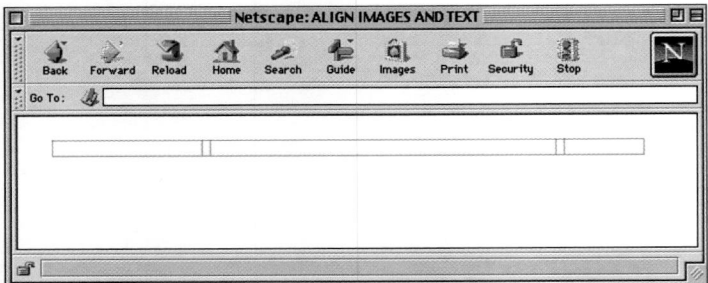

A 3-column, 2-gutter table.

Duplicate the table, creating three identical structures.

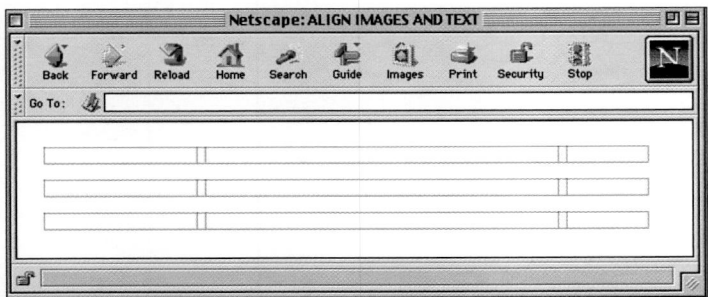

Three identical tables.

Modify your HTML to match the following code:

1 Begin your HTML as you normally would:

```
<HTML>
<HEAD>
<TITLE>ALIGN IMAGES AND TEXT</TITLE>
</HEAD>
<BODY BGCOLOR="#FFFFFF" TEXT="#000000">
<BR>
```

2 Center your page's content:

```
<CENTER>
```

3 Create your first table (500-pixels wide) and set the border visibility to 1 (or visible):

```
<TABLE WIDTH=500 CELLPADDING=0 CELLSPACING=0 BORDER=1>
<TR>
<TD WIDTH=125 BGCOLOR="#990000" VALIGN=TOP ALIGN=RIGHT><FONT FACE="ARIAL"
COLOR="#FFFFFF" SIZE=3><STRONG>Notes: </STRONG></FONT></TD>
<TD WIDTH=5> </TD>
<TD WIDTH=300 VALIGN=TOP ALIGN=LEFT><FONT FACE="ARIAL" COLOR="#999999">
Here are some notes that I have put together to serve as a demonstration
for this web design technique.</FONT></TD>
<TD WIDTH=5> </TD>
<TD WIDTH=65> </TD>
</TR>
</TABLE>
```

4 Create your second table; be sure to fill in empty table data cells with nonbreaking spaces ( ) so that they do not collapse on Netscape browsers:

```
<TABLE WIDTH=500 CELLPADDING=0 CELLSPACING=0 BORDER=1>
<TR>
<TD WIDTH=125> </TD>
<TD WIDTH=5> </TD>
<TD WIDTH=300> </TD>
<TD WIDTH=5> </TD>
<TD WIDTH=65> </TD>
</TR>
</TABLE>
```

5 Create your third table:

```
<TABLE WIDTH=500 CELLPADDING=0 CELLSPACING=0 BORDER=1>
<TR>
<TD WIDTH=125> </TD>
<TD WIDTH=5> </TD>
```

```
<TD WIDTH=300> </TD>
<TD WIDTH=5> </TD>
<TD WIDTH=65> </TD>
</TR>
</TABLE>
```

6 Finish centering your page's content and end your HTML:

```
</CENTER>
</BODY>
</HTML>
```

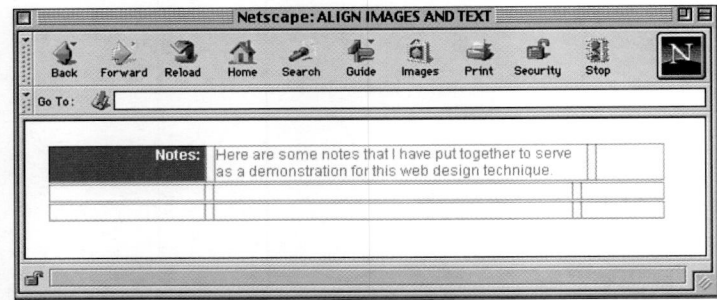

Notice the table "collapse" in the third column of the first row.

Adding a Spacer GIF

In the preceding HTML, something is missing. A spacer GIF would fix the apparent `<TD>` cell collapse occurring in the third column of the first row. Spacer GIFs help maintain the `<TD>` width so that no other cells can impede upon it. Notice the following HTML, where the `"spacer.gif"` file has been added:

```
<TABLE WIDTH=500 CELLPADDING=0 CELLSPACING=0 BORDER=1>
<TR>
<TD WIDTH=125 BGCOLOR="#990000" VALIGN=TOP ALIGN=RIGHT>
<FONT FACE="ARIAL" COLOR="#FFFFFF" SIZE=3>
<STRONG>Notes: </STRONG></FONT></TD>
<TD WIDTH=5> </TD>
<TD WIDTH=300 VALIGN=TOP ALIGN=LEFT><FONT FACE="ARIAL"
COLOR="#999999">Here are some notes that I have put together to serve
as a demonstration for this web design technique.</FONT></TD>
<TD WIDTH=5> </TD>
<TD WIDTH=65><IMG SRC="spacer.gif" WIDTH=1 HEIGHT=1 VSPACE=5
HSPACE=32></TD>
</TR>
```

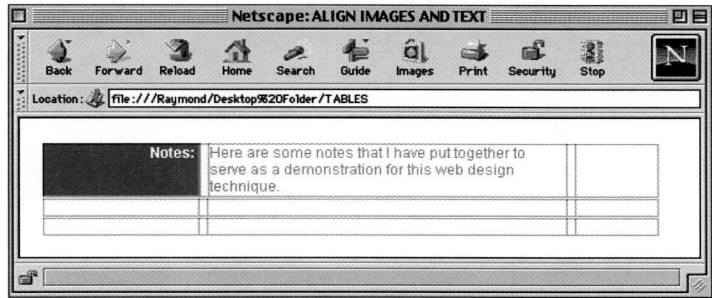

Table data cell collapse fixed with the placement of a spacer GIF.

Adding More Data to the Table

As more data is added to the table, a need arises to align the next paragraph of text with an image in the left column. How can we ensure that the text lines up perfectly with the image we place within another column? Easy—begin both in an entirely new table, keeping the look and feel of the first table consistent so that the average viewer cannot tell that we changed tables—nor will it matter if it's done transparently.

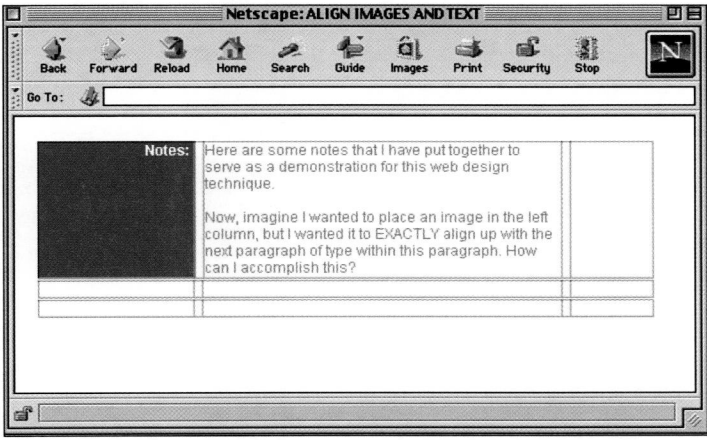

143

More data is added to the table.

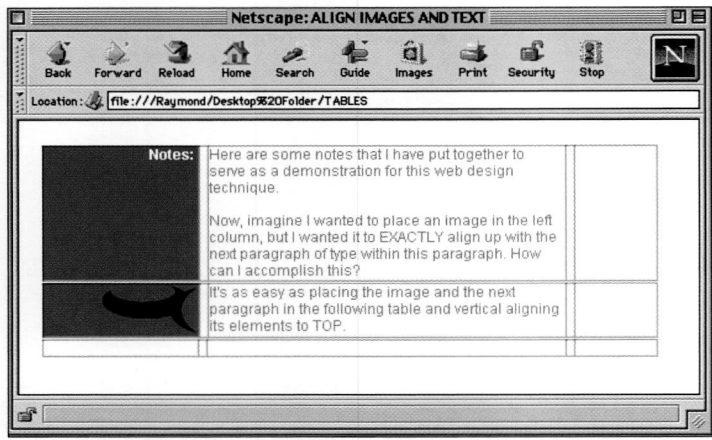

New paragraph aligned with an image in the left column.

Creating Space

The preceding figure demonstrates a perfect alignment of the next paragraph of type with an image in the left column. However, we need to create space between the last paragraph and the new one. This is accomplished by adding an entire table between the old and new tables, to keep the look and feel consistent once again.

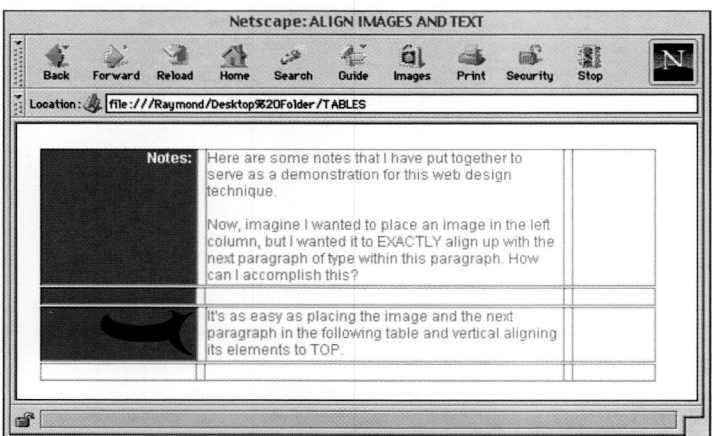

Space added between the tables to maintain white space consistency.

Finishing the Page

Lastly, we will add a copyright notice and create an entirely black table at the bottom of the data to contain and section the work off, symbolizing a visual end to the page.

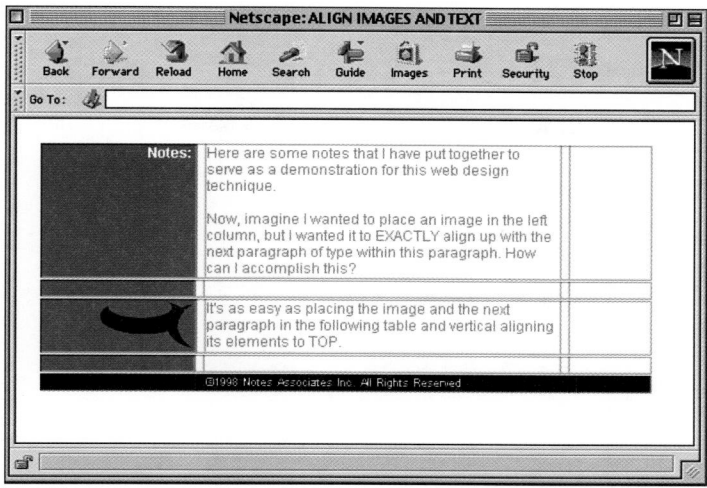

Black bar is added at the bottom.

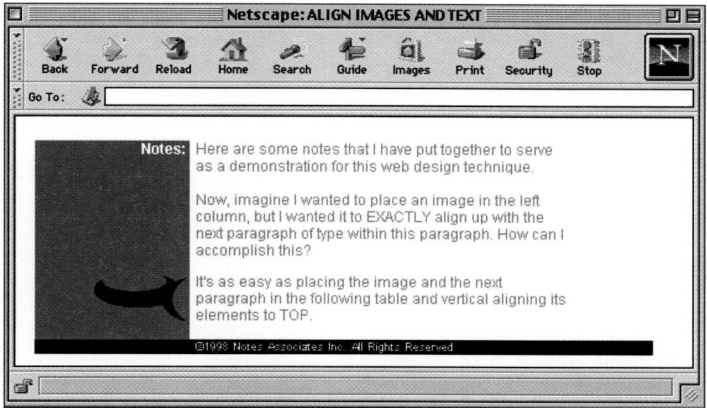

Black bar is added at the bottom and borders are turned off.

Here is the final HTML code, based on the preceding figure and the HTML introduced earlier:

```
<HTML>
<HEAD>
<TITLE>ALIGN IMAGES AND TEXT</TITLE>
</HEAD>
<BODY BGCOLOR="#FFFFFF" TEXT="#000000">
<BR>
<CENTER>
```

1 Turn borders off (or set them to invisible) by specifying 0 instead of 1:

```
<TABLE WIDTH=500 CELLPADDING=0 CELLSPACING=0 BORDER=0>
```

2 Fill your table data cells with content and test out the resulting page on your browser:

```
<TR>
<TD WIDTH=125 BGCOLOR="#990000" VALIGN=TOP ALIGN=RIGHT>
<FONT FACE="ARIAL" COLOR="#FFFFFF" SIZE=3>
<STRONG>Notes: </STRONG></FONT></TD>

<TD WIDTH=5> </TD>

<TD WIDTH=300 VALIGN=TOP ALIGN=LEFT><FONT FACE="ARIAL"
COLOR="#999999">

Here are some notes that I have put together to serve as a
demonstration for this web design technique.<BR><BR>Now, imagine I
wanted to place an image in the left column, but I wanted it to
EXACTLY align up with the next paragraph of type within this
paragraph. How can I accomplish this?

</FONT></TD>

<TD WIDTH=5> </TD>

<TD WIDTH=65><IMG SRC="spacer.gif" WIDTH=1 HEIGHT=1 VSPACE=5
HSPACE=32></TD>

</TR>
</TABLE>
<TABLE WIDTH=500 CELLPADDING=0 CELLSPACING=0 BORDER=0>
<TR>
<TD WIDTH=125 BGCOLOR="#990000"> </TD>

<TD WIDTH=5> </TD>

<TD WIDTH=300> </TD>

<TD WIDTH=5> </TD>

<TD WIDTH=65> </TD>

</TR>
</TABLE>
<TABLE WIDTH=500 CELLPADDING=0 CELLSPACING=0 BORDER=0>
<TR>
```

3 Notice that the table data cell background colors (BGCOLOR) are coded consistently between table data rows to maintain a unified look between all tables:

```
<TD WIDTH=125 BGCOLOR="#990000" VALIGN=TOP ALIGN=RIGHT><IMG
SRC="image.gif" WIDTH=79 HEIGHT=43></TD>

<TD WIDTH=5> </TD>

<TD WIDTH=300 VALIGN=TOP ALIGN=LEFT><FONT FACE="ARIAL"
COLOR="#999999">

It's as easy as placing the image and the next paragraph in the fol-
lowing table and vertical aligning its elements to TOP.

</FONT></TD>

<TD WIDTH=5> </TD>
```

```
<TD WIDTH=65><IMG SRC="spacer.gif" WIDTH=1 HEIGHT=1 VSPACE=5
HSPACE=32></TD>
</TR>
</TABLE>
<TABLE WIDTH=500 CELLPADDING=0 CELLSPACING=0 BORDER=0>
<TR>
<TD WIDTH=125 BGCOLOR="#990000"> </TD>
<TD WIDTH=5> </TD>
<TD WIDTH=300> </TD>
<TD WIDTH=5> </TD>
<TD WIDTH=65> </TD>
</TR>
</TABLE>
<TABLE WIDTH=500 CELLPADDING=0 CELLSPACING=0 BORDER=0>
<TR>
<TD WIDTH=125 BGCOLOR="#000000"><IMG SRC="spacer.gif" WIDTH=1 HEIGHT=1
VSPACE=5 HSPACE=62></TD>
<TD WIDTH=5 BGCOLOR="#000000"> </TD>
<TD WIDTH=300 BGCOLOR="#000000"><FONT FACE="ARIAL" COLOR="#FFFFFF"
SIZE=1>©1998 Notes Associates Inc. All Rights Reserved</FONT></TD>
<TD WIDTH=5 BGCOLOR="#000000"> </TD>
<TD WIDTH=65 BGCOLOR="#000000"> </TD>
</TR>
</TABLE>
</CENTER>
</BODY>
</HTML>
```

Tables have offered an unprecedented amount of flexibility and design freedom for the Web developer and will continue to do so until the next "great" technology emerges. ●

147

Create Nested Tables

Use this technique to:

- **Achieve full control of image and type placement.** By placing tables within tables (referred to as "nesting"), you can create structured "pockets" of information within your table cells—great for callout boxes.

- **Create a multi-column bordered structure.** Design borders by combining background-colored data cells and nested tables.

Nesting tables basically refers to the act of placing a table within another table. When nesting tables, place the new table within the <TD></TD> tags of another table. This way you can nest tables within tables within tables.

Be warned, however, that nesting tables can cause major delays in the display of your page. Many browsers do not display the page until all the table data is loaded and the end of the table tag is reached as the browser scans the page HTML. Pages containing severely nested tables can take forever to load. You should test any pages in which you nest tables with a 28.8 modem to see the impact (if any) the technique poses to your site.

Creating a Simple Nested Table

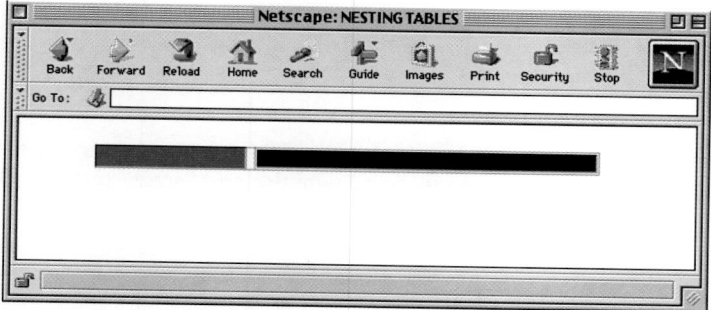

A simple nested table within the third column of the main table.

You can create the nesting example in the preceding figure with the following HTML:

1 Begin your HTML as you normally would:

```
<HTML>
<HEAD>
```

```
<TITLE>NESTING TABLES</TITLE>
</HEAD>
<BODY BGCOLOR="#FFFFFF" TEXT="#000000">
<BR>
```

2 Center your page's content by using the <CENTER> tag:

```
<CENTER>
```

3 Create a 400-pixel-wide table with a border of 1 so you can see how it looks on the page (later you can eliminate the border by setting it back to 0):

```
<TABLE WIDTH=400 CELLPADDING=0 CELLSPACING=0 BORDER=1>
<TR>
```

4 Create colored table data cells (remember to place a nonbreaking space or spacer GIF within the cells that are to remain blank):

```
<TD WIDTH=125 BGCOLOR="#990000"> </TD>
<TD WIDTH=5> </TD>
```

5 Nest a table within the third column (simply create an entire new table by using the <TABLE> tag):

```
<TD WIDTH=270><TABLE WIDTH=270 CELLPADDING=0 CELLSPACING=0 BORDER=1>
  <TR>
  <TD WIDTH=270 BGCOLOR="#000000"> </TD>
  </TR>
```

6 Be sure to *close* your new table tag when you're done nesting the table:

```
  </TABLE>
</TD>
</TR>
```

7 Close your original table:

```
</TABLE>
```

8 End your HTML as you normally would:

```
</CENTER>
</BODY>
</HTML>
```

149

Creating Multiple Nested Tables

Try the following HTML code as an exercise in creating multiple nested tables, starting with simple and moving to more complex:

1 Begin your HTML as you normally would:

```
<HTML>
<HEAD>
<TITLE>NESTING TABLES</TITLE>
</HEAD>
<BODY BGCOLOR="#FFFFFF" TEXT="#000000">
<BR>
```

2 Center your page's content:

```
<CENTER>
```

3 Create your first table (400 pixels wide, with borders set to 1 so that you can see what's going on when the page is previewed in your browser):

```
<TABLE WIDTH=400 CELLPADDING=0 CELLSPACING=0 BORDER=1>
```

4 Create some content within your master table, breaking it up into table data cells:

```
<TR>
<TD WIDTH=125 BGCOLOR="#990000"> </TD>
<TD WIDTH=5> </TD>
```

5 Nest your first table within the third column (you can experiment by nesting your table within another column):

```
<TD WIDTH=270><TABLE WIDTH=270 CELLPADDING=0 CELLSPACING=0 BORDER=1>
    <TR>
    <TD WIDTH=270 BGCOLOR="#000000"> </TD>
    </TR>
```

6 Close your first nested table and move on:

```
    </TABLE>
</TD>
</TR>
```

7 Close your initial table:

```
</TABLE>
```

8 Create a space between your first table and the second by placing a <BR> tag between the two (otherwise, they stick together):

```
<BR>
```

9 Begin a second table, almost identical to the one above it (this time, experimenting with multiple table data cells with differing background color schemes within the nested table):

```
<TABLE WIDTH=400 CELLPADDING=0 CELLSPACING=0 BORDER=1>
<TR>
<TD WIDTH=125 BGCOLOR="#990000"> </TD>
<TD WIDTH=5> </TD>
```

10 Nest your new table within the third column of your main table:

```
<TD WIDTH=270><TABLE WIDTH=270 CELLPADDING=0 CELLSPACING=0 BORDER=1>
```

11 Create two table data cells within this nested table, altering their background colors:

```
    <TR>
    <TD WIDTH=135 BGCOLOR="#00CC00"> </TD>
    <TD WIDTH=135 BGCOLOR="#CC0033"> </TD>
    </TR>
```

12 Close your nested table:

```
    </TABLE>
</TD>
</TR>
```

13 Close your main table:

```
</TABLE>
<BR>
```

14 Begin your third and last table, again setting the width to 400 pixels and its border to 1.

```
<TABLE WIDTH=400 CELLPADDING=0 CELLSPACING=0 BORDER=1>
<TR>
<TD WIDTH=125 BGCOLOR="#990000"> </TD>
<TD WIDTH=5> </TD>
```

15 This time, when you create your nested table, create two rows of table data cells with varying background colors. Do you see how this kind of layout can enable you to position text and images within a single table?

```
<TD WIDTH=270><TABLE WIDTH=270 CELLPADDING=0 CELLSPACING=0 BORDER=1>
    <TR>
    <TD WIDTH=135 BGCOLOR="#00CC00"> </TD>
    <TD WIDTH=135 BGCOLOR="#CC0033"> </TD>
    </TR>
    <TR>
    <TD WIDTH=135 BGCOLOR="#006699"> </TD>
    <TD WIDTH=135 BGCOLOR="#CCCC00"> </TD>
    </TR>
```

16 Close your nested table:

```
    </TABLE>
</TD>
</TR>
```

17 Close your main table:

```
</TABLE>
```

18 Finish centering your page's contents:

```
</CENTER>
```

19 End your HTML:

```
</BODY>
</HTML>
```

The preceding code yields the following when run in your browser:

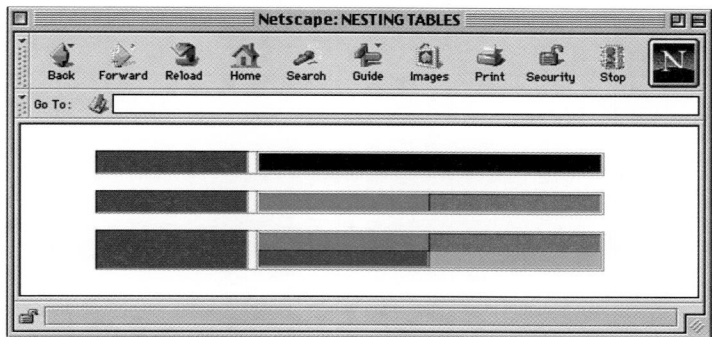

Multiple nested tables exercise.

Controlling Type Placement and Flow

Use nested tables to create a template with the capability to fully control typographic layout. Begin with the following code, which yields the table seen in the following figure:

```
<HTML>
<HEAD>
<TITLE>NESTING TABLES</TITLE>
</HEAD>
<BODY BGCOLOR="#FFFFFF" TEXT="#000000">
<BR>
<CENTER>
<TABLE WIDTH=400 CELLPADDING=5 CELLSPACING=0 BORDER=1>
<TR>
<TD WIDTH=125 BGCOLOR="#990000"> </TD>
<TD WIDTH=5 BGCOLOR="#990000"> </TD>
```

153

```
<TD WIDTH=270 BGCOLOR="#000000"><TABLE WIDTH=270 CELLPADDING=0
CELLSPACING=0 BORDER=1>
    <TR>
    <TD WIDTH=270 COLSPAN=2 BGCOLOR="#000000"> </TD>
    </TR>
    <TR>
    <TD WIDTH=135 BGCOLOR="#FFCC33"> </TD>
    <TD WIDTH=135 BGCOLOR="#000000"> </TD>
    </TR>
    </TABLE>
</TD>
</TR>
</TABLE>
</CENTER>
</BODY>
</HTML>
```

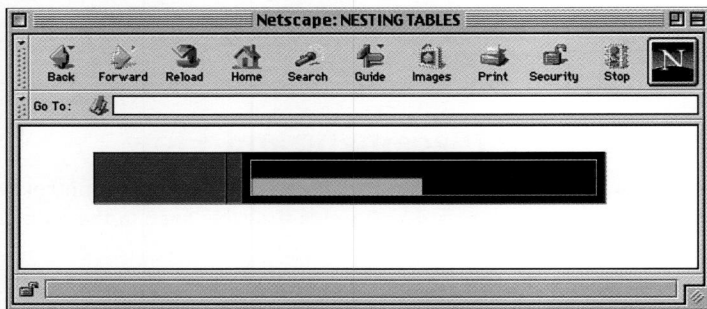

Nesting table data cells to control type flow.

Next, set the background to black and eliminate browser offset by setting your MARGINWIDTH, MARGINHEIGHT, LEFTMARGIN, and TOPMARGIN <BODY> attributes to 0. Although the preceding only works on 4.0 browsers, it's the only way to truly eliminate browser offset and achieve this effect. The following code yields the effect shown in the following figure:

```
<HTML>
<HEAD>
<TITLE>NESTING TABLES</TITLE>
</HEAD>
<BODY MARGINWIDTH=0 MARGINHEIGHT=0 LEFTMARGIN=0 TOPMARGIN=0
BGCOLOR="#000000" TEXT="#FFFFFF">
<TABLE WIDTH=400 CELLPADDING=5 CELLSPACING=0 BORDER=1>
<TR>
```

```
<TD WIDTH=125 BGCOLOR="#990000"> </TD>
<TD WIDTH=5 BGCOLOR="#990000"> </TD>
<TD WIDTH=270 BGCOLOR="#000000"><TABLE WIDTH=270 CELLPADDING=0
CELLSPACING=0 BORDER=1>
    <TR>
    <TD WIDTH=270 COLSPAN=2 BGCOLOR="#000000"> </TD>
    </TR>
    <TR>
    <TD WIDTH=135 BGCOLOR="#FFCC33"> </TD>
    <TD WIDTH=135 BGCOLOR="#000000"> </TD>
    </TR>
    </TABLE>
</TD>
</TR>
</TABLE>
</BODY>
</HTML>
```

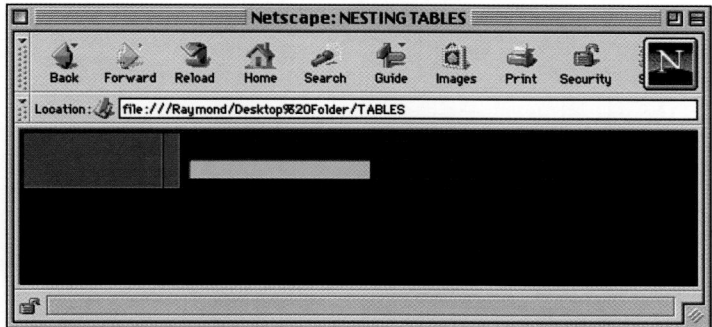

Eliminating browser offset.

Creating a Bordered Structure

Modifying the previous HTML code slightly, insert the body copy and create a border
around the table containing text (using the <TD> BGCOLOR attribute):

```
<HTML>
<HEAD>
<TITLE>NESTING TABLES</TITLE>
</HEAD>
<BODY MARGINWIDTH=0 MARGINHEIGHT=0 LEFTMARGIN=0 TOPMARGIN=0
BGCOLOR="#000000" TEXT="#FFFFFF">
```

```
<TABLE WIDTH=450 CELLPADDING=0 CELLSPACING=0 BORDER=0>
<TR>
<TD WIDTH=125 VALIGN=TOP BGCOLOR="#990000"><FONT FACE="VERDANA"
COLOR="#FFCC33" SIZE=5><STRONG>   HOT<BR>
      gossip</FONT></STRONG></TD>
<TD WIDTH=275 BGCOLOR="#000000"><TABLE WIDTH=270 CELLPADDING=0
CELLSPACING=5 BORDER=0>
    <TR>
    <TD WIDTH=275 COLSPAN=3 BGCOLOR="#000000"><FONT FACE="VERDANA"
SIZE=2>
Imagine a body of text that features the hottest gossip about the
web and those who build it. Now imagine having to read through all
of it just to get to the meaty, juicy stuff that you're dying for -
only to be bored with useless rhetoric and unintelligible lingo.
<BR> </FONT></TD>
    </TR>
    <TR>
    <TD WIDTH=132 ALIGN=CENTER BGCOLOR="#FFCC33"><FONT FACE="VERDANA"
COLOR="#000000" SIZE=4><I>"Here's what<BR>you need<BR>to
know!"</I></FONT></TD>
    <TD WIDTH=3 BGCOLOR="#000000"> </TD>
    <TD WIDTH=140 BGCOLOR="#000000"><FONT FACE="VERDANA" SIZE=2>
Thanks to the thoughtful designers of this little online "gossip"
rag, all you have to do is check out the call-out box to the left
for the latest hot scoop without having to read all of this boring
text.
</FONT></TD>
    </TR>
    </TABLE>
</TD>
<TD WIDTH=50 BGCOLOR="#990000"> </TD>
</TR>
<TR>
<TD WIDTH=125 BGCOLOR="#990000"> </TD>
<TD WIDTH=275 BGCOLOR="#990000"> </TD>
<TD WIDTH=50 BGCOLOR="#990000"> </TD>
</TR>
</TABLE>
</BODY>
</HTML>
```

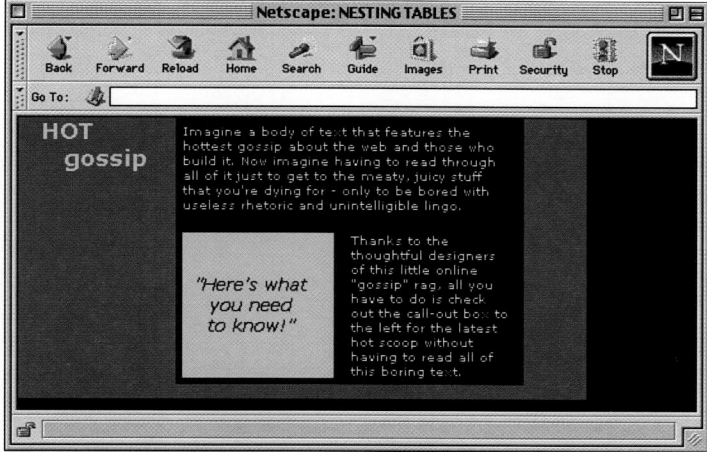

Final nested table with the text callout example.

As you can see in the preceding figure, if used in moderation, nested tables within data cells can be an effective means of laying out text with the capability to control background color for specific callout text. ●

Resize Tables Dynamically

Use this technique to:

- **Automatically respond as the viewer resizes the browser window.** You can create tables that dynamically scale up or down, based on user demand, fully utilizing the real estate on your screen.

- **Please your viewers.** Whether accessing your site at 640×480 or 1024×768, your viewers will not miss a pixel if you deliver dynamic pages that resize to suit most platforms and screen sizes—including TV.

Using Percentages

The secret to creating dynamically responsive tables is to use percentages instead of fixed pixel widths for table- and data-cell widths.

In the HTML that follows, note the percentages and how they are used. Giving a table a 100 percent width gives it the same width as the current browser width. Therefore, if the browser window is made larger or smaller, the table reacts accordingly. The only way this technique will work throughout is if it is incorporated consistently throughout your tables and data cells. Every width must be specified in relative percentages.

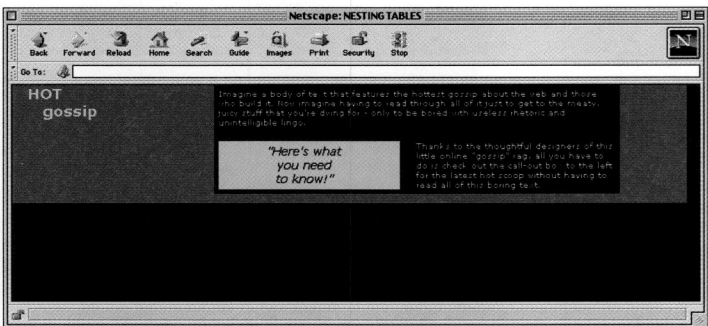

A fully stretched-out browser window with a dynamically responsive table.

Code the following HTML and test it in your browser. Will you achieve a similar result to that presented in the preceding figure?

1 Begin your HTML as you normally would:

```
<HTML>
<HEAD>
<TITLE>NESTING TABLES</TITLE>
</HEAD>
```

2 Try to eliminate browser offset for those on 4.0 or better browsers by adding the MARGINWIDTH/HEIGHT and LEFT/TOP MARGIN attributes within your <BODY> tag (this additional code is ignored by older browsers):

```
<BODY MARGINWIDTH=0 MARGINHEIGHT=0 LEFTMARGIN=0 TOPMARGIN=0
BGCOLOR="#000000" TEXT="#FFFFFF">
```

3 Create a table and, instead of setting a pixel width, set a width of 100 percent, which makes the table as wide as the browser window:

```
<TABLE WIDTH=100% CELLPADDING=0 CELLSPACING=0 BORDER=0>
<TR>
```

4 You must continue the process of setting percentage widths throughout *every* table data cell element. If you don't, you'll have unpredictable results. In this case, you want the first table data cell to take up 30 percent of the entire table width. As you can guess, the rest of the data cells must account for the remaining 70 percent of the table width:

```
<TD WIDTH=30% VALIGN=TOP ALIGN=CENTER BGCOLOR="#990000">
<FONT FACE="VERDANA" COLOR="#FFCC33" SIZE=5>
<STRONG>   HOT<BR>      
gossip</FONT></STRONG></TD>
```

5 The next table data cell takes up 60 percent of the entire table width, leaving 10 percent up for grabs. Within this table data cell, you nest another table. Note here that its width must be set to 100 percent, so that it occupies 100 percent of the table data cell, which occupies 60 percent of the *main* table. This technique can be a bit confusing, which is one of the reasons it's rarely seen on the Web:

```
<TD WIDTH=60% BGCOLOR="#000000"><TABLE WIDTH=100% CELLPADDING=0
CELLSPACING=5 BORDER=0>
    <TR>
```

6 Within the nested table are two rows, the first of which contains a table data cell that takes up 100 percent of the table width—easily:

```
    <TD WIDTH=100% COLSPAN=3 BGCOLOR="#000000"><FONT FACE="VERDANA"
SIZE=2>Imagine a body of text that features the hottest gossip about the
Web and those who build it. Now imagine having to read through all of it
just to get to the meaty, juicy stuff that you're dying for - only to be
bored with useless rhetoric and unintelligible lingo.<BR> </FONT></TD>
    </TR>
    <TR>
```

7 The second table row consists of three table data cells—one taking up 48 percent of the table width, another taking up two percent, and the last taking up 50 percent for a total of 100 percent—yes, some math is involved:

```
    <TD WIDTH=48% ALIGN=CENTER BGCOLOR="#FFCC33"><FONT FACE="VERDANA"
COLOR="#000000" SIZE=4><I>"Here's what<BR>you need<BR>to
know!"</I></FONT></TD>
    <TD WIDTH=2% BGCOLOR="#000000"> </TD>
```

159

```
<TD WIDTH=50% BGCOLOR="#000000"><FONT FACE="VERDANA"
SIZE=2>Thanks to the thoughtful designers of this little online "gos-
sip" rag, all you have to do is check out the callout box to the
left for the latest hot scoop without having to read all this boring
text.</FONT></TD>
    </TR>
```

8 Close your nested table:

```
    </TABLE>
</TD>
```

9 Here's that last table data cell, defining the remaining 10 percent of the main table layout:

```
<TD WIDTH=10% BGCOLOR="#990000"> </TD>
</TR>
```

10 Add a bit of color to the bottom of your table by creating empty table data cells with colored backgrounds:

```
<TR>
<TD WIDTH=30% BGCOLOR="#990000"> </TD>
<TD WIDTH=60% BGCOLOR="#990000"> </TD>
<TD WIDTH=10% BGCOLOR="#990000"> </TD>
</TR>
```

11 Close your main table and end your HTML:

```
</TABLE>
</BODY>
</HTML>
```

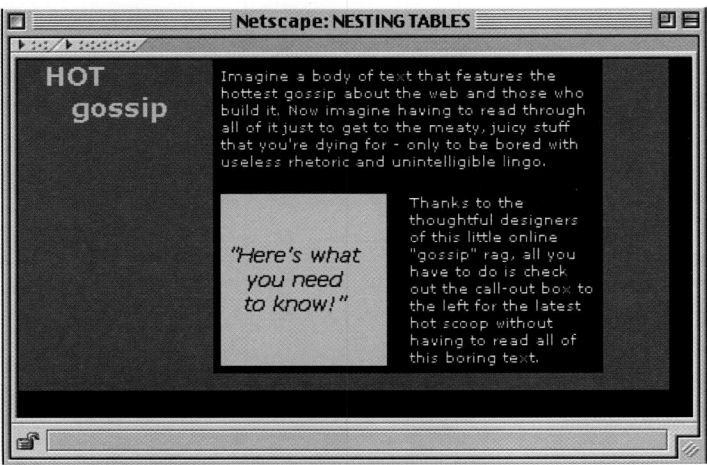

Further display of dynamic responsiveness.

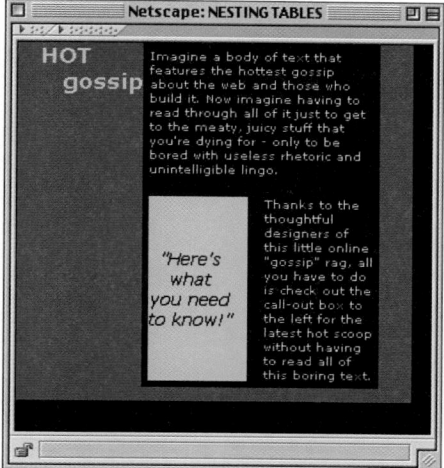

Even further display of dynamic responsiveness.

Dynamically responsive tables are exciting to use and visitors are often floored by their ability to reformat data and images on-the-fly. However, the designer looking for ultimate control over his or her creation often avoids this technique. One of the main reasons why dynamically responsive tables don't go *quite* to the edge of browser windows is browser offset. Although the elimination of browser offset is easy enough, as implemented in the <BODY> tag of the preceding code, it does not work with older browsers, which imposes a limitation on using this technique.

In addition, because the tables are sized by percentage and not explicit pixel-based widths, the browser sometimes rounds the figure up or down to the nearest width, based on the current browser window size. This sometimes tends to leave page layouts a bit short of the browser window size (this is more apparent when the browser window is stretched out considerably). In the future, as more control variables are introduced for this technique, perhaps more designers will embrace it. ●

PART V

Magic with Frames

Web designers have long had a love-hate relationship with frames. When frames were introduced in 1996, people abused them by dividing up their sites into tiny little sections of individually scrolling content.

This created a "frames backlash" that turned many people off of the technology. Designers considered frames ugly and unsophisticated due to the visible borders they created.

Much has changed since 1996. Frame borders can now be hidden to help Web designers create a seamless look and feel. If used carefully and with forethought, frames can add an unprecedented amount of control for Web designers wanting to separate navigation from content, while giving the user a sense of stability in terms of navigation.

Create a No-Frames Option

Use this technique to:

- **Avoid alienating your viewers.** Let your viewers know if their browser does not support frames, or create an alternative non-framed site for those who would rather not deal with frames.

- **Provide an upgrade path.** Displaying a no-frames alternative page to viewers with older browsers enables them to upgrade their browser (if you provide the upgrade links). Some surfers have no idea that their browser is outdated. You can help them get with the program.

If your site uses frames, chances are that you will have no problem delivering your content to most of the users out there. The most recent browsers (beginning with Netscape 2.0+, IE 3.0+, WebTV, and AOL 3.0+) all support frames technology. However, some browsers (such as Internet Explorer) enable viewers to turn off frames, whereas most older browsers do not support frames. If you do not provide an alternative to your framed site, some visitors get a blank page upon arrival.

Creation Options

You have two options when creating a no-frames alternative:

1 Design a browser warning (or upgrade) page

2 Design an entire non-framed version of your site

Depending on the amount of time and resources at your disposal, you can cover all the bases by designing a framed *and* non-framed version of your site. Most developers, however, do not have the resources necessary to constantly update and maintain two entirely different versions of the same Web site. Therefore, many opt to create a warning page that notifies those using non-frames-capable browsers of an upgrade path.

Forwarding Users to an Alternative Page

To make your no-frames alternative page or site available to older browsers (or those who have turned frames off), insert <NOFRAMES></NOFRAMES> tags after your <FRAMESET></FRAMESET> tags. Between your <NOFRAMES></NOFRAMES> tags, you might insert HTML text or a META refresh tag that forwards your non-frames-capable viewers to an alternative page (or site).

The following code is an excerpt from the frames-based *click here* Web site's `index.html` home page located at `http://www.rpirouz.com/click`. Note how the `<NOFRAMES></NOFRAMES>` tags are implemented here:

1 Begin your HTML as you normally would:

```
<HTML>

<HEAD>

<TITLE>Click Here.</TITLE>
```

2 Insert META NAME content to help place your page within search engines:

```
<META NAME="keywords" CONTENT="creative, online advertising, interactive
developer, design, graphic design, advertising, banner, banner ads, click-
through, interface, interactive, click here, lynda weinman, raymond
pirouz, pirouz, raymond">

<META NAME="description" CONTENT="Click Here [ISBN 1562057928], written by
Raymond Pirouz and developed with Lynda Weinman, takes you beyond 'cool,'
'hip,' and 'killer' and shows you how conceptual, strategic, targeted
visual communication can be used to create web sites that bring users back
time and again. This valuable guide features a philosophical approach to
web design—building on foundations and emphasizing creativity and utili-
ty. Rather than focusing on the 'how-to's,' Click Here covers the 'why-
to's' - and serves as a priceless reference long after the technologies
involved are obsolete.">

</HEAD>
```

3 Begin establishing your framed page contents:

```
<FRAMESET FRAMEBORDER=NO BORDER=0 FRAMESPACING=0 ROWS="60,*">
```

```
<FRAME SRC="navs.htm" NAME="clicktop" MARGINWIDTH=0 MARGINHEIGHT=0
SCROLLING=NO>
<FRAME SRC="contents.htm" NAME="clickbot" SCROLLING=YES>

</FRAMESET>
```

4 Begin talking to browsers that don't support frames by using the
<NOFRAMES> tag:

```
<NOFRAMES>
```

5 Within these tags, you can either create your warning page or use a META
Refresh function to send users to a specific warning page, in this case,
noframes.html:

```
<META HTTP-EQUIV="refresh" CONTENT="5; URL=noframes.html">
```

6 End your <NOFRAMES> tag:

```
</NOFRAMES>
```

7 End your HTML:

```
</BODY>
```

```
</HTML>
```

As you can see in the preceding code, the <META> tag is used to send those who
cannot display framed sites to a page called noframes.html within five seconds
after the page is loaded.

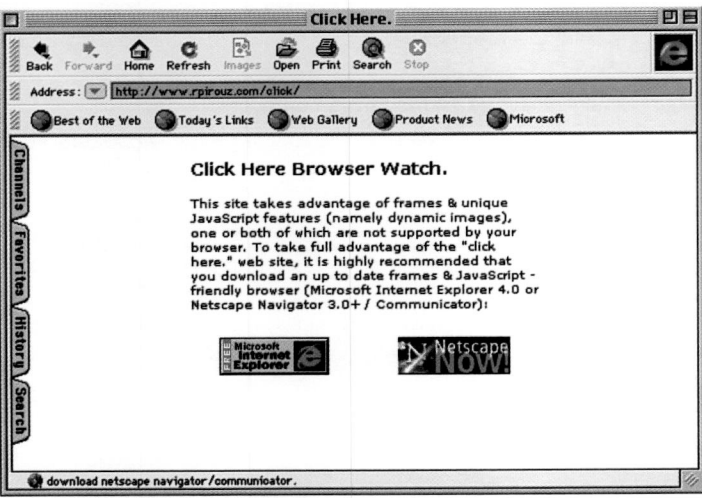

Browser Watch *page for the* click here *Web site.*

Creating the Page

The *Browser Watch* page illustrated here was designed by using the following HTML:

1 Begin your HTML as you normally would:

```
<HTML>

<HEAD>

<TITLE>Click Here.</TITLE>
```

2 Add your META NAME content to help get listed within search engines:

```
<META NAME="keywords" CONTENT="creative, online advertising, interactive
developer, design, graphic design, advertising, banner, banner ads, click-
through, interface, interactive, click here, lynda weinman, raymond
pirouz, pirouz, raymond">

<META NAME="description" CONTENT="Click Here [ISBN 1562057928], written by
Raymond Pirouz and developed with Lynda Weinman, takes you beyond 'cool,'
'hip,' and 'killer' and shows you how conceptual, strategic, targeted
visual communication can be used to create Web sites that bring users back
time and again. This valuable guide features a philosophical approach to
web design—building on foundations and emphasizing creativity and utili-
ty. Rather than focusing on the 'how-to's,' Click Here covers the 'why-
to's' - and serves as a priceless reference long after the technologies
involved are obsolete.">

</HEAD>
```

3 Set your BODY background color as well as LINK and TEXT colors:

```
<BODY BGCOLOR="#ffffff" LINK = "#333300" ALINK = "#333300" VLINK =
"#cccc00" TEXT = "#000000">
```

4 Center your page's contents:

```
<CENTER>
```

5 Create a table to house your content and give the cells some "air" by setting the CELLSPACING to 10:

```
<TABLE WIDTH=300 CELLPADDING=0 CELLSPACING=10 BORDER=0>
<TR>
<TD WIDTH=300 COLSPAN=2>
```

167

6 Establish the fonts that you'd like your audience to see, setting their sizes. Here you can explain that an upgrade path is available and that your viewer's browser is somehow incapable of displaying your site or is too old:

```
<FONT FACE="Verdana,Arial,Helvetica,Courier New,Courier"
SIZE=1><H3>Click Here Browser Watch.</H3>
```

```
<FONT SIZE=2>This site takes advantage of frames and unique
JavaScript features (namely dynamic images), one or both of which is
not supported by your browser. To take full advantage of the "click
here" Web site, it is highly recommended that you download an up-to-
date frames and JavaScript-friendly browser (Microsoft Internet
Explorer 4.0 or Netscape Navigator 3.0+ / Communicator):<BR><BR>
</FONT>
</TD>
</TR>
```

7 Provide the upgrade paths by linking to them using graphic icons:

```
<TD WIDTH=150 ALIGN=CENTER><A HREF="http://www.microsoft.com/ie/down-
load" onMouseOver="window.status='download internet explorer 4.0.';
return true"><IMG WIDTH="88" HEIGHT="31" SRC="ie.gif" ALT="Internet
Explorer" BORDER=0></a></td>
```

```
<TD WIDTH=150 ALIGN=CENTER><A HREF="http://www.netscape.com/download"
onMouseOver="window.status='download netscape navigator/communica-
tor.'; return true"><IMG WIDTH="90" HEIGHT="31" SRC="N.GIF"
ALT="Netscape Navigator" BORDER=0></A></TD>
</TD>
</TR>
```

8 End your table and stop centering the page's contents:

```
</TABLE>
```

```
</CENTER>
```

9 End HTML:

```
</BODY>
```

```
</HTML>
```

Notice that the page (refer to the first figure in this section) provides upgrade paths (to IE 4.0 and Netscape 4.0) so that those with older browsers can obtain newer versions. Although it is not required for you to provide this service, it is considered good netiquette and is common practice among most Web sites. ●

Create a Single-Frame Site

Use this technique to:

- **Eliminate browser offset.** Get rid of those pesky invisible borders created by Internet Explorer and Netscape browsers.

- **Hide your Web site's directory structure.** No matter where your viewers are within your site, they always see http://www.yoursite.com, not http://www.yoursite.com/yourfolder/anotherfolder/index.html.

Just because you specify a <FRAMESET> in order to use frames technology on your site doesn't mean that you literally have to display *multiple* frames. By using a 100% value followed by a ",*" in the ROWS attribute of your <FRAMESET> tag, you can specify a single-frame Web site, as shown in the following:

```
<FRAMESET FRAMEBORDER=NO BORDER=0 FRAMESPACING=0 ROWS="100%,*">
```

The preceding code tells HTML to create a framed site that takes up 100 percent of the page. The * indicates that the second frame can take up the rest of the page (which does not exist because the first frame is taking up 100 percent of the page, making the second frame void).

Hide Your Site's Directory Structure

One of the advantages of creating a single-frame Web site is that it enables you to hide your site's directory structure from your visitors. For instance, when you arrive at a site's home page, the URL you normally see goes something like this: http://www.sitename.com/index.html. When arriving at a single frame site, the URL you see, no matter where you are within the site, is http://www.sitename.com. How can this be advantageous?

If you always want your visitors to enter your site from your home page, this is a good technique to incorporate. Sometimes people tend to bookmark a certain page deep within a site and never go back to your home page (which is where most Web sites are updated regularly). Unless the newest information about your site is located on each and every page, those users miss out on the newest happenings in bypassing your home page.

If you incorporate the single-frame technique, some people might complain that they cannot bookmark certain pages within your site. Although this can be frustrating, bookmarking is not possible in *any* rendition of framed sites (single or multi-framed). The inability to bookmark pages is one of the weaknesses of incorporating frames, but its benefits more than outweigh this one flaw that is bound to be fixed in an upcoming browser update.

Eliminate Browser Offset

Another advantage to creating a single-frame site (this applies to multiple-frame sites as well) is the elimination of browser offset. Netscape and Microsoft's invisible internal screen border can easily be removed within a framed environment, although it's more easily done with Internet Explorer than Netscape Navigator:

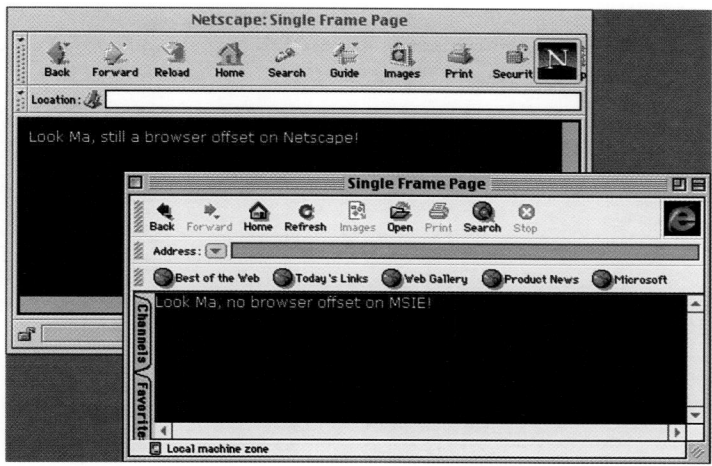

Although the single frame quickly eliminates browser offset in Internet Explorer, the border is still apparent in Netscape Navigator.

Eliminate Browser Offset in Internet Explorer

The following HTML proved successful in eliminating browser offset from the Internet Explorer browser, but not from Netscape Navigator:

1 Begin your HTML as you normally would:

```
<HTML>

<HEAD>

<TITLE>Single Frame Page</TITLE>

</HEAD>
```

2 Create a framed page, consisting of a single frame by specifying ROWS as
"100%, *". This basically tells the browser to create a single frame taking up
100 percent of the page:

```
<FRAMESET FRAMEBORDER=NO BORDER=0 FRAMESPACING=0 ROWS="100%,*">
```

3 Set your frame source as your home page:

```
<FRAME SRC="home.html" NAME="home" SCROLLING=YES>
```

4 End your FRAMESET:

```
</FRAMESET>
```

5 Create a NOFRAMES option, sending those without frames capabilities to
another page:

```
<NOFRAMES>
```

```
<META HTTP-EQUIV="refresh" CONTENT="5; URL=noframes.html">
```

```
</NOFRAMES>
```

6 End your HTML:

```
</BODY>
```

```
</HTML>
```

Eliminate Browser Offset for Netscape Navigator

To eliminate browser offset within a single frame for Netscape Navigator, you must
include the MARGINWIDTH=0 and MARGINHEIGHT=0 attributes within the <FRAME> tag
of your <FRAMESET>, as demonstrated here:

1 Begin your HTML and code it exactly:

```
<HTML>
```

```
<HEAD>
```

```
<TITLE>Single Frame Page</TITLE>
```

```
</HEAD>
```

```
<FRAMESET FRAMEBORDER=NO BORDER=0 FRAMESPACING=0 ROWS="100%,*">
```

2 The only change occurs here, where you need to add the `MARGINWIDTH`/`HEIGHT` attributes to the `<FRAME>` tag so that Netscape browsers eliminate browser offset:

```
<FRAME SRC="home.html" NAME="home" MARGINWIDTH=0 MARGINHEIGHT=0
SCROLLING=YES>

</FRAMESET>

<NOFRAMES>

<META HTTP-EQUIV="refresh" CONTENT="5; URL=noframes.html">

</NOFRAMES>

</BODY>

</HTML>
```

The preceding HTML results in the elimination of browser offset within a single-frame environment, as depicted in the following figure.

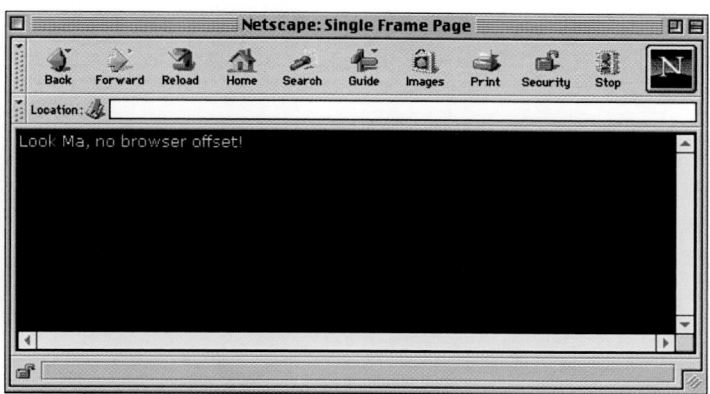

Browser offset eliminated within Netscape Navigator. ●

Force Frames

Use this technique to:

- **Avoid getting framed.** Force framed sites to open a new window for your site, instead of loading it within their frame structure.

- **Always appear in frames.** Force your framed pages to bring up your framed site if visitors try to access them.

By using JavaScript, you can control certain aspects of how your framed site is displayed. If a frame-based Web site links to your frame-based site and targets your site to appear within one of its frames, the result can be haphazard at best. Your site would then appear within a single frame of another framed site. Many errors can occur at this time—not to mention that it can also get pretty ugly. This is referred to as "getting framed."

The following figure is a good example of what a "framed" Web site looks like. As you can see, the R35 Web site is divided into two frames—one on top and the other on bottom.

The R35 direct Web site "framed" under the R35 Web site.

If a link from the top frame calls the R35 direct site to the bottom frame, all breaks loose because the R35 direct Web site also uses frames. Because the R35 direct site is not designed to be viewed within another Web site, a piece of JavaScript code must be implemented within its `index.html` file to avoid this situation.

Avoid Getting Framed

Fortunately, it's pretty simple to avoid getting framed. Simply place the following code within the <HEAD></HEAD> tags of your main HTML file (usually index.html):

```
<SCRIPT LANGUAGE="JavaScript">
<!--

if (parent.location.href != window.location.href) parent.location.href=
window.location.href;

//-->
</SCRIPT>
```

The script basically says that if the framed page is opened within a page (or frame) that isn't its parent, it sends this window to a brand-new page so that its parent is the main page. In other words, this script forces your site to appear in a brand-new window if a framed site tries to link to your framed site.

Using the R35 direct Web site as the example, the following figure illustrates what would happen if a site using frames tries to link to it and forces it to appear within one of its frames.

The R35 direct Web site, avoiding getting framed.

With the JavaScript code above implemented, the R35 direct Web site does not appear within another framed site—it's that simple.

Limiting Access to Framed Pages

What if someone tries to access one of the pages within your framed site? Let's say that you have designed a site with multiple frames and you have a frame on the right containing some images. Generally, any viewer can choose to open that particular frame in a new window and create a bookmark to that particular frame. If you do not want visitors to access individual frames within your site and instead want them to browse your site in its entirety, you can force the frame to load a particular page (usually the index.html) if someone tries to access it directly:

```
<SCRIPT LANGUAGE="JavaScript">
<!--//

if (top == self) self.location.href="index.html";

//-->
</SCRIPT>
```

The preceding script, when placed within the <HEAD></HEAD> tags of your framed pages, forces your visitor's browser to go to a certain page if this page is accessed directly. It basically says that if the user has landed at this page directly, take the user to another page (in this case, index.html). An alternate way to accomplish this is to create a page called warning.html or something similar, where you let your visitor know that you would prefer it if the site were browsed in its entirety, and then offer a link to your framed home page.

To further illustrate the "warning" example, take a look at the following figure.

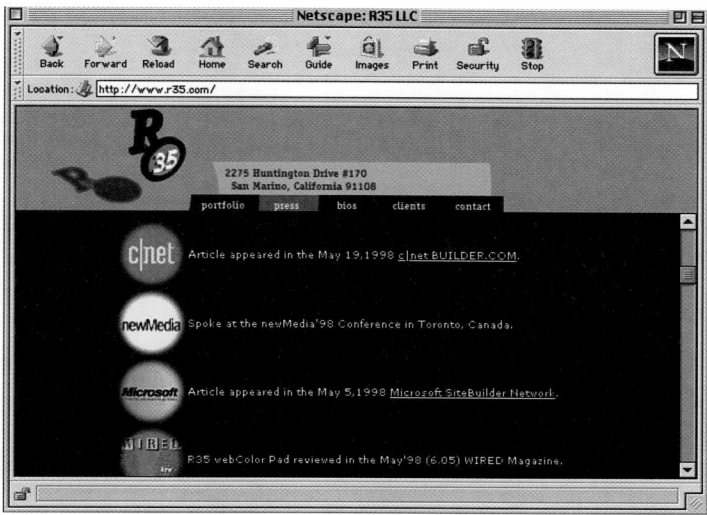

The R35 Web site with the "press" page selected.

Here, the "press" page within the R35 Web site has been selected and displayed in the bottom frame. This is how the R35 press page is designed to be accessed. If users decide to access the "press" page directly, bypassing the framed R35 Web site structure, they are greeted by the warning page illustrated in the following figure.

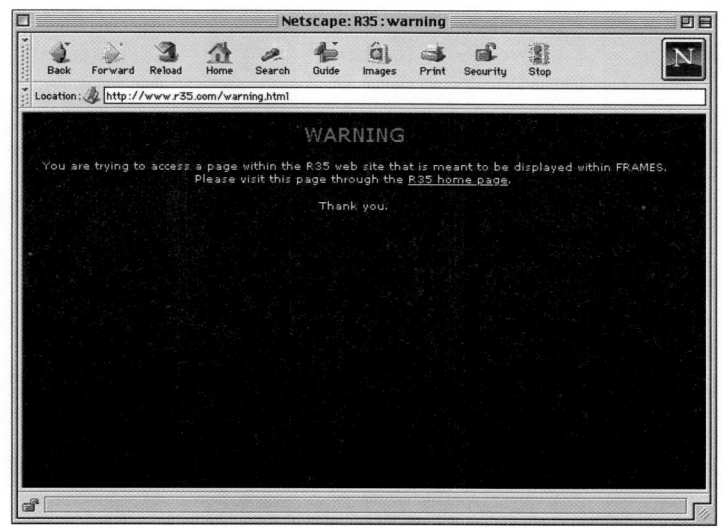

The R35 Web site warning page for those trying to access pages designed to be viewed within the framed structure.

To ensure that users can't bypass your framed site structure, take the following steps:

1 Incorporate the JavaScript into your framed page. In the preceding R35 example, the "press" page has the following JavaScript coded within its `<HEAD></HEAD>` tags:

```
<SCRIPT LANGUAGE="JavaScript">
<!--//

if (top == self) self.location.href="warning.html";

//-->

</SCRIPT>
```

2 Create a warning page, allowing viewers to link to your Web site's framed home page, from which the same document can be retrieved by using the frames structure:

```
<HTML>

<HEAD>

<TITLE>R35 : warning</TITLE>

</HEAD>

<BODY BGCOLOR="#000000" LINK="#ffffff" VLINK="#ffffff"
ALINK="#ffffff" TEXT="#999999">

<CENTER>

<FONT FACE="VERDANA, ARIAL, HELVETICA" COLOR="#FF0000" SIZE=5>
WARNING</FONT>

<BR><BR>
```

3 Make sure you tell your viewers why they have been sent to this page and provide a link to your site's framed home page:

```
<FONT FACE="VERDANA, ARIAL, HELVETICA" COLOR="#FFFFFF" SIZE=2>You are try-
ing to access a page within the R35 web site that is meant to be displayed
within FRAMES. Please visit this page through the <A
HREF="http://www.r35.com">R35 home page</A>.</FONT>

<BR><BR>

<FONT FACE="VERDANA, ARIAL, HELVETICA" COLOR="#FFFFFF" SIZE=2>Thank
you.</FONT>

</CENTER>

</BODY>

</HTML>
```

To see this technique in action, point your browser to http://www.r35.com/press.htm. You will see the warning page and be prompted to access the Web site through its framed home page. ●

Design Frames Within Frames

Use this technique to:

- **Design unique framed page layout combinations.** Give your layout more flexibility by exploring several variations.

- **Create distinct information regions.** Develop information regions that remain consistent and perform tasks independent of other frames.

- **Maximize your onscreen real-estate.** Make full use of your screen by making images or content appear in pre-established locations within your frame structure.

- **Access more than one frame.** Present the results of some links in one frame and others in a separate frame. This technique is great for comparisons and contrasts.

Frames enable you to create modular regions wherein images and text can be positioned with precision. Before you get into placing frames within frames (or nesting frames), quickly review basic frames layout techniques:

There are two ways to lay out basic frames:

1. Using rows–Frames are introduced vertically—one after another.

2. Using columns–Frames are introduced horizontally—next to one another.

Basic Frames Layout

The basic two-frame page consists of three files:

1. `index.html`—Contains the `<FRAMESET></FRAMESET>` tags (which point to the framed pages), as well as the `<NOFRAMES></NOFRAMES>` tags (which point to the alternate page or site for browsers that do not display frames).

2. First framed page–The first of two framed pages.

3. Second framed page–The second framed page.

The following three HTML files were used to create the basic frames structure depicted in the following figure:

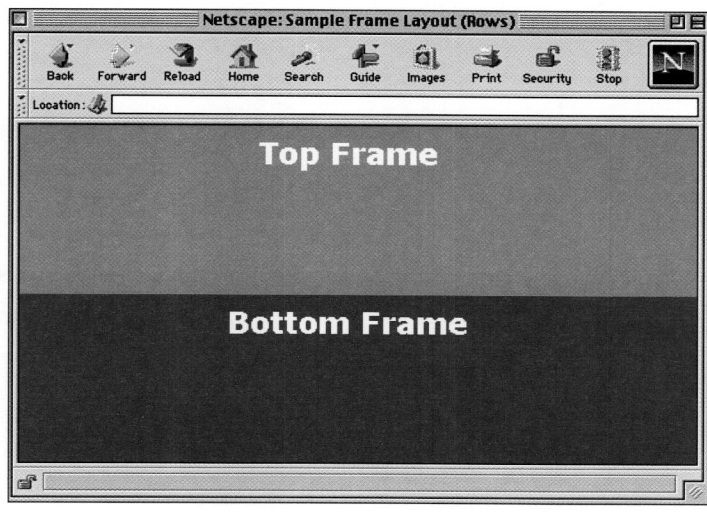

Basic frames layout using rows.

The `index.html` File

This is the main HTML page that defines the frames structure by using the <FRAMESET> tag. Make sure to offer a <NOFRAMES> alternative for older browsers:

```
<HTML>

<HEAD>

<TITLE>Sample Frame Layout (Rows)</TITLE>

</HEAD>

<FRAMESET FRAMEBORDER=NO BORDER=0 FRAMESPACING=0 ROWS="50%,50%">

<FRAME SRC="top.html" NAME="top" SCROLLING=AUTO>
<FRAME SRC="bottom.html" NAME="bottom" SCROLLING=AUTO>

</FRAMESET>

<NOFRAMES>

<META HTTP-EQUIV="refresh" CONTENT="5; URL=noframes.html">
```

```
</NOFRAMES>

</BODY>

</HTML>
```

The `top.html` File

This file is called by the `index.html` page and houses the contents for the top frame:

```
<HTML>

<HEAD>

<TITLE>Single Frame Page (TOP)</TITLE>

</HEAD>

<BODY LEFTMARGIN=0 TOPMARGIN=0 BGCOLOR="#FF6600" LINK = "#ffffff"
ALINK = "#ffffff" VLINK = "#ffffff" TEXT = "#ffffff">

<CENTER>

<FONT FACE="VERDANA"><H1>Top Frame</H1></FONT>

</CENTER>

</BODY>

</HTML>
```

The `bottom.html` File

This file is called by the `index.html` page and houses the contents for the bottom frame:

```
<HTML>

<HEAD>

<TITLE>Single Frame Page (BOTTOM)</TITLE>

</HEAD>

<BODY LEFTMARGIN=0 TOPMARGIN=0 BGCOLOR="#330099" LINK = "#ffffff"
ALINK = "#ffffff" VLINK = "#ffffff" TEXT = "#ffffff">
```

```
<CENTER>

<FONT FACE="VERDANA"><H1>Bottom Frame</H1></FONT>

</CENTER>

</BODY>

</HTML>
```

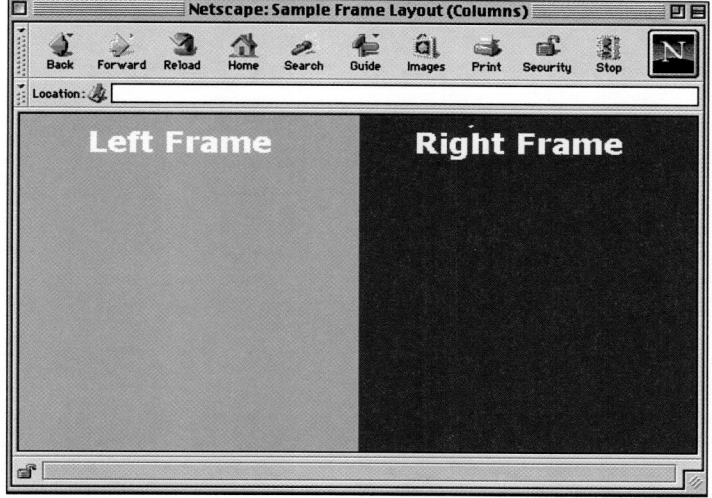

Basic frames layout using columns.

The following three HTML files were used to create the basic frames structure depicted in the preceding figure.

The index.html File

This is the main HTML page that defines the frames structure by using the `<FRAMESET>` tag. Make sure to offer a `<NOFRAMES>` alternative for older browsers:

```
<HTML>

<HEAD>

<TITLE>Sample Frame Layout (Columns)</TITLE>

</HEAD>

<FRAMESET FRAMEBORDER=NO BORDER=0 FRAMESPACING=0 COLS="50%,50%">
```

```
<FRAME SRC="left.html" NAME="left" SCROLLING=AUTO>
<FRAME SRC="right.html" NAME="right" SCROLLING=AUTO>

</FRAMESET>

<NOFRAMES>

<META HTTP-EQUIV="refresh" CONTENT="5; URL=noframes.html">

</NOFRAMES>

</BODY>

</HTML>
```

The left.html File

This file is called by the index.html page and houses the contents for the left frame:

```
<HTML>

<HEAD>

<TITLE>Single Frame Page (LEFT)</TITLE>

</HEAD>

<BODY LEFTMARGIN=0 TOPMARGIN=0 BGCOLOR="#CCCC00" LINK = "#ffffff"
ALINK = "#ffffff" VLINK = "#ffffff" TEXT = "#ffffff">

<CENTER>

<FONT FACE="VERDANA"><H1>Left Frame</H1></FONT>

</CENTER>

</BODY>

</HTML>
```

The `right.html` File

This file is called by the `index.html` page and houses the contents for the right frame:

```
<HTML>

<HEAD>

<TITLE>Single Frame Page (RIGHT)</TITLE>

</HEAD>

<BODY LEFTMARGIN=0 TOPMARGIN=0 BGCOLOR="#336633" LINK = "#ffffff" ALINK =
"#ffffff" VLINK = "#ffffff" TEXT = "#ffffff">

<CENTER>

<FONT FACE="VERDANA"><H1>Right Frame</H1></FONT>

</CENTER>

</BODY>

</HTML>
```

Nesting Frames

Once you get the basic idea of frames down, nesting frames within frames is a breeze. Nesting occurs when you place a <FRAMESET> tag within another <FRAMESET> tag in place of a <FRAME> tag.

 Whenever you create a <FRAMESET> **tag, always be sure to close it off with a** </FRAMESET> **tag. Often, designers nest frames within frames by adding an extra** <FRAMESET> **tag, forgetting to add the backslash, which results in a blank Web page and furious temple rubbing.**

185

Take a look at the HTML used to create the illustration in the following figure.

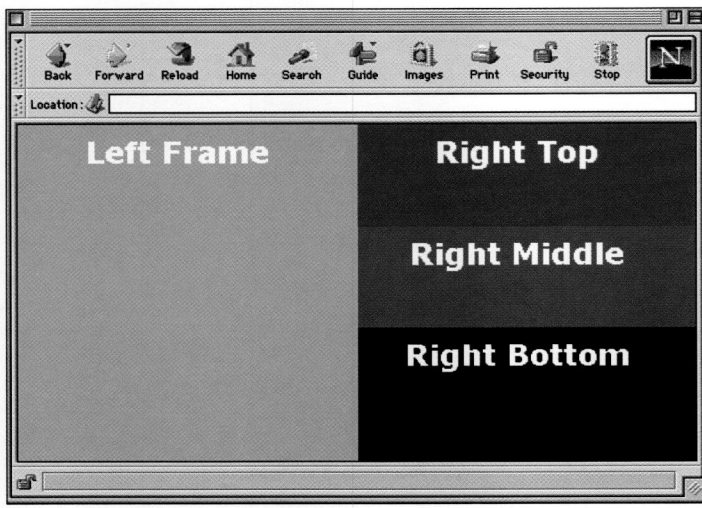

Nesting frames within frames.

Pay close attention to how the <FRAMESET> tags are configured:

1 Begin your HTML as you normally would:

```
<HTML>

<HEAD>

<TITLE>Nesting Frames within Frames</TITLE>

</HEAD>
```

2 Create your initial frameset, defining a two-column page split 50/50 down the center:

```
<FRAMESET FRAMEBORDER=NO BORDER=0 FRAMESPACING=0 COLS="50%,50%">
```

3 Define your left column as an HTML page:

```
<FRAME SRC="left.html" NAME="left" SCROLLING=AUTO>
```

4 For your right column, nest three frames within it by establishing a new frameset, dividing up the column into three rows:

```
    <FRAMESET FRAMEBORDER=NO BORDER=0 FRAMESPACING=0
ROWS="30%,30%,40%">
    <FRAME SRC="right_t.html" NAME="right_top" SCROLLING=AUTO>
    <FRAME SRC="right_m.html" NAME="right_middle" SCROLLING=AUTO>
    <FRAME SRC="right_b.html" NAME="right_bottom" SCROLLING=AUTO>
```

5 Make sure to CLOSE your frameset *twice*—once for the original frameset and another time for the nested frameset:

```
    </FRAMESET>
</FRAMESET>
```

6 Provide a NOFRAMES alternative:

```
<NOFRAMES>

<META HTTP-EQUIV="refresh" CONTENT="5; URL=noframes.html">

</NOFRAMES>
```

7 End your HTML:

```
</BODY>

</HTML>
```

As you can see in the preceding HTML, accomplishing this effect requires five HTML pages:

- index.html, left.html—**Left frame**
- right_t.html—**Right top page**
- right_m.html—**Right middle page**
- right_b.html—**Right bottom page**

The other four pages follow.

The left.html File

This file is called by the index.html page and houses the contents for the left frame:

```
<HTML>

<HEAD>

<TITLE>Nested Example Left Page</TITLE>

</HEAD>

<BODY LEFTMARGIN=0 TOPMARGIN=0 BGCOLOR="#CCCC00" LINK = "#ffffff" ALINK =
"#ffffff" VLINK = "#ffffff" TEXT = "#ffffff">

<CENTER>
```

```
<FONT FACE="VERDANA"><H1>Left Frame</H1></FONT>

</CENTER>

</BODY>

</HTML>
```

The `right_t.html` File

This file is called by the `index.html` page and houses the contents for the top-right frame:

```
<HTML>

<HEAD>

<TITLE>Nested Example Right Top Page</TITLE>

</HEAD>

<BODY LEFTMARGIN=0 TOPMARGIN=0 BGCOLOR="#336633" LINK = "#ffffff"
ALINK = "#ffffff" VLINK = "#ffffff" TEXT = "#ffffff">

<CENTER>

<FONT FACE="VERDANA"><H1>Right Top</H1></FONT>

</CENTER>

</BODY>

</HTML>
```

The `right_m.html` File

This file is called by the `index.html` page and houses the contents for the middle-right frame:

```
<HTML>

<HEAD>

<TITLE>Nested Example Right Middle Page</TITLE>

</HEAD>
```

```
<BODY LEFTMARGIN=0 TOPMARGIN=0 BGCOLOR="#990000" LINK = "#ffffff" ALINK =
"#ffffff" VLINK = "#ffffff" TEXT = "#ffffff">

<CENTER>

<FONT FACE="VERDANA"><H1>Right Middle</H1></FONT>

</CENTER>

</BODY>

</HTML>
```

The right_b.html File

This file is called by the index.html page and houses the contents for the bottom-right frame:

```
<HTML>

<HEAD>

<TITLE>Nested Example Right Bottom Page</TITLE>

</HEAD>

<BODY LEFTMARGIN=0 TOPMARGIN=0 BGCOLOR="#000000" LINK = "#ffffff" ALINK =
"#ffffff" VLINK = "#ffffff" TEXT = "#ffffff">

<CENTER>

<FONT FACE="VERDANA"><H1>Right Bottom</H1></FONT>

</CENTER>

</BODY>

</HTML>
```

189

Frames are a powerful technology and when you master them you will be able to design Web sites that take full advantage of the onscreen real-estate. For some real-world examples, check out these very well-designed framed sites on the Web:

- Macromedia (http://www.macromedia.com)

- High Five (http://www.highfive.com) ●

Create Border Graphics by Using Frames

Use this technique to:

- **Create a border graphic around a center frame.** Border graphics can add a distinct personality to your site.

- **Center your site's main frame window at all times.** As your viewers resize the browser window, your Web site always remains nested within colorful border graphics.

Get Creative!

Getting creative with frames can yield some pretty cool results. For example, you can use frames to design a "fake" border around your site's main content frame. Take a look at the following illustration as an example:

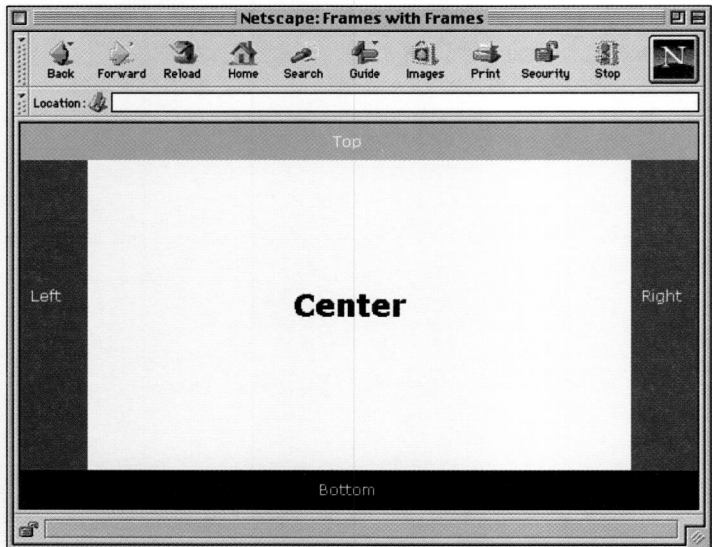

Create a border by using frames.

What if you want to use background images to create your own custom border graphics? You can accomplish this by calling background images within each of the border HTML pages.

Vertical border background graphic.

Horizontal border background graphic.

The GIF border graphics in the preceding figures represent images that can be called as background tiling GIFs with which custom border graphics can be made. You can experiment with different GIF border graphics to match the design of your Web site.

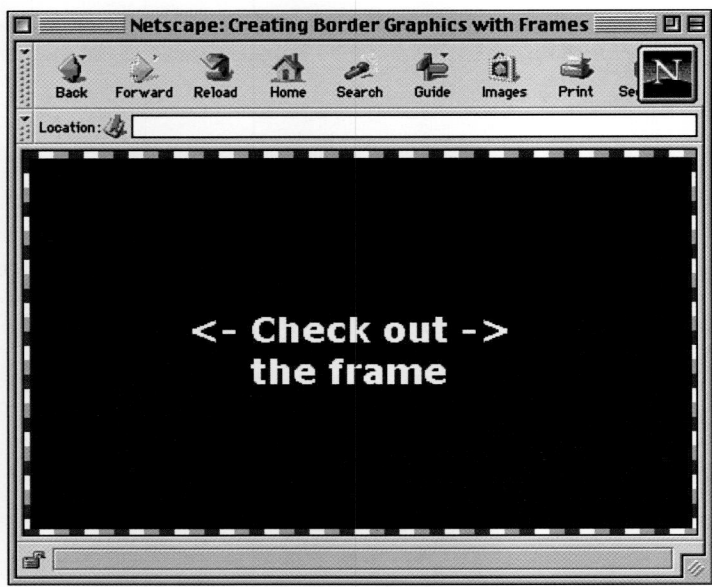

A "fake" border created by using frames and background-tiled GIFs.

The following six HTML files were used to create the image illustrated in the preceding figure.

The `index.html` File

In the following code, notice that the left, center, and right frames are nested within the second row of the <FRAMESET> (three rows total).

I Begin your HTML as you normally would:

```
<HTML>

<HEAD>

<TITLE>Creating Border Graphics with Frames</TITLE>

</HEAD>
```

2 Establish your FRAMESET and divide your page into three main rows: 2 percent for each border area and 96 percent for the main page's contents:

```
<FRAMESET FRAMEBORDER=NO BORDER=0 FRAMESPACING=0 ROWS="2%,96%,2%">
```

3 Define your top frame's HTML page:

```
<FRAME SRC="top.html" NAME="top" SCROLLING=0>
```

4 Break your middle (96%) row into three columns by adding a nested FRAMESET within your original FRAMESET: 1% for left and right borders and 98% for the center (all the while defining each unit's HTML page):

```
<FRAMESET FRAMEBORDER=NO BORDER=0 FRAMESPACING=0 COLS="1%,98%,1%">
<FRAME SRC="left.html" NAME="left" SCROLLING=0>
<FRAME SRC="center.html" NAME="center" SCROLLING=AUTO>
<FRAME SRC="right.html" NAME="right" SCROLLING=0>
```

5 End the nested FRAMESET:

```
</FRAMESET>
```

6 Define your bottom frame's HTML page:

```
<FRAME SRC="bottom.html" NAME="bottom" SCROLLING=0>
```

7 End the main FRAMESET:

```
</FRAMESET>
```

8 Offer a NOFRAMES option:

```
<NOFRAMES>

<META HTTP-EQUIV="refresh" CONTENT="5; URL=noframes.html">

</NOFRAMES>
```

9 End your HTML:

```
</BODY>

</HTML>
```

193

The `top.html` File

This file is called by the `index.html` page and houses the contents for the top border frame:

```
<HTML>

<HEAD>

<TITLE>Top Frame</TITLE>

</HEAD>

<BODY BACKGROUND="horizontal.gif">

</BODY>

</HTML>
```

The `left.html` File

This file is called by the `index.html` page and houses the contents for the left border frame:

```
<HTML>

<HEAD>

<TITLE>Left Frame</TITLE>

</HEAD>

<BODY BACKGROUND="vertical.gif">

</BODY>

</HTML>
```

The center.html File

This file is called by the index.html page and houses the contents for the center (main content) frame:

```
<HTML>

<HEAD>

<TITLE>Center Page</TITLE>

</HEAD>

<BODY BGCOLOR="#333300" LINK = "#ffffff" ALINK = "#ffffff" VLINK =
"#ffffff" TEXT = "#FFFFFF">

<CENTER>
<BR><BR><BR><BR><BR><BR><BR><BR>

<FONT FACE="VERDANA"><H1>&#60;- Check out -&#62;<BR>the frame</H1></FONT>

</CENTER>

</BODY>

</HTML>
```

The right.html File

This file is called by the index.html page and houses the contents for the right border frame:

```
<HTML>

<HEAD>

<TITLE>Right Frame</TITLE>

</HEAD>

<BODY BACKGROUND="vertical.gif">

</BODY>

</HTML>
```

The `bottom.html` File

This file is called by the `index.html` page and houses the contents for the bottom border frame:

```
<HTML>

<HEAD>

<TITLE>Bottom Frame</TITLE>

</HEAD>

<BODY BACKGROUND="horizontal.gif">

</BODY>

</HTML>
```

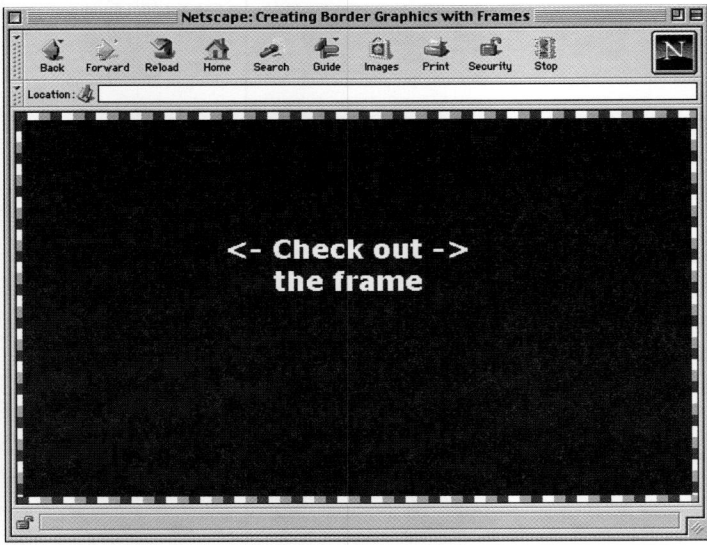

The border remains consistent even if the browser window is extended.

To see a good example of this technique used on the Web, check out the WebMonster site at `http://www.webmonster.net`. ●

Design Frames for Navigation

Use this technique to:

- **Avoid having to reload navigation graphics at every page.** You can decrease the amount of time it takes the pages of your site to load if you confine the navigation to a frame separate from the dynamic content.

- **Give the user a sense of security.** Enhance your viewer's browsing experience by making all the site's links available at all times.

One of the most useful aspects of frames is that it helps enhance Web site navigation. By keeping the site's navigation within a consistent frame that is always available to the viewer, you can improve your site's usability, thereby promoting repeat visits.

Using a Two-Frame Structure

The *click here.* Web site, shown here, incorporates a two-frame structure specifically designed to enhance navigation.

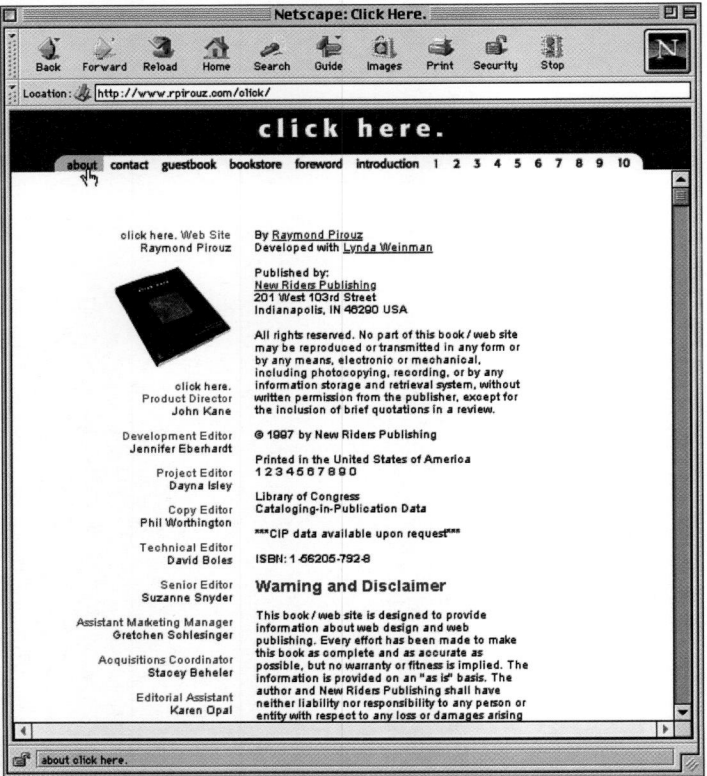

The click here. *Web site's "about" page.*

By placing the 17 GIF image links within a constant frame that does not change every time the bottom frame does, the Web site saves users at least 15–30 seconds per page (when compared to placing all GIF navigation images on every page when designing a navigational structure that makes use of JavaScript rollovers and JavaScript's preload function).

As depicted in the preceding figure, when a user selects a navigation link in the top frame, the target page loads in the bottom frame and the top navigation frame remains unchanged (except for the JavaScript rollovers that occur within the top frame).

The following `index.html` page specifies a two-frame page, allotting 60 pixels to the top frame and the remaining browser window (as depicted by the *) to the bottom frame:

1 Begin your HTML as you normally would, adding META NAME tags to enhance search engine placement:

```
<HTML>

<HEAD>

<TITLE>Click Here.</TITLE>

<META NAME="keywords" CONTENT="creative, online advertising, interactive
developer, design, graphic design, advertising, banner, banner ads, click-
through, interface, interactive, click here, lynda weinman, raymond
pirouz, pirouz, raymond">

<META NAME="description" CONTENT="Click Here [ISBN 1562057928], written by
Raymond Pirouz and developed with Lynda Weinman, takes you beyond 'cool,'
'hip,' and 'killer' and shows you how conceptual, strategic, targeted
visual communication can be used to create Web sites that bring users back
time and again. This valuable guide features a philosophical approach to
Web design—building on foundations and emphasizing creativity and utili-
ty. Rather than focusing on the 'how-to's,' Click Here covers the 'why-
to's' - and serves as a priceless reference long after the technologies
involved are obsolete."></HEAD>
```

199

2 Define your <FRAMESET> to two rows (or two columns—as your needs might vary), remembering that you can set a pixel or percentage width for one of the rows/columns and an * for the other to indicate that it should fill up the remaining space:

```
<FRAMESET FRAMEBORDER=NO BORDER=0 FRAMESPACING=0 ROWS="60,*">
```

3 Establish the pages that appear within the frames and name the frames so that you can refer back to them with the TARGET attribute within your <A HREF> tags:

```
<FRAME SRC="navs.htm" NAME="clicktop" MARGINWIDTH=0 MARGINHEIGHT=0
SCROLLING=NO>
<FRAME SRC="contents.htm" NAME="clickbot" SCROLLING=YES>

</FRAMESET>
```

4 Offer a NOFRAMES alternative:

```
<NOFRAMES>

<META HTTP-EQUIV="refresh" CONTENT="5; URL=noframes.htm">

</NOFRAMES>
```

5 End HTML:

```
</BODY>

</HTML>
```

The Navigation Without Frames

The following figure illustrates how the navigation page is layed out. Notice the tiling background image, cback2.gif.

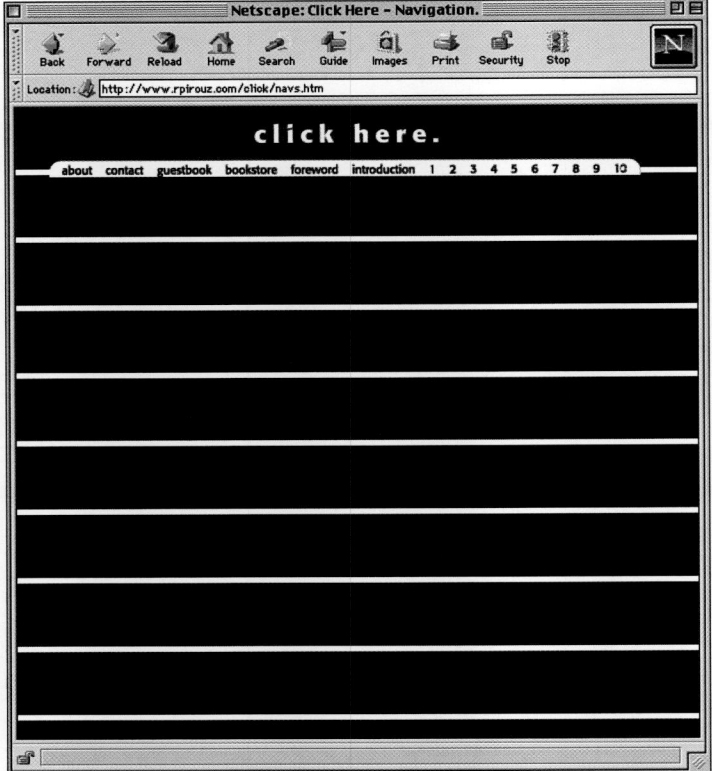

The click here. *navigation page without frames.*

Each link is targeted to the bottom window, named "clickbot," as illustrated by the following HTML:

```
<A HREF="about.htm" onMouseOver = "imgOn('img1');window.status='about click
here.'; return true" onMouseOut = "imgOff('img1')" target="clickbot"
onClick = "imgOff('img1')">
```

Although the preceding line of code uses some JavaScript for the rollovers, pay close attention to the target="clickbot" attribute within the <A HREF> tag. This little snippet of HTML forces the browser to call the linked page to the frame named "clickbot," which in this case is the bottom frame of the *click here*. Web site.

For another very graphic and easily navigable example of navigation within frames, check out the Godzilla Web site at http://www.godzilla.com. ●

Target Multiple Frames with JavaScript

Use this technique to:

- **Cause a link to change two frames at one time.** Using JavaScript, you can click one link and have two or three frames change at once!

- **Enhance your frame-based navigation.** Let your users know their place within your site by updating your navigation frame along with the content frame.

Updating Multiple Frames

By using JavaScript, you can cause one link to update two or more frames at once. Implementing this technique is quite simple. Take a look at the following JavaScript code:

1 Establish JavaScript within your HTML document's `<HEAD></HEAD>` tags:

```
<SCRIPT LANGUAGE="JavaScript">
<!--//
```

2 Create a function (in this case, called X, but you can call it whatever you like) and call two or more variables (in this case, x, y, and z), which are described shortly:

```
function X(xURL,yURL,zURL) {

  parent.x.location.href=xURL;
  parent.y.location.href=yURL;
  parent.z.location.href=zURL;

}

//-->
</SCRIPT>
```

3 To customize the script for your needs, replace X, x, y, and z with the following:

X = the function name you assign (changeURLs)

x = the frame 1 name (assigned to each individual frame in the index.html page)

y = the frame 1 name (assigned to each individual frame in the index.html page)

z = the frame 1 name (assigned to each individual frame in the index.html page)

For example, if you have a four-frame site and want to make three frames update after clicking a link in the first frame, here's how you'd set up the code:

1 Establish JavaScript within your document's `<HEAD></HEAD>` tags:

```
<SCRIPT LANGUAGE="JavaScript">
<!--//
```

2 Define your function and variables:

```
function changeThree(secondURL,thirdURL,fourthURL) {

  parent.second.location.href=secondURL;
  parent.third.location.href=thirdURL;
  parent.fourth.location.href=fourthURL;

}


//-->
</SCRIPT>
```

Please note that "second," "third," and "fourth" are the frame "names" assigned within the page's `index.html` `<FRAMESRC>` `<FRAME>` tag as such:

```
<FRAMESET FRAMEBORDER=NO BORDER=0 FRAMESPACING=0 ROWS="10%,30%,30%,30%">
    <FRAME SRC="navigation.html" NAME="first" SCROLLING=YES>
    <FRAME SRC="1.html" NAME="second" SCROLLING=YES>
    <FRAME SRC="2.html" NAME="third" SCROLLING=YES>
    <FRAME SRC="3.html" NAME="fourth" SCROLLING=YES>
</FRAMESET>
```

To tell JavaScript to update all three frames with one link, code your `<A HREF>` tags like so:

```
<A
HREF="JavaScript:changeThree('page1.html',page2.html','page3.html')">link
that changes 3 frames at once</A>
```

Notice that in the preceding `<A HREF>` tag, JavaScript is told to update the page named "second" with `page1.html`, "third" with `page2.html`, and "fourth" with `page3.html`.

The R35 Web site located at `http://www.r35.com` uses this technique to update the navigation frame (on top) as well as the content frame (on bottom) every time a link is clicked.

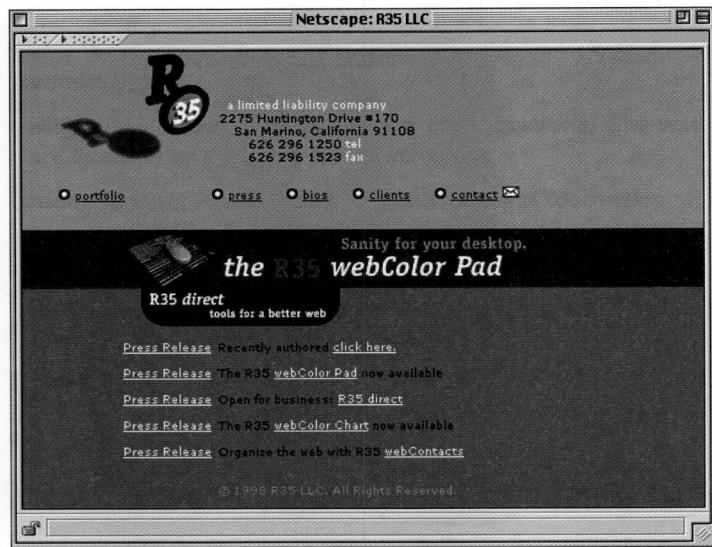

The R35 Web site.

The following figure demonstrates what happens to the top frame when the "bios" link is selected. As you can see, the top frame, along with the bottom frame, is updated.

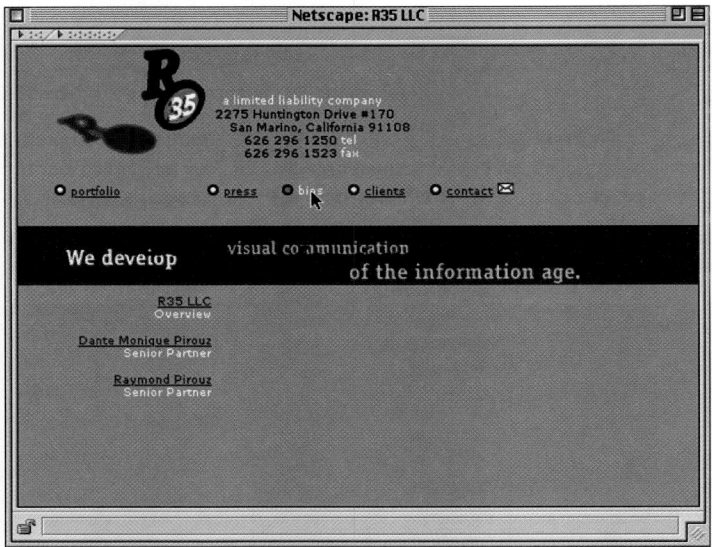

The R35 Web site with the "bios" link selected.

What makes this technique effective is that the top frame is updated to reflect that the user is now in the "bios" section. This is represented by the fact that "bios" is no longer clickable and its circle indicator is lit. The technique of updating navigation frames works well to enhance the navigation experience and provide the user with one extra level of feedback.

For another online example of frames, JavaScript and navigation techniques, pay `http://www.eyecandy.org` a visit. ●

PART VI

Magic with Windows

Ever since the 2.0 version of Netscape Navigator and the 3.0 version of Internet Explorer, designers have had the ability to force new browser windows to open for their visitors.

Some designers have used the open window technology to treat their home pages as launch pads, opening windows to display graphics or other pages with rigidly controlled parameters.

Other designers have used the technology to create "remote-control" windows that assist the user in navigating through the Web site. A majority of designers, however, have been opening new windows for links that take the user away from their site (so that their site will always remain in the background and available to the user).

Ultimately, no matter how the technology has been used, the ability to open new windows (while distracting and confusing to some) has given Web designers an extra ounce of "control" over the delivery of the Web experience.

Open New Windows with HTML
TARGET

Use this technique to:

- **Open new windows without using JavaScript or any extra code.**
  By simply using HTML, you can force a new browser window to open
  when a user clicks a link.

- **Open new windows for viewers who have disabled JavaScript.** This
  HTML technique does the trick with or without a JavaScript-enabled
  browser.

Although much of the open window technology requires the use of JavaScript
code, there *is* a way to force new windows to open by using simple HTML code.

HTML Versus JavaScript

Why use simple HTML when you can use JavaScript?

1 JavaScript may cause older browsers, slower platforms, or RAM-hungry systems to crash.

2 HTML is much easier to implement than JavaScript.

The simple HTML that makes opening new windows possible is the TARGET
attribute, commonly used within frames. This attribute enables you to point linked
URLs to a frame or browser window referred to by a name. By using the
TARGET="_blank" attribute within your <A HREF> tag, you force your linked URL to
appear within a brand-new browser window (using the reserved name, _blank, as a
setting for brand-new, empty default browser windows).

The only drawback to using simple HTML when opening new windows is that no
customization is possible. The resulting HTML-generated open window is generally
as large as the window that contained the initial link. It also contains all the default
browser window elements such as buttons, the location window, and so on.

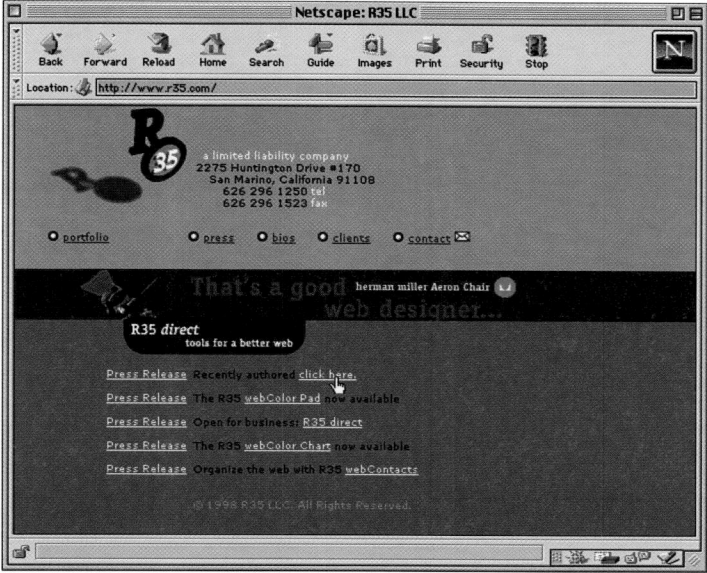

The R35 Web site uses simple HTML to open new browser windows.

The preceding figure demonstrates a link on the R35 Web site that uses the simple HTML open window technique. The R35 Web site uses the HTML-based open window technique when no window customization is required to display the page that is being linked to.

Coding the HTML

To open new windows by using simple HTML, code your <A HREF> tags like so:

```
<A HREF="http://www.yourURL.com" TARGET="_blank">your linked text</A>
```

209

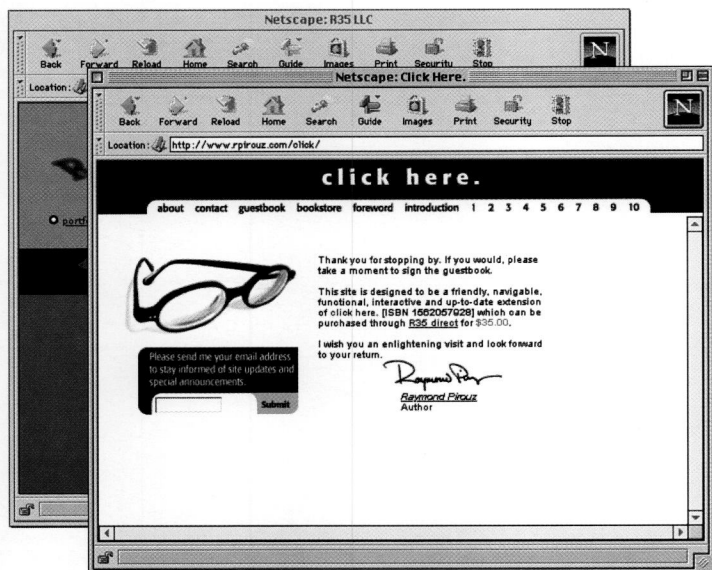

New browser window opened by using HTML.

The underscore character "_" (Shift plus Dash) must be used when specifying the "blank" TARGET. Here's how the technique is used within the R35 page's bottom frame to force the *click here.* site to open in a new window:

```
<A HREF="http://www.rpirouz.com/click/" TARGET="_blank"
onMouseOver="window.status='visit the click here site.'; return
true;">click here.</A>
```

Notice that JavaScript has been incorporated here to force the status bar to display the message within single quotes, but the only piece of code forcing the new window is the TARGET="_blank" attribute.

Check out some more Web sites that use simple HTML to create new windows for their links:

- Communication Arts (http://www.commarts.com)

- Internet Professional Publishers Association (http://www.ippa.org) ●

Open and Close Windows with JavaScript

Use this technique to:

- **Open new windows with ultimate control.** You can specify exactly how wide and tall your new window should be—but that's not all. By using JavaScript, you can tell your browser whether or not to display the menu buttons and status bar below—total control.

- **Enable users to close newly opened windows with one click.** Let your viewers close the new window as easily as you opened it for them.

If you're interested in making your new windows a certain dimension—or if you don't want them to display the default browser buttons and location boxes—you'll need to enhance your HTML with some JavaScript.

Open New Windows

To open new windows by using JavaScript, declare your code within the `<HEAD></HEAD>` tags of your HTML page like so:

```
<SCRIPT LANGUAGE="JavaScript">
<!--//
function openWindow() {
window.open("","windowname",'toolbar=0,location=0,scrollbars=1,width=5
00,height=500,resizable=1');
}
//-->
</SCRIPT>
```

The preceding JavaScript declares a function called `openWindow`, which further defines certain parameters within the parentheses following the JavaScript `window.open` command:

- `""`   This is the URL location, which you don't need to fill in, because you'll be defining it later in the `<A HREF>` tag.

- `"windowname"`   This is the name you give the window. You'll need to name your `window.open` function so that you can target it later in your HTML.

- `toolbar=0`   This means that the toolbar buttons on your browser (Back, Forward, Reload, Home, and so on) should not be visible (I would denote that they *should* be visible). As well, you can use "yes" or "no" instead of "1" or "0" to specify this—words are often easier to remember than numbers.

- `location=0`   This tells JavaScript not to show the location window, which is located under the toolbar, displaying the current URL location.

- `scrollbars=1`   This tells JavaScript to show scrollbars (if they are required—0 would denote *not* showing scrollbars).

- `width` and `height`   These tell JavaScript how large or small the new window should be (in pixels).

- `resizable=1`   This means that the user can resize the window by dragging its lower-right corner (0 denotes that the window is *not* resizable).

As you can see by this list of parameters, you can control many aspects of a new window's appearance.

Calling the JavaScript Function

To call the JavaScript function, code your `<A HREF>` tag like so:

```
<A HREF="http://www.newpage.com" onClick=openWindow()
TARGET="windowname">Your Linking Text or Image Here</A>
```

Implementing the preceding painless JavaScript code enables you to gain a fair amount of control with regard to how your linked pages are delivered to your audience.

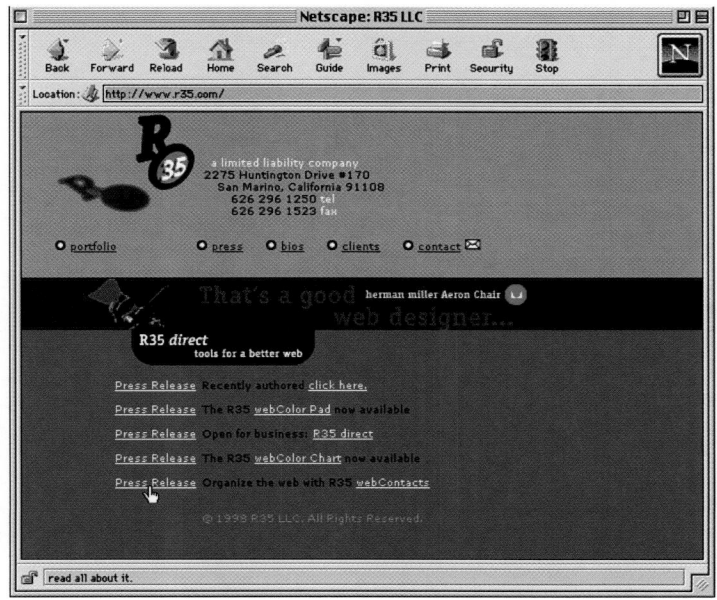

The R35 Web site with a link that calls a more controlled, JavaScript-based new window.

213

On the R35 Web site, for example, the press release links in the bottom frame use a JavaScript `open.window` function to create new windows that simply display the press releases. Upon clicking a "press release" link from the R35 Web site, users are presented with a new window similar in structure to the following figure.

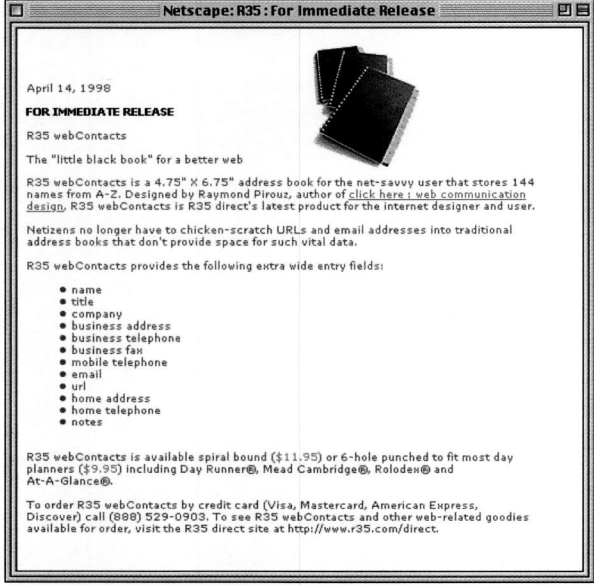

The R35 press release window without a toolbar, location window, or scrollbar.

As you can see in the preceding figure, R35's press release page doesn't display any toolbars, location windows, or a status bar and is free from a scrollbar because its predefined 500-pixel window height accommodates all the page's content on the Macintosh. PC viewers will probably get a scrollbar on this page, because the PC tends to display type larger than the Macintosh, thereby creating a more lengthy page.

Advantages to Opening New Windows

The are many advantages to opening new windows. The following two figures demonstrate one of the most common uses of the technique—to display a more detailed, close-up version of a small image.

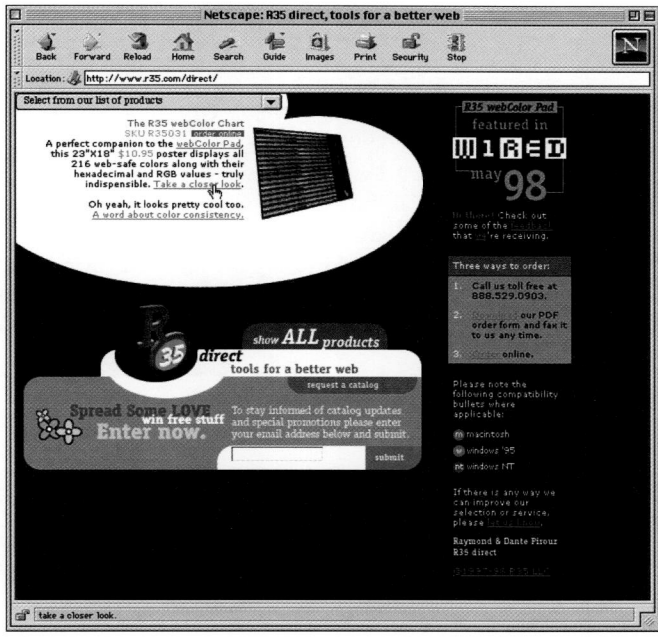

The R35 direct page also uses JavaScript to open windows.

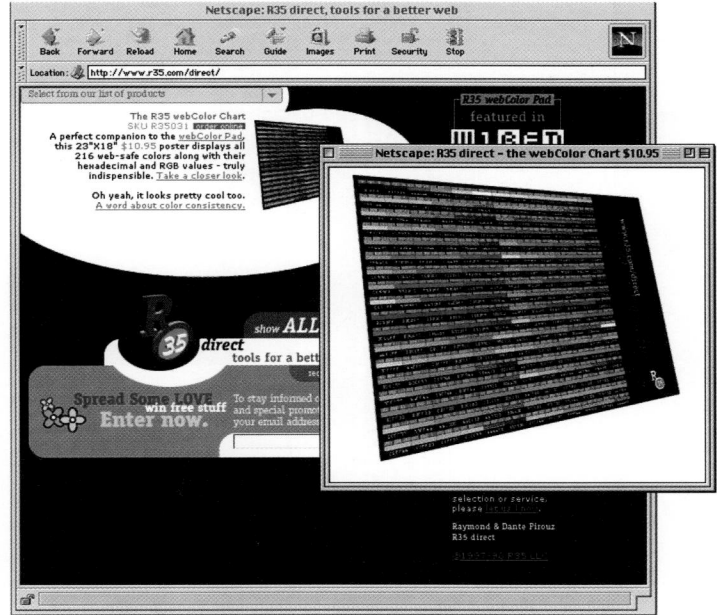

Use the JavaScript window open technique to display a larger version of a small image.

Why not just show the larger image in the first place? Two reasons:

1 Bandwidth—Smaller images take much less time to load and display.

2 Layout limitations—You can only display so much information on a Web page and still adhere to an underlying design foundation that holds the page together.

These two factors, coupled with JavaScript's ease of implementation and browser-wide compatibility, make a good case for using the JavaScript window open technique to show larger close-ups of small images to those who are interested in seeing them.

Positioning New Windows

What if you want to make your new window appear at a specific location on your user's screen? Well, it's possible and the following code works on both Internet Explorer and Netscape Navigator 4.0. All you really have to do is add the `left` and `top` attributes to your JavaScript `openWindow` function like so:

```
<SCRIPT LANGUAGE="JavaScript">
<!--//
function openWindow() {
window.open("","windowname",'toolbar=0,location=0,scrollbars=1,width=5
00,height=500,resizable=1, left=150, top=100');
}
//-->
</SCRIPT>
```

In this example, the new window is forced to appear 150 pixels from the left and 100 pixels from the top of your viewer's screen. Because the code will not cause errors for older browsers, it's safe to use and implement.

Close Windows

By using JavaScript, you not only can *open* windows, you can *close* them as well. It's really quite simple:

```
<A HREF=JavaScript:onClick=self.close()>Close this window</A>
```

That's all there is to it. This simple piece of code tells JavaScript that when the user clicks the hyperlink (or linked image), the window from which the click originated should close. ●

217

Design a Launch Pad Home Page

Use this technique to:

- **Totally control the Web experience.** By designing a launch pad home page, you control every aspect of the site—from new window dimensions to whether or not they contain menu bars. By using this technique, you can create a custom Web site experience for your visitors.

- **Always keep your home page in the background.** This technique keeps your home page accessible to your viewers, who never really *leave* your home page.

- **Open an unlimited array of layout potential.** By using your home page as a launch pad, you don't have the layout limitations imposed by single-window home pages because each new window can expand on a different topic with its own unique layout, leaving the other windows accessible at all times.

By using the power and flexibility of JavaScript, you can design a very unconventional home page with lots of surprises in store for your visitors. There are two kinds of launch pad home pages:

1 Those that cause new windows to open when users click links.

2 Those that automatically launch new windows when the home page loads.

New Windows on Demand

A launch pad home page is simply this: a home page from which every link opens a new window, leaving the home page in the background. Pushed one step further, it can be this: a unique home page experience that does not rely on common conventions of Web design to lead the viewer deeper.

The following figure is not your usual home page—it's a top view of a golf course!

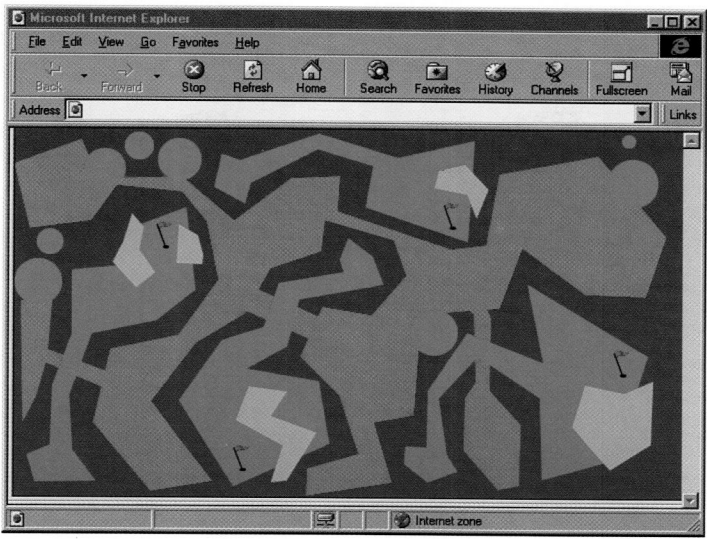

An unconventional home page based on a golf course.

Imagine, however, that you are a golf course owner wanting to create an online presence for your establishment. By making each hole in the course into a link, you can create new windows to open, each describing a certain aspect of your Web site and business. By creating an icon of a clubhouse, you can force an online store to open up in a new window, selling golf clubs and other golf-related merchandise.

The golf course with new windows opened.

The launch pad Web site can be treated as a thematic entity, such as the golf course Web site, or it can be approached differently. What's important here is that the launch pad Web site treats the common design, layout, header placement, and navigation issues differently than the standard one-page Web site. For those willing to take the JavaScript open-window technique one step further, the launch pad concept is a good place to start.

Auto-Loading New Windows

Another way to display a multi-page launch pad Web site is to automatically display a series of new windows once the home page has loaded.

This technique is handled quite simply in HTML. Within your <HEAD></HEAD> tags, you must provide your JavaScript declaration:

```
<SCRIPT LANGUAGE="JavaScript">
<!--//
function openPages()
{
window.open("http://www.URL#1.com","window1",'toolbar=0,
location=0,scrollbars=0,width=300,height=300, resizable=0');

window.open("http://www.URL#2.com","window2",'toolbar=0,
location=0,scrollbars=0,width=300,height=300, resizable=0');

window.open("http://www.URL#3.com","window3",'toolbar=0,
location=0,scrollbars=0,width=300,height=300, resizable=0');
}
//-->
</SCRIPT>
```

The preceding code tells JavaScript that when the openPages function is called, it should open three different pages, each 300 × 300 pixels in size, named window1, window2, and window3, located at the URLs designated within the code.

In order to make the new windows appear as soon as the home page loads, you must add the onLoad attribute within your <BODY> tag as such:

```
<BODY BGCOLOR="#XXXXXX" LINK="# XXXXXX " VLINK="# XXXXXX " ALINK="# XXXXXX
" TEXT="# XXXXXX " onLoad="openPages()">
```

This tells JavaScript that as soon as the page loads, it should launch the openPages function.

No matter how you decide to implement the launch pad technique, it can add a unique touch to your Web site. ●

Open Remote Navigation Windows

Use this technique to:

- **Enhance your site's navigation.** Create a window specifically to help your user navigate throughout your site. This technique is beneficial in that it provides a constantly visible and available means of navigation independent of what's going on in the main window.

- **Create more room for content on your page.** By creating a "remote control," you can remove the navigation from your main content window, giving you much more flexibility and room for your content and layout.

The remote navigation window is the simplest and most utilitarian application of the JavaScript open-window technique.

> **TIP** This technique requires two pages to function properly. The first is your home page (or the page from which you would like your remote control to launch) and the second is your remote control page. In other words, you'll need two HTML documents—one for your main page and another for your remote control page.

There are two kinds of remote navigation windows:

1 Those that automatically appear when the page loads.

2 Those that are called through a link in the home page.

Making the Remote Control Appear Automatically

In order to take full advantage of a navigation window, it's important to immediately offer it to your visitors, instead of hoping that they will find the link that launches it. Creating the remote window is quite simple. You'll need to code some JavaScript within your main document (or the page from which the remote control will be forced to open).

First, define your JavaScript function within your HTML page's `<HEAD></HEAD>` tags:

```
<SCRIPT LANGUAGE="JavaScript">
<!--//

function openRemote()
{
window.open("http://www.remoteURL.com","remote",'toolbar=0,
location=0,scrollbars=0,width=200,height=350,resizable=0');
}


//-->
</SCRIPT>
```

The preceding code tells JavaScript that when the `openRemote` function is called, it should open a 200-pixel-wide by 350-pixel-tall window without a toolbar, location window, or scrollbars, without allowing it to be resizable.

In order to make the remote window appear as soon as the home page loads, you must add the `onLoad` attribute within your `<BODY>` tag:

```
<BODY BGCOLOR="#XXXXXX" LINK="# XXXXXX " VLINK="# XXXXXX " ALINK="# XXXXXX
" TEXT="# XXXXXX " onLoad="openRemote()">
```

This code tells JavaScript that as soon as the page loads, it should launch the remote navigation window.

The following figure demonstrates one way to handle remote-window navigation.

An online golf page with a remote navigation window.

223

As you can see, no navigation links appear within the main Web page. Hence, the design within this page is more fluid and less restricted to a certain portion of the page to make room for the navigation. As you can imagine, the possibilities are endless.

Coding and Using the Remote Control Page

In order to allow your remote page to control your main Web page, you need to seek the aid of JavaScript. First, define your JavaScript function within your remote navigation page's <HEAD></HEAD> tags:

```
<SCRIPT LANGUAGE="JavaScript">
<!--//

function gotoSite(site) {
    if (site != "") {
        opener.document.location=site
    }
}

//-->
</SCRIPT>
```

The preceding code tells JavaScript that when the gotoSite function is called, it should force the document that opened it (opener.document.location) to go to the specified URL.

Easy enough? There's one more step. Within your <A HREF> tag, you must specify your target URL as such:

```
<a href="JavaScript:gotoSite('http://www.pageURL.com')">link</a>
```

The above JavaScript forces your large Web site window to go to the URL that you specify.

For more information on using JavaScript to build new windows, visit cnet's informative BUILDER.COM Web site located at http://www.builder.com and check out their cool "Window builder" tool at:

```
http://www.builder.com/Programming/Kahn/092497/toolwb.html?st.bl.fd.co
ol5
```

Also, don't forget to take a look at WebCoder.com's awesome selection of JavaScript tips and tricks at http://www.webcoder.com. ●

PART VII

Magic with Type

Web typography is the most limiting aspect of Web design. For starters, Web designers are limited to dealing with a handful of fonts, whereas print design allows for a selection limited only by type-vendor offerings and job budgets.

Beyond the font availability issues, platform inconsistencies exist (specified <FONT> tag sizes display larger on PCs than on Macs), along with scale and positioning issues.

The future of Web typography looks bright given the full adoption and implementation of Cascading Style Sheets (CSS—currently available only to 4.0+ browsers), which allows for pixel-perfect type specification, absolute positioning, layering, and much, much more.

For now, several Web-type treatment techniques have evolved to give Web designers some freedom to specify and manipulate online typography until future technologies are embraced by the masses.

Specifying Fonts with HTML

Use this technique to:

- **Deliver a consistent look across platforms.** Whether designing for Macintosh audiences, PC viewers, or both, you're limited to specifying a handful of typefaces for mass consumption. Knowing which ones to use can keep the look of your page consistent across platforms.

- **Control how type is displayed to a majority of viewers.** Using the HTML <FONT> tag, you can specify the size and color of your typeface and remain confident that the results will be fairly consistent across platforms and browsers.

Despite its many limitations, HTML contains several key tags that enable Web designers to maintain a certain level of sanity. One of these is the <FONT> tag, and knowing how to use it will help you deliver somewhat consistent typography across the many platforms.

Specifying Size

The following code will give you an idea of the various sizes available with the <FONT> tag:

```
<HTML>

<HEAD>

<TITLE>Type Test</TITLE>

</HEAD>

<BODY BGCOLOR="#000000" TEXT="#FFFFFF">

<FONT FACE="VERDANA, ARIAL, HELVETICA" SIZE=1>This is size
1</FONT><BR><BR>
<FONT FACE="VERDANA, ARIAL, HELVETICA" SIZE=2>This is size
2</FONT><BR><BR>
<FONT FACE="VERDANA, ARIAL, HELVETICA" SIZE=3>This is size
3</FONT><BR><BR>
<FONT FACE="VERDANA, ARIAL, HELVETICA" SIZE=4>This is size
4</FONT><BR><BR>
<FONT FACE="VERDANA, ARIAL, HELVETICA" SIZE=5>This is size
5</FONT><BR><BR>
<FONT FACE="VERDANA, ARIAL, HELVETICA" SIZE=6>This is size
6</FONT><BR><BR>
<FONT FACE="VERDANA, ARIAL, HELVETICA" SIZE=7>This is size
7</FONT><BR><BR>

</BODY>

</HTML>
```

Take a close look at the following two figures and you'll notice something odd—the PC tends to display fonts quite larger in some cases than does the Macintosh when using the same HTML!

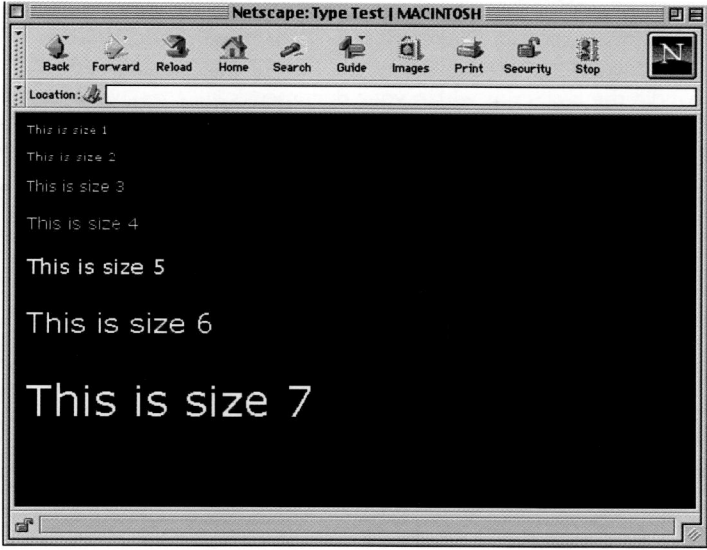

Testing font sizes on the Macintosh.

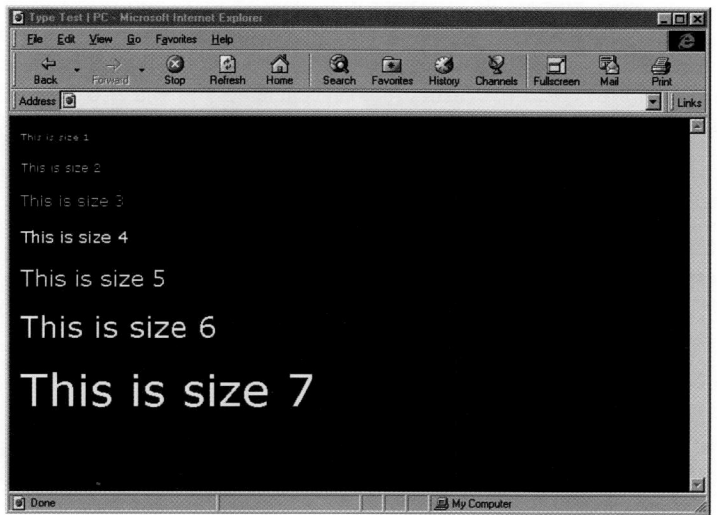

Testing font sizes on the PC.

This is something you should take into consideration when designing your pages. One way to work around this flaw is to use JavaScript to detect your user's machine type (Mac or PC) and display font sizes specific to the way that machine renders them. For example, let's say you have a page in which you would like PC users to see your fonts at size 5, and Macintosh users to see your fonts at size 4. You can set the BASEFONT of the entire page to these particular sizes. The <BASE-FONT> tag tells HTML to set all fonts within your page to a specific size. Here's how we'd handle the JavaScript within your document's <HEAD></HEAD> tags:

```
<SCRIPT LANGUAGE="JavaScript">
    if (navigator.appVersion.indexOf("Mac") > 1){
    document.write('<BASEFONT SIZE="4">');
    }
    else {
    document.write('<BASEFONT SIZE="5">');
    }
</SCRIPT>
```

That's all there is to it. The above code tells JavaScript that if the machine is a Mac, it should set the BASEFONT for the document to size 4. Otherwise, it should set the BASEFONT size for the page to size 5 (this would also be true for UNIX machines and all other non-Mac systems).

Specifying Fonts

As a Web type designer, your ability to specify fonts with HTML is limited to but a few of the more commonly prevalent typefaces on Macs and PCs. On the Mac, some of the more common fonts are Helvetica, Courier, Palatino, and Times. If you have installed Microsoft's Internet Explorer or have downloaded Microsoft's free fonts from http://www.microsoft.com/typography, you will also have Verdana and Arial at your disposal.

On the PC, you will generally find the fonts Verdana, Arial, Helvetica, Courier New, Palatino, and Times New Roman installed.

As you can see, the Mac and PC share a pretty consistent set of general fonts that you can specify in HTML and be sure that they will appear for your viewer. On UNIX machines, you will generally only find Helvetica and Times; hence, your selection is limited further if you're designing for that platform as well.

To specify consistent fonts across platforms, design your site listing your favorite common font within your <FONT> tag, also offering alternate choices just in case users don't have access to your font of choice. Here's how:

```
<FONT FACE="Verdana, Arial, Helvetica" SIZE="X" COLOR="#XXXXXX">
```

In the preceding example, the font Verdana is the font your viewer's browser looks for first. If Verdana is not available, the browser then looks for Arial and so on down the line until it finds a font with which to display the page.

Testing for Fonts

What if none of these fonts is available to the system? How can you specify fonts and ensure that your viewers will see something similar, even though they may not have the font you specified? If your viewers have PCs, chances are that they will see what their browser defaults to (generally a serif face). If your viewers are on Macs, however, you can specify the generic serif or sans-serif font faces within your <FONT> tag based on the kind of look you want your site to have. If the Mac-based browser cannot find the faces you initially requested, it will then find the closest serif or sans-serif alternative.

For example, if you're laying out a sans-serif page, consider the following:

```
<FONT FACE="Verdana, Arial, Helvetica, SANS-SERIF">
```

If your visitor doesn't have Verdana, chances are she has Arial or Helvetica. Otherwise, her browser will select a sans-serif face to show. In the following figure, note that the Sans-Serif default face is Helvetica. If Helvetica were not available, the browser would have chosen another sans-serif face.

Testing for sans-serif fonts.

If you're laying out a serif page, consider the following:

```
<FONT FACE="Palatino, Times, Times New Roman, SERIF">
```

Testing for serif fonts.

Again, both Mac and PC users probably have Palatino installed, but if not, Mac users default to Times (the default serif face), while PC users see Times New Roman (or their browsers select a serif face to display).

Code the following sans-serif and serif font tests and see what appears in your browser:

```
<HTML>

<HEAD>

<TITLE>Sans-Serif Font Test</TITLE>

</HEAD>

<BODY BGCOLOR="#000000" TEXT="#FFFFFF">

<CENTER>

<FONT FACE="VERDANA" SIZE=7>Verdana</FONT><BR><BR>
<FONT FACE="ARIAL" SIZE=7>Arial</FONT><BR><BR>
```

```
<FONT FACE="HELVETICA" SIZE=7>Helvetica</FONT><BR><BR>
<FONT FACE="SANS-SERIF" SIZE=7>Sans-Serif</FONT><BR><BR>

</CENTER>

</BODY>

</HTML>
```

Here is the serif font test:

```
<HTML>

<HEAD>

<TITLE>Serif Font Test</TITLE>

</HEAD>

<BODY BGCOLOR="#000000" TEXT="#FFFFFF">

<CENTER>

<FONT FACE="PALATINO" SIZE=7>Palatino</FONT><BR><BR>
<FONT FACE="TIMES NEW ROMAN" SIZE=7>Times New Roman</FONT><BR><BR>
<FONT FACE="TIMES" SIZE=7>Times</FONT><BR><BR>
<FONT FACE="SERIF" SIZE=7>Serif</FONT><BR><BR>

</CENTER>

</BODY>

</HTML>
```

231

If you have a Mac as well as a PC, check out the code in both machines and compare the results. Experiment with changing the FONT FACE to a font specific to your system, then remove the font from your system font-set, and see what happens when you reload the page. ●

Specifying Fonts with Cascading Style Sheets

Use this technique to:

- **Apply styles to entire paragraphs of text.** You can use Cascading Style Sheets to apply a certain color, weight, and size to entire paragraphs of type without having to deal with the limitations of the <FONT> tag.

- **Gain more control when specifying font size.** Go beyond HTML's limited sizing specifications and use conventions common to word processing, desktop publishing, and vector graphics software.

Cascading Style Sheets (CSS) is the savior of online Web typography. Unfortunately, only 4.0 or better browsers can take advantage of the technology, and it will take a bit of time before the "masses" climb onto the 4.0 bandwagon. Nevertheless, there is no reason why you shouldn't get your feet wet and start experimenting with the awesome power of CSS.

> **TIP** This section is a quick **CSS** primer and in no way attempts to delve into the entire subject matter. Several good books have been written on **CSS**, and there are a dozen Web sites littering the Internet with **CSS** resources bursting from their virtual seams. Use this section to experiment with the technology. Once you're hooked, check out the references at the end of this section for further exploration.

Creating Styles

If you've played around with JavaScript implementation, you'll quickly get the hang of how to specify and use CSS. Much like JavaScript, CSS can either be defined within HTML's <HEAD></HEAD> tags or be used within your code. In this example, you'll define CSS within the <HEAD></HEAD> tags to specify *styles* of type. In CSS, styles refer to sections of type that have a specific look, size, color, or any other attribute given to them when initially defined within the <HEAD></HEAD> tags. For this example, you will create three styles:

- A sans-serif, 18-point face with a 24-point leading (the space between the lines of type).

- A serif, 18-point italic face with 24-point leading.

- A serif, 24-point bold face (for the title).

Begin Your CSS Declaration

Here's how it's done:

1 Code your HTML as usual:

```
<HTML>
```

```
<HEAD>

<TITLE>Calling Fonts with Cascading Style Sheets</TITLE>
```

2 Begin your CSS declaration, telling the browser that you're creating Cascading Style Sheets and that older browsers should ignore the code:

```
<STYLE type="text/css">
<!--
```

3 So far, so good. Next, apply a background color to the document:

```
body {
background: #333300
}
```

Adding Style Declarations

The next step is to add your style declarations.

I Begin your first style declaration. The name given to this style is bodycopy, but notice that CSS requires a period before the name (don't forget that in your code). Within the bodycopy declaration, the font-face is set, along with the size, line-height (or leading), and font color:

```
.bodycopy    {
font-family: Verdana, Arial, Helvetica;
font-size: 18pt;
line-height: 24pt;
color: #999966
}
```

2 The second style declaration is named alternate:

```
.alternate    {
font-family: Palatino, Times New Roman, Times;
font-style: italic;
font-size: 18pt;
line-height: 24pt;
color: #999966
}
```

3 The third style declaration—used for titles—is called sectionhead:

```
.sectionhead   {
font-family: Verdana, Arial, Helvetica;
font-weight: bold;
font-size: 24pt;
color: #FFFFFF
}
```

> **TIP** You can call the styles anything you like, as long as you refer to them by name later in your HTML.

4 End your Style Sheets declaration within the <HEAD> tag:

```
-->
</STYLE>

</HEAD>

<BODY>
```

Create the Title Element and Body Copy

Use the <DIV> tag to create the title element and use <SPAN> to create the body copy.

1 In CSS, <DIV> is used to define an element, while <SPAN> defines elements within <DIV> tags. Create your title element by using a <DIV> tag and calling it by name, using class="sectionhead":

```
<DIV class="sectionhead">Introducing CSS</DIV>
```

> **TIP** Note that you do not use the period (.) when calling the DIV class.

2 Next create the body copy. The great thing about CSS is that you can simply change the way text looks by calling another class within <DIV></DIV> tags by using <SPAN>:

```
<DIV class="bodycopy">Isn't CSS great? Not only can I set my font
colors, sizes, weights and leading only once, I also get to change
them...<SPAN class="alternate">on the fly without having to re-code
all the time.</SPAN></DIV>
```

3 End your <BODY> and <HTML> tags as usual:

```
</BODY>

</HTML>
```

Putting It All Together

Here's the code in its entirety:

```
<HTML>

<HEAD>

<TITLE>Calling Fonts with Cascading Style Sheets</TITLE>

<STYLE type="text/css">
<!--

   body {
   background: #333300
}

   .bodycopy    {
   font-family: Verdana, Arial, Helvetica;
   font-size: 18pt;
   line-height: 24pt;
   color: #999966
}

   .alternate    {
   font-family: Palatino, Times New Roman, Times;
   font-style: italic;
   font-size: 18pt;
   line-height: 24pt;
   color: #999966
}

   .sectionhead   {
   font-family: Verdana, Arial, Helvetica;
   font-weight: bold;
```

```
      font-size: 24pt;
      color: #FFFFFF
   }


   -->
   </STYLE>

   </HEAD>

   <BODY>
   <DIV class="sectionhead">Introducing CSS</DIV>
   <DIV class="bodycopy">Isn't CSS great? Not only can I set my font
   colors, sizes, weights and leading only once, I also get to change
   them...<SPAN class="alternate">on the fly without having to re-code
   all the time.</SPAN></DIV>

   <BR><BR>

   </BODY>

   </HTML>
```

The following figure is the result of the preceding CSS code. Feel free to experiment with font sizing, leading, color choices, and font-families to see variations on your browser.

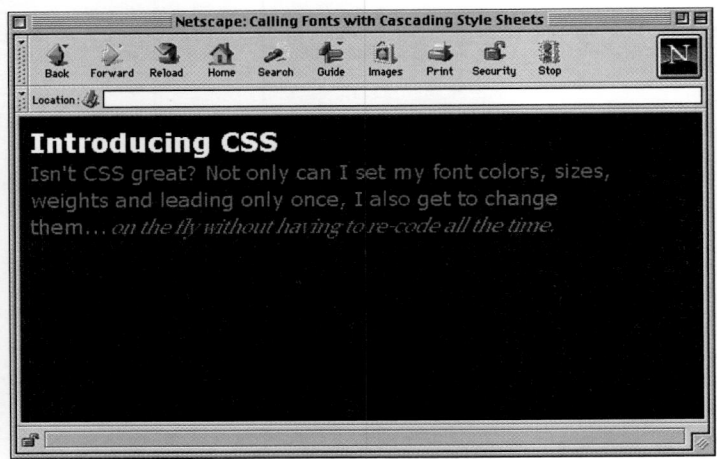

Using CSS to call fonts and define typographic style.

To learn more about this very detailed system of online type specification, surf to the following Web sites for further information:

World Wide Web Consortium on CSS: `http://www.w3.org/Style/`

Web Review's *Creating Your First Style Sheet*:
`http://webreview.com/97/10/10/style/index.html` ●

Position and Layer Type with CSS

Use this technique to:

- **Specify absolute placement for your text.** Specify exactly where your text is to appear for your viewer without having to manage tables or spacer GIFs.

- **Create multiple layers on which type can *float*.** Using Cascading Style Sheets, you can achieve quick-loading layered typography without using a single image!

- **Design more flexible layouts.** Overcome the layout limitations imposed by simple HTML and single-layer placement restrictions.

It is highly recommended that you read the previous section, "Specifying Fonts with Cascading Style Sheets," before you read this section, as the following builds on techniques introduced there.

Layering Typographic Elements

Beyond simply specifying fonts, sizes, and styles, CSS enables the Web designer to position type on multiple layers with pixel-perfect precision. CSS uses the term "z-index" when referring to Web page layers. Z-index refers to the Z-axis that rises above and below the plain on which the X and Y axis are located. Using the z-index, CSS can place type on different levels (or planes) to create a layered type effect.

When absolutely positioning typographic elements, CSS looks for a "top" location and a "left" location (usually specified in pixels). For example, if you want text to begin 30 pixels down from the top edge of the browser window and 60 pixels in from the left edge, you would specify a "top" value of 30 and a "left" value of 60 pixels.

The following figure represents a sample of what you can accomplish by using layering and absolute positioning.

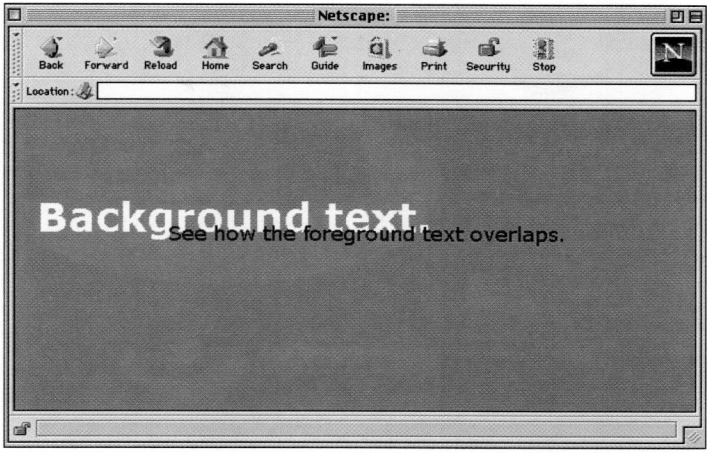

Layering type with CSS.

The text "Background text" is on a different layer, and is, in fact, one layer below the text "See how the foreground text overlaps." Here is how you can accomplish this effect by using CSS:

1 Begin coding your HTML as usual:

```
<HTML>

<HEAD>
```

2 Declare Cascading Style Sheets:

```
<STYLE type="text/css">
<!--
```

3 Set your body background color:

```
    body {
    background: #999966
}
```

4 Define a "background" text style. This layer begins 75 pixels down from the top edge of the screen and 20 pixels in from the left edge, as specified by the `top` and `left` values. Notice also that this layer resides on z-index: 1. Layer numbers represent their positions within the layer hierarchy. For example, layer 4 would be in front of layer 3, so any type on layer 4 would overlap type on layer 3 if placed within proximity of one another.

```
    .background    { position: absolute;
    top: 75px;
    left: 20px;
    z-index: 1;
```

239

```
    font-family: Verdana, Arial, Helvetica;
    font-weight: bold;
    font-size: 36pt;
    color: #ffffff
}
```

5 Define a "foreground" text style. Notice that this layer begins 101 pixels down from the top edge of the browser window and comes in 135 pixels from the left edge. This layer resides on z-index number 2, so you know that type on this layer overlaps any type on z-index number 1:

```
.foreground  { position: absolute;
top: 101px;
left: 135px;
z-index: 2;
font-family: Verdana, Arial, Helvetica;
font-size: 18pt;
color: #333300
}
```

6 End your style declaration:

```
-->
</STYLE>

</HEAD>
```

7 Begin your <BODY> tag and specify your <DIV> tag classes, based on your initial CSS declarations in step 2:

```
<BODY>

<DIV class="background">Background text.</DIV>

<DIV class="foreground">See how the foreground text overlaps.</DIV>
```

8 Close up your <BODY> and <HTML> tags:

```
</BODY>

</HTML>
```

As you can see in this code, after you declare the absolute position of your type and its z-index, all you need to do is specify it within your body by using <DIV> tags and type away, knowing that your type will appear *as you specified it* within 4.0 and higher browsers.

Putting It All Together

Here is the entire code:

```
<HTML>

<HEAD>

<STYLE type="text/css">
<!--

    body {
    background: #999966
}

    .background    { position: absolute;
    top: 75px;
    left: 20px;
    z-index: 1;
    font-family: Verdana, Arial, Helvetica;
    font-weight: bold;
    font-size: 36pt;
    color: #ffffff
}

    .foreground    { position: absolute;
    top: 101px;
    left: 135px;
    z-index: 2;
    font-family: Verdana, Arial, Helvetica;
    font-size: 18pt;
    color: #333300
}

-->
</STYLE>

</HEAD>

<BODY>

<SPAN class="background">Background text.</SPAN>

<SPAN class="foreground">See how the foreground text overlaps.</SPAN>

</BODY>

</HTML>
```

If you are interested in creating more effects with CSS, check out the resources listed at the end of the section named "Specifying Fonts with Cascading Style Sheets." ●

Creating Nonunderlined Text Links with CSS

Use this technique to:

- **Create unique text links.** Remove unsightly underlined links from your page and design a cleaner text layout, leaving color as the only hypertext link indicator.

- **Design more visually pleasing typographic navigation.** Using Cascading Style Sheets to specify links, you can create nonunderlined links without having to resort to images and image maps.

Before you continue with this section, it is highly recommended that you read the section titled, "Specifying Fonts with Cascading Style Sheets," as the following builds on techniques introduced there.

Applying Styles

With Cascading Style Sheets, you can apply styles to virtually any aspect of HTML, whether they are tags (such as <P> or <DIV>) or other HTML attributes such as active and visited links.

One aspect of HTML that I know many designers would change if they could is the fact that hyperlinks are underlined. Although underlining helps to visually point out hyperlinks, it is generally considered typographically weak and unattractive. The same kind of attention can be drawn to type by using other decorative treatments such as weight and color.

For example, in the following figure, notice how plain and relatively simplistic the standard underlined link appears.

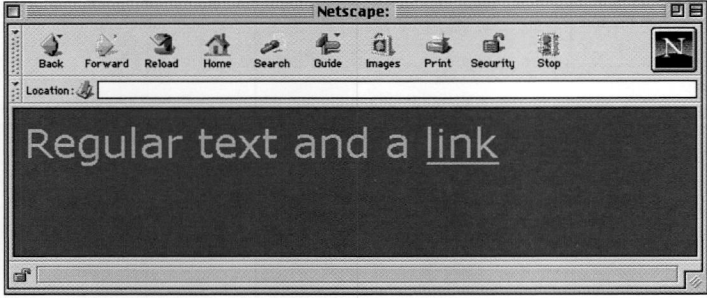

The standard less-than-attractive underlined link.

The following figure represents an HTML hyperlink that is *not* underlined. As you can see, even though it's not underlined, the word "link" *does* stand out and attracts the eye due to its heavier weight as well as its bright color.

Creating nonunderlined links with CSS.

This variation is a much more unique approach at delivering hyperlinked text. In order to avoid any confusion, however, it is strongly suggested that all your "links" share the same attributes (in other words, all should be the same font, same color and same weight—bold, regular or italic) to maintain consistency.

Turning Off Link Underlining

Here's how you can use CSS to turn link underlining off:

1 Begin with HTML as usual:

```
<HTML>

<HEAD>
```

2 Declare your CSS and background image color:

```
<STYLE type="text/css">
<!--

    body {
    background: #0033FF
}
```

243

3 Define your A:LINK style:

```
A:LINK {
font-family: Verdana, Arial, Helvetica;
font-weight: bold;
text-decoration: none;
font-size: 36pt;
color: #FFFFFF
}
```

Notice that the text-decoration variable is introduced in step 3, and none is chosen, which means not underlined.

4 Define the CSS style for your body copy:

```
.bodycopy   {
font-family: Verdana, Arial, Helvetica;
font-size: 36pt;
color: #99CCFF
}
```

5 End the CSS declaration and begin your HTML body:

```
-->
</STYLE>

</HEAD>

<BODY>
```

6 Assign your bodycopy style to a paragraph tag (<P>) and link within it (as you usually would). This time, however, the result will be a nonunderlined link:

```
<P CLASS="bodycopy">Regular text and a <A
HREF="http://www.link.com">link</A></P>
```

7 Close your <BODY> and <HTML> tags:

```
</BODY>
```

Experiment with font colors and sizes, and try to incorporate nonunderlined linked text within different CSS styles that you can define on your own. Here's the code in its entirety:

```
<HTML>

<HEAD>

<STYLE type="text/css">
<!--

    body {
    background: #0033FF
}

    A:LINK {
    font-family: Verdana, Arial, Helvetica;
    font-weight: bold;
```

```
    text-decoration: none;
    font-size: 36pt;
    color: #FFFFFF
}


    .bodycopy   {
    font-family: Verdana, Arial, Helvetica;
    font-size: 36pt;
    color: #99CCFF
}

-->
</STYLE>

</HEAD>

<BODY>

<P CLASS="bodycopy">Regular text and a <A
HREF="http://www.link.com">link</A></P>

</BODY>

</HTML>
```

Please remember that CSS is a very complex and detailed add-on to HTML. If you are interested in creating more effects using CSS, it is highly recommended that you check out the resources listed at the end of the section named "Specifying Fonts with Cascading Style Sheets." ●

Wrap Type Around Images

Use this technique to:

- **Create more interesting layouts.** Integrate type and images to create a magazine-like editorial look.

- **Work around HTML layout restrictions.** Design typography that defies conventional HTML layout limitations.

Designing Web typography is not limited to type alone. Most of the time, you will need to lay out and design type in relation to images or other graphics. Generally, HTML does not enable you to specify where a graphic can be placed in relation to type.

Typographic Layout Limitations of Conventional HTML

Imagine having to integrate the image in the following figure into your Web page, forcing type to wrap around it.

A snake in the desert.

Typically, in order to place an image along with some text on a page, you would code HTML like so:

```
<HTML>

<HEAD>

<TITLE>Snake in the Desert</TITLE>
```

```
</HEAD>

<BODY BGCOLOR="#CC9966" TEXT="#000000">

<CENTER>

<IMG SRC="snake.gif" WIDTH=300 HEIGHT=300><FONT FACE="VERDANA" SIZE=3>Snake
in the desert.</FONT>

</CENTER>

</BODY>

</HTML>
```

As you can see in the following figure (the visual representation of the above HTML), there is no way to strategically guide text around images without some kind of underlying structure with which to house and control the flow of objects.

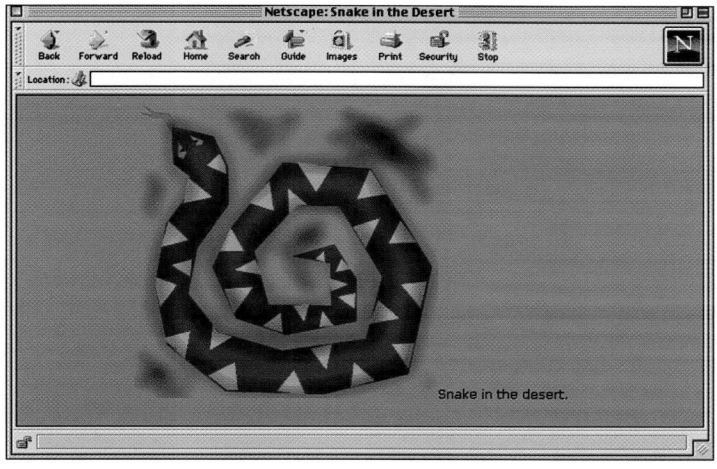

Without structure, it's hard to control the flow of text around images.

Using Tables to Enhance Layout

By using tables, you can gain firm control over how your image lays out within your page's body of text. As you can see in the following figure, a five-column, 600-pixel table has been designed to house both text and images to create a text-wrap effect.

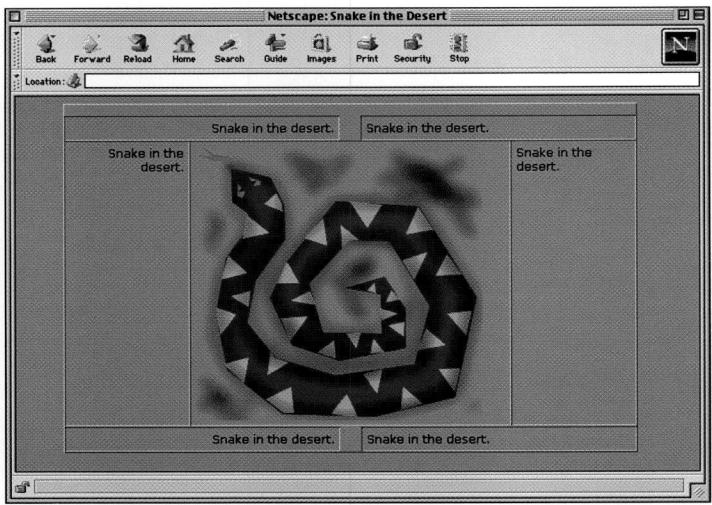

Gain text-wrap control by using tables.

Here are the specifications for the table:

```
<TABLE WIDTH=600 CELLPADDING=5 CELLSPACING=0 BORDER=1>
<TR>
<TD WIDTH=145></TD>
<TD WIDTH=145></TD>
<TD WIDTH=10></TD>
<TD WIDTH=145></TD>
<TD WIDTH=145></TD>
```

As you can see in the code, CELLPADDING has been set to 5 so that there is some breathing room between the columns separating text fields. Use the following HTML to create a table structure similar to that in the preceding figure:

1 Begin your HTML as you normally would:

```
<HTML>

<HEAD>

<TITLE>Snake in the Desert</TITLE>

</HEAD>

<BODY BGCOLOR="#CC9966" TEXT="#000000">
```

2 Center your page's content:

```
<CENTER>
```

3 Begin a 600-pixel-wide table, giving it some air by setting the CELLPADDING to 5 pixels. Also, set your BORDER to 1 so that you can see the table as you lay it out and test it on your browser. When you're done coding the page, you can set this value back to 0.

```
<TABLE WIDTH=600 CELLPADDING=5 CELLSPACING=0 BORDER=1>
```

4 Establish your first table data row, giving it five columns:

```
<TR>
<TD WIDTH=145></TD>
<TD WIDTH=145></TD>
<TD WIDTH=10></TD>
<TD WIDTH=145></TD>
<TD WIDTH=145></TD>
</TR>
```

5 Begin laying out your page within your second table data row, letting the first act as the table's master layout. Notice that you'll use the COLSPAN attribute within the <TD> tag to span content across multiple columns:

```
<TR>
<TD WIDTH=290 VALIGN=BOTTOM ALIGN=RIGHT COLSPAN=2><FONT FACE="VERDANA"
SIZE=3>Snake in the desert.</FONT></TD>
<TD WIDTH=10></TD>
<TD WIDTH=290 VALIGN=BOTTOM ALIGN=LEFT COLSPAN=2><FONT FACE="VERDANA"
SIZE=3>Snake in the desert.</FONT></TD>
</TR>
```

6 In your third table data row, you can bring in your image so it appears centered amongst all the other table data cells containing text. Notice that your image will span three columns, while the text within the <TD> cells takes up one column each (for a total of five columns):

```
<TR>
<TD WIDTH=145 VALIGN=TOP ALIGN=RIGHT><FONT FACE="VERDANA" SIZE=3>Snake in
the desert.</FONT></TD>
<TD WIDTH=300 COLSPAN=3><IMG SRC="snake.gif" WIDTH=300 HEIGHT=300></TD>
<TD WIDTH=145 VALIGN=TOP ALIGN=LEFT><FONT FACE="VERDANA" SIZE=3>Snake in
the desert.</FONT></TD>
</TR>
```

7 Close out the bottom of your page by adding more text in a new table data row:

```
<TR><TD WIDTH=290 VALIGN=BOTTOM ALIGN=RIGHT COLSPAN=2><FONT
FACE="VERDANA" SIZE=3>Snake in the desert.</FONT></TD>
<TD WIDTH=10></TD>
<TD WIDTH=290 VALIGN=BOTTOM ALIGN=LEFT COLSPAN=2><FONT FACE="VERDANA"
SIZE=3>Snake in the desert.</FONT></TD>
</TR>
```

8 Close your table, finish centering your page's content, and end the HTML:

```
</TABLE>

</CENTER>

</BODY>

</HTML>
```

In the preceding code, notice that the image in the middle table row (`<TR>`) has a COLSPAN of 3, which forces it to sit perfectly in the center of the composition.

As you can see in the following figure, filling in the columns with text fills out the composition nicely and creates a pretty good text-wrap effect.

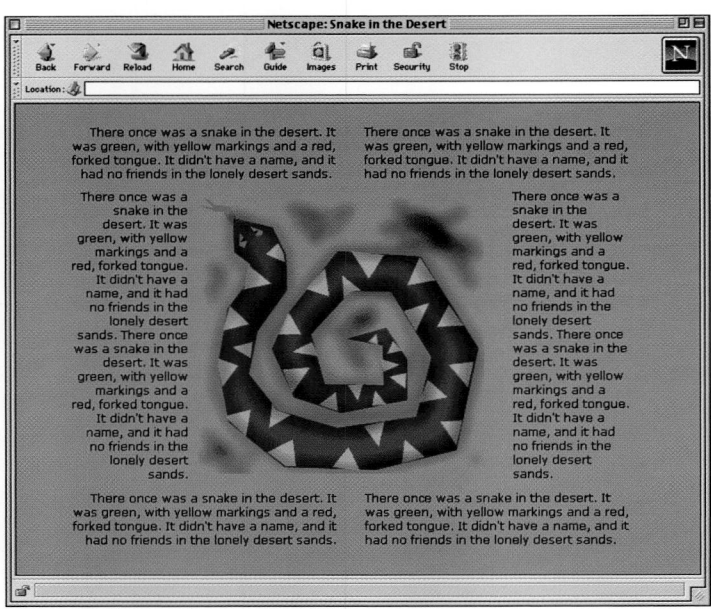

The final text-wrap effect with all the columns filled in.

When creating this kind of composition, take the following into consideration:

- Design the image with the page's background color in mind. If you create an image that seamlessly fits within the page, you achieve a more interesting text-wrap effect.

- HTML is *not* QuarkXPress or PageMaker. When using this text-wrap effect, columns of type do not automatically flow into one another. This is a "fake" solution that is otherwise not available to Web designers, so plan out how to evenly distribute your text among the columns. ●

Create Lists by Using Graphics Instead of HTML Bullets

Use this technique to:

- **Create attractive lists.** Instead of using conventional bullets (•) to enhance lists, get creative by using small images and tables.

- **Overcome the limitations imposed by the** <UL> **and** <OL> **tags.** Not only do the <OL> and <UL> tags create lists that take lots of room, they also offer very few (if any) customization options.

HTML's Restrictive <UL> and <OL> Tags

Two of the most restrictive aspects of HTML typography are the <UL> and <OL> tags, which determine the way HTML lays out ordered and bulleted lists. Although they are convenient to code, the resulting imagery leaves much to be desired and is not customizable. Check out the following HTML and see for yourself:

```
<HTML>

<HEAD>

<TITLE><OL> & <UL> Tags</TITLE>

</HEAD>

<BODY BGCOLOR="#6600FF" TEXT="#FFFFFF">

<FONT FACE="VERDANA" SIZE="5">The Typical Ordered List:<BR><BR>
<OL>
<LI>First Item</LI>
<LI>Second Item</LI>
<LI>Third Item</LI>
<LI>Fourth Item</LI>
</OL>
<BR>
The Typical Unordered List:<BR><BR>
<UL>
<LI>First Item</LI>
<LI>Second Item</LI>
<LI>Third Item</LI>
<LI>Fourth Item</LI>
```

```
</UL>
</FONT>

</BODY>

</HTML>
```

When viewed in a browser, the preceding code results in the following figure.

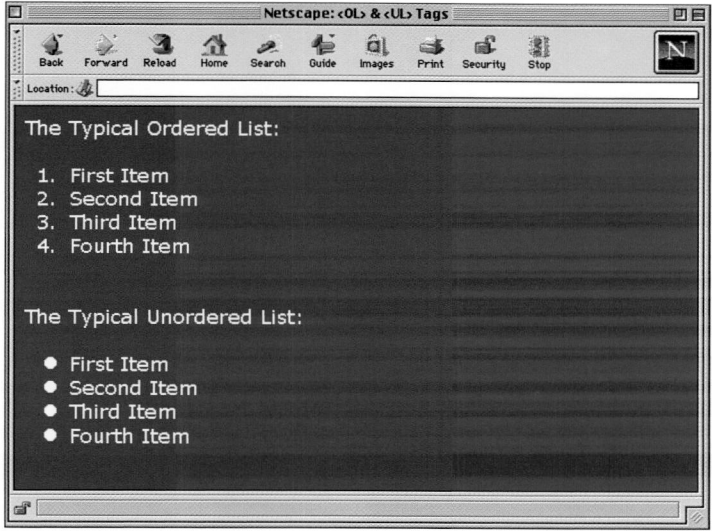

<OL> and <UL> tags.

As you can see, it's a rather bland way of displaying lists. What if you want to color your numbers yellow, while keeping your text white? Sorry—not possible with the <OL> and <UL> tags.

Creating Graphically Enhanced Lists

To graphically enhance your lists, you need to design small shapes or numerals (depending on how you want to display your lists) in your favorite image-editing program, save them out as GIFs, and then implement them within a tables layout to achieve "fake" ordered/bulleted lists, as illustrated in the following figure.

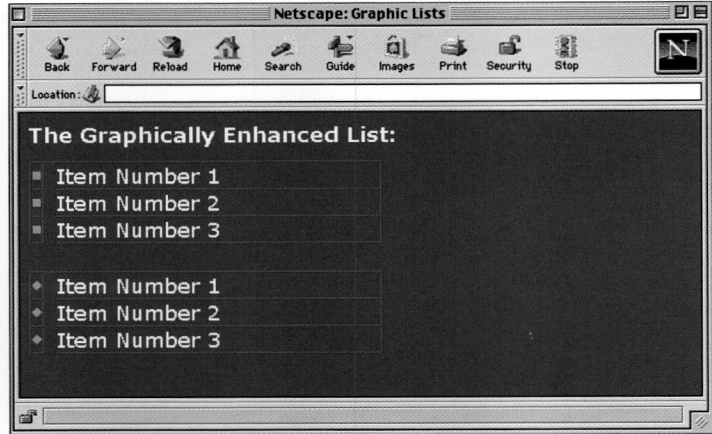

Graphically enhanced lists.

As you can see by the visible tables in the preceding figure, the tables are comprised of three columns:

- A first column for the bulleted graphic or colored numeral GIF

- A second column for white space to divide up the graphic from the list item

- A third column to house the list item

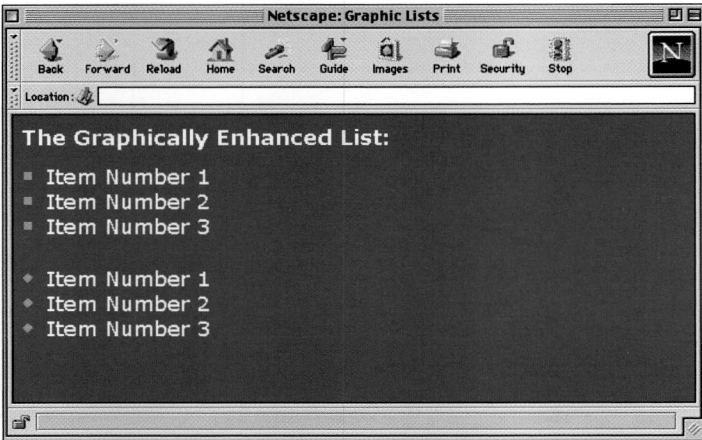

Graphically enhanced lists with table borders off.

By turning table borders off, you can achieve graphic-bulleted or numbered lists—a visually pleasing alternative to the <UL> and <OL> tags. Try it for yourself. To create graphically enhanced lists, use the following HTML, designing 9×9 pixel images or colored numerals to identify your list items.

Using a Square GIF Image

In the following example, a square GIF image is used.

1 Begin your HTML as you normally would:

```
<HTML>

<HEAD>

<TITLE>Graphic Lists</TITLE>

</HEAD>

<BODY BGCOLOR="#6600FF" TEXT="#FFFFFF">

<FONT FACE="VERDANA" SIZE="5"><STRONG>The Graphically Enhanced
List:</STRONG></FONT>
<BR><BR>
```

2 Create a 300-pixel table to house your data:

```
<TABLE WIDTH=300 CELLPADDING=0 CELLSPACING=0 BORDER=0>
<TR>
```

3 Place your graphic bullet (in this case `square.gif`) within the table's first data cell:

```
<TD WIDTH=9><IMG SRC="square.gif" WIDTH=9 HEIGHT=9></TD>
```

4 Create some room between the graphic bullet and its corresponding text with another table data cell:

```
<TD WIDTH=11></TD>
```

5 Create a third table data cell to house the text associated with your first bullet:

```
<TD WIDTH=280><FONT FACE="VERDANA" SIZE="5">Item Number 1</FONT></TD>
</TR>
```

6 Begin a new table data row and continue the above steps two more times so that you end up with three graphic bullets with three sets of corresponding text:

```
<TR>
<TD WIDTH=9><IMG SRC="square.gif" WIDTH=9 HEIGHT=9></TD>
<TD WIDTH=11></TD>
<TD WIDTH=280><FONT FACE="VERDANA" SIZE="5">Item Number 2</FONT></TD>
</TR>
```

255

```
<TR>
<TD WIDTH=9><IMG SRC="square.gif" WIDTH=9 HEIGHT=9></TD>
<TD WIDTH=11></TD>
<TD WIDTH=280><FONT FACE="VERDANA" SIZE="5">Item Number 3</FONT></TD>
</TR>
```

7 End your table:

```
</TABLE>
```

Using a Diamond GIF Image

In the following example, a diamond GIF image is used.

1 Create some room between the two tables by adding two hard returns:

```
<BR><BR>
```

2 Create a second 300-pixel wide table:

```
<TABLE WIDTH=300 CELLPADDING=0 CELLSPACING=0 BORDER=0>
<TR>
```

3 Place your graphic within the table's first data cell, but this time choose a diamond or other shape:

```
<TD WIDTH=9><IMG SRC="diamond.gif" WIDTH=9 HEIGHT=9></TD>
```

4 Create some room between the graphic bullet and its corresponding text with another table data cell:

```
<TD WIDTH=11></TD>
```

5 Create a third table data cell to house the text associated with your diamond bullet:

```
<TD WIDTH=280><FONT FACE="VERDANA" SIZE="5">Item Number 1</FONT></TD>
</TR>
```

6 Begin a new table data row and continue adding two more diamond bullets and text for a total of three diamond bullets with three sets of corresponding text:

```
<TR>
<TD WIDTH=9><IMG SRC="diamond.gif" WIDTH=9 HEIGHT=9></TD>
<TD WIDTH=11></TD>
<TD WIDTH=280><FONT FACE="VERDANA" SIZE="5">Item Number 2</FONT></TD>
</TR>
<TR>
<TD WIDTH=9><IMG SRC="diamond.gif" WIDTH=9 HEIGHT=9></TD>
```

```
<TD WIDTH=11></TD>
<TD WIDTH=280><FONT FACE="VERDANA" SIZE="5">Item Number 3</FONT></TD>
</TR>
</TABLE>
```

7 End your HTML and test the page in your browser:

```
</BODY>

</HTML>
```

The possibilities are endless when it comes to choosing what type of image to use when identifying your list items. This technique can help you overcome HTML's default list settings and enable your lists to fall within the look and feel guidelines you have established for your Web site. ●

Create Structured Type by Using Columns

Use this technique to:

- **Position your typography within multiple columns.** Achieve an editorial-style typographic look for your Web site.

- **Bring order to your page and enhance typographic layouts.** By structuring an organized means of typographic delivery, you enhance the overall look of the page.

Tables have dramatically enhanced how Web designers work with type on the page. Using tables, you can specify multicolumn layouts that not only help to organize your content but also ease visual strain by grouping type into smaller columns rather than large chunks.

The Nonbreaking Space ( )

Before we go into the columns technique, I want to introduce you to one of HTML's wonders—the nonbreaking space or   in HTML code. Some of you might not have been introduced to this little snippet of code due to its subtle nature. At first glance, the nonbreaking space will go unnoticed by the average user in search of the "hottest" HTML tip or trick. Surprisingly, the nonbreaking space is one of the most easy-to-implement, useful, underutilized pieces of code. To use it within your HTML, all you have to do is specify it instead of keying in the space bar. For example:

```
<HTML>
<BODY BGCOLOR="#000000" TEXT="#FFFFFF">
<FONT FACE="VERDANA" SIZE=4>
<P>There will be a space here.</P>
</FONT>
</HTML>
```

At first glance, the words space here look like a single word containing a major typo. However, if you drop the above line into your HTML, you will see that a space will appear between the words space and here as depicted in the following figure.

Space created using the HTML code for nonbreaking space.

What if you want to add two or more spaces between the words? Try to code in the following HTML:

```
<HTML>
<BODY BGCOLOR="#000000" TEXT="#FFFFFF">
<FONT FACE="VERDANA" SIZE=4>
<P>There will be two spaces  here.</P>
</FONT>
</HTML>
```

As you can see here, you need to key in two spaces between the words spaces and here to obtain two spaces between the words. Take a look at the following figure to see the outcome of this code.

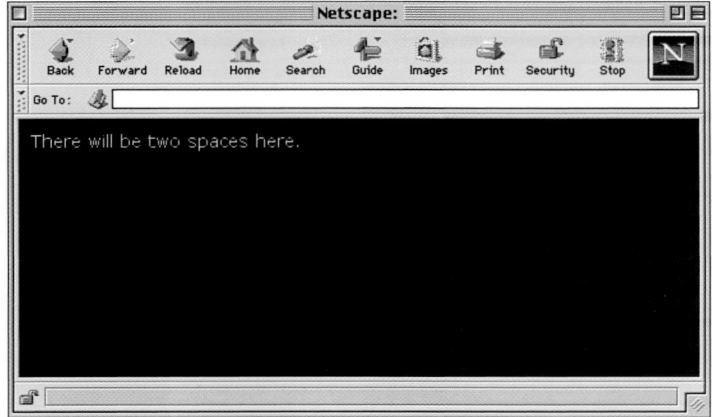

Only one space created using the keyboard's space bar.

As you can see in this figure, using the space bar to create many spaces between words will only result in ONE space—no more. This does not hold true if you use the <PRE> tag, but in any other tag, adding more than one space bar character does not result in multiple spaces when your page is filtered through HTML.

The nonbreaking space character ( ) is the only way to obtain multiple spaces between words when not using the <pre> tag. Here's how you can change that last piece of HTML to add the multiple spaces:

```
<HTML>
<BODY BGCOLOR="#000000" TEXT="#FFFFFF">
<FONT FACE="VERDANA" SIZE=4>
<P>There will be two spaces  here.</P>
</FONT>
</HTML>
```

The preceding code results in the following figure. As you can see, two spaces are between the words spaces and here as a result of using the nonbreaking space character.

Multiple spaces created using the nonbreaking space code.

The   code can also be used within tables. To find out how to take advantage of this piece of code within tables, check out the section within this book entitled "Define White Space."

Creating the Columns Template

When designing your multicolumn table, always begin with a template, separating columns with small gutters, which help give the columns of type some breathing room.

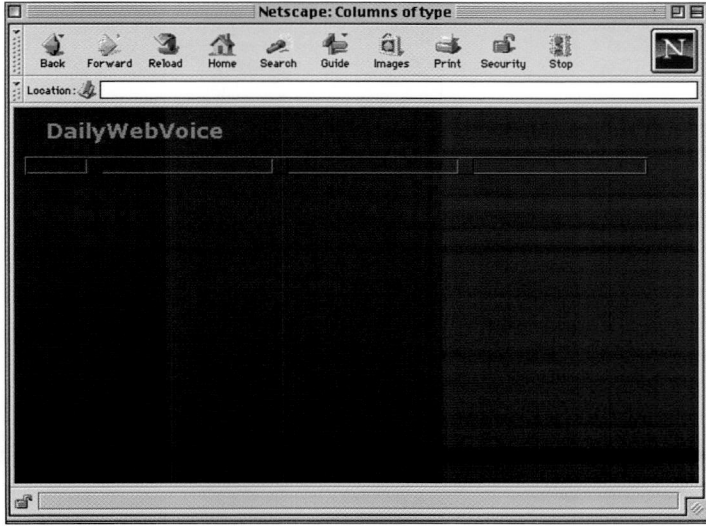

Begin with a template.

To create the template shown in the preceding figure, follow these steps:

1 Begin your HTML as usual:

```
<HTML>

<HEAD>

<TITLE>Columns of type</TITLE>

</HEAD>

<BODY BGCOLOR="#663300" TEXT="#CC9966">

<FONT FACE="VERDANA"
SIZE="5"><STRONG>   DailyWebVoice</STRONG></FONT>
<BR><BR>
```

2 Create a 530-pixel wide table containing 7 columns: a left column at 50 pixels, 3 gutters at 10 pixels each, and 3 text columns at 150 pixels each. Set the table's border to 1 so that you can see this structure. You need to use nonbreaking spaces within your table data cells in order for the table to appear on your screen (Netscape browsers):

```
<TABLE WIDTH=530 CELLPADDING=0 CELLSPACING=0 BORDER=1>
<TR>
<TD WIDTH=50> </TD>
```

```
<TD WIDTH=10></TD>
<TD WIDTH=150> </TD>
<TD WIDTH=10></TD>
<TD WIDTH=150> </TD>
<TD WIDTH=10></TD>
<TD WIDTH=150> </TD>
</TR>
</TABLE>
```

3 End your HTML:

```
</BODY>

</HTML>
```

Notice that the preceding HTML defines a 7-column table, 3 used as gutters, 3 used to hold type, and the first used for white space.

Filling in the Columns

Filling in the columns is as easy as filling in the preceding HTML with your type. The result is illustrated in the following figure.

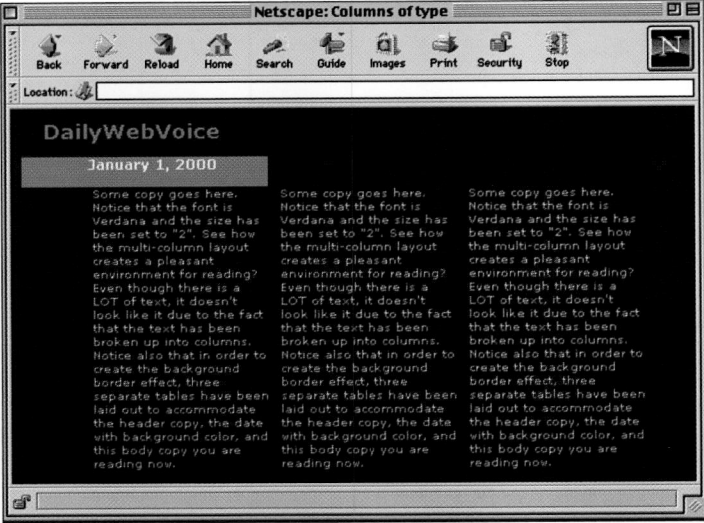

A three-column, structured grid housing an article.

Notice how the first column (serving as white space) helps to push the text to the right, aligning it nicely past the article title. This creates a visual, stair-step effect that helps lead the eye from the article title, down the date and into the body, which starts under the date and continues down and then right—one by one through each column. When designing your columns of type, be careful not to make your columns too skinny so that they cause overly long pages. Long, skinny columns make for difficult browsing. Try to maintain a balance between column width and length to minimize unnecessary scrolling.

The following is the complete code used to create what you see in the preceding figure (note the BGCOLOR attribute within the <TD> tags that created the table data cell background colors). It is based on the HTML code introduced earlier and builds upon it:

1 Begin your HTML:

```
<HTML>

<HEAD>

<TITLE>Columns of type</TITLE>

</HEAD>

<BODY BGCOLOR="#663300" TEXT="#CC9966">
```

2 Establish a FONT FACE, SIZE, and STYLE for your title:

```
<FONT FACE="VERDANA"
SIZE="5"><STRONG>   DailyWebVoice</STRONG></FONT>
<BR><BR>
```

3 Create your 530-pixel wide table, setting the border to 0 so that it is not visible:

```
<TABLE WIDTH=530 CELLPADDING=0 CELLSPACING=0 BORDER=0>
<TR>
```

4 Set background colors for your table data cells to create a more unifying effect between the cells, making sure to include the nonbreaking space within blank table data cells:

```
<TD WIDTH=50 BGCOLOR="#CC9966"> </TD>
<TD WIDTH=5 BGCOLOR="#CC9966"> </TD>
<TD WIDTH=150 BGCOLOR="#CC9966"><FONT FACE="VERDANA" SIZE="3"
COLOR="#FFFFFF"><STRONG>January 1, 2000</STRONG></FONT></TD>
<TD WIDTH=5></TD>
<TD WIDTH=150> </TD>
<TD WIDTH=5></TD>
<TD WIDTH=150> </TD>
</TR>
</TABLE>
```

5 Create entirely empty tables to create space between your content without losing the table data cell colors between the columns and rows:

```
<TABLE WIDTH=530 CELLPADDING=0 CELLSPACING=0 BORDER=0>
<TR>
<TD WIDTH=50 BGCOLOR="#CC9966"> </TD>
<TD WIDTH=10 BGCOLOR="#CC9966"> </TD>
<TD WIDTH=150 BGCOLOR="#CC9966"> </TD>
<TD WIDTH=10></TD>
<TD WIDTH=150> </TD>
<TD WIDTH=10></TD>
<TD WIDTH=150> </TD>
</TR>
</TABLE>
```

6 Create a table to house the main content of the page using the same previous table data cell structure to maintain consistency:

```
<TABLE WIDTH=530 CELLPADDING=0 CELLSPACING=0 BORDER=0>
<TR>
<TD WIDTH=50> </TD>
<TD WIDTH=10> </TD>
<TD WIDTH=150><FONT FACE="VERDANA" SIZE="2" COLOR="#FFFFFF">Some copy
goes here. Notice that the font is Verdana and the size has been set
to "2". See how the multi-column layout creates a pleasant environ-
ment for reading? Even though there is a LOT of text, it doesn't
look like it due to the fact that the text has been broken up into
columns. Notice also that in order to create the background border
effect, three separate tables have been layed out to accommodate the
header copy, the date with background color, and this body copy you
are reading now.</FONT></TD>
<TD WIDTH=10> </TD>
<TD WIDTH=150><FONT FACE="VERDANA" SIZE="2" COLOR="#FFFFFF">Some copy
goes here. Notice that the font is Verdana and the size has been set
to "2". See how the multi-column layout creates a pleasant environ-
ment for reading? Even though there is a LOT of text, it doesn't
look like it due to the fact that the text has been broken up into
columns. Notice also that in order to create the background border
effect, three separate tables have been layed out to accommodate the
header copy, the date with background color, and this body copy you
are reading now.</FONT></TD>
<TD WIDTH=10> </TD>
<TD WIDTH=150><FONT FACE="VERDANA" SIZE="2" COLOR="#FFFFFF">Some copy
goes here. Notice that the font is Verdana and the size has been set
to "2". See how the multi-column layout creates a pleasant environ-
ment for reading? Even though there is a LOT of text, it doesn't
look like it due to the fact that the text has been broken up into
columns. Notice also that in order to create the background border
effect, three separate tables have been layed out to accommodate the
header copy, the date with background color, and this body copy you
are reading now.</FONT></TD>
</TR>
</TABLE>
```

7 End your HTML:

```
</BODY>

</HTML>
```

Take a look at some other Web sites that use columns to structure and organize their HTML typographic layouts:

- the {fray} (`http://www.fray.com`)
- atlas magazine (`http://www.atlasmagazine.com`) ●

PART VIII

Magic with Forms

Web designers often shy away from using forms because they look so predefined, standard, and sterile.

Ironically, truly successful Web sites are not only attractive and interactive—they are also functional. Nine times out of ten, a Web site's functionality is made possible through the use of forms.

Despite their generic appearance, forms *can* be made to look attractive if creatively integrated within the overall graphic structure of the page. Mastering the art of Web design using forms enables you to take the average Web page beyond inter-activity, giving it true functionality.

Incorporating Color and Graphics into Forms

Use this technique to:

- **Develop form-field containers.** Add structure to the way your form fields are layed out.

- **Design a unique look and feel for your forms.** Make the forms portion of your page look and feel the same as the rest of your site.

- **Integrate forms into your Web site's design aesthetic.** Forms don't have to be boring—livening them up with color and graphic images enhances your page's overall design aesthetic.

Incorporating forms into your Web page is no different than incorporating images or text. Forms are elements that must be thoughtfully placed for maximum impact. Unlike graphics or text, which might or might not require interaction, forms always require some sort of interaction with the user. Because of this, you must pay even more attention to forms when it comes to their design and integration into the established graphic page structure.

Designing Forms

When designing forms, consider the following points:

- Use tables to structure an underlying grid in which form fields and HTML text will be placed.

- Use the BGCOLOR attribute of table data (<TD>) cells to create color behind your form fields.

- Make sure that the look and feel of your forms stays consistent within your overall Web site design aesthetic.

- When possible, incorporate GIFs or JPEGs into your form structure to make it less sterile.

The following figure is an Adobe Photoshop file demonstrating a form-field container. Form-field containers are graphics that are cut up into smaller GIF files and later brought into an HTML table layout. Within the table, a form field is incorporated along with the graphics to create a more visual form instead of the HTML text alternative.

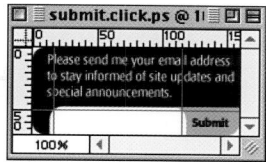

The click here. *updates request box. In Photoshop, guides are brought out to section off the graphic so that it can be cut into sections and saved as separate GIF files for placement within a table.*

The following figure shows the form-field container within the context of the *click here.* Web site home page. Notice that the field container is a table nested within the site's first major table data cell.

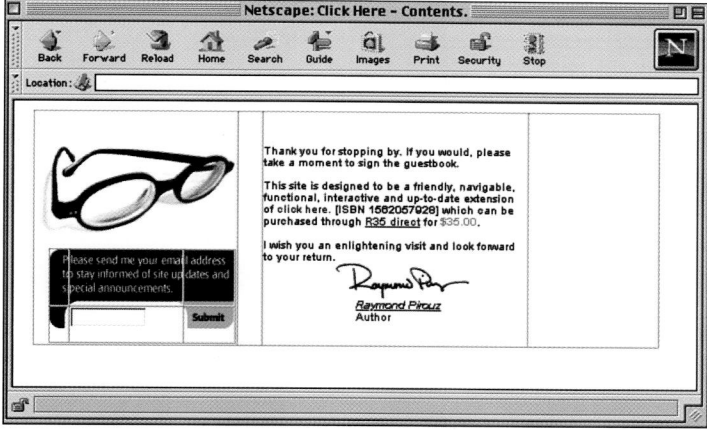

The click here. *updates request box within the site structure.*

Create a Form-Field Container

To create your form-field container, follow these steps:

1. Begin with an Adobe Photoshop graphic that you section off into fields, keeping a blank portion available for the form field, as in the first figure (center bottom of the image).

2. After your large graphic has been saved as several small GIFs, create an HTML table to house the graphic form-field container components and call your images within the code using <IMG> tags.

3. Within the table data cell that your form field is to be inserted, create your <FORM> field and test the results on your browser.

Writing the Code

The following HTML is excerpted from the *click here.* Web site
(`http://www.rpirouz.com/click`) and demonstrates how the form-field container
in the preceding figure is coded into the page:

```
<TABLE WIDTH=160 CELLPADDING=0 CELLSPACING=0 BORDER=0>


<TR>


<TD WIDTH=16><IMG WIDTH=16 HEIGHT=51 SRC="A1.GIF" ALT="PLEASE SEND ME
YOUR EMAIL ADDRESS TO STAY INFORMED OF SITE UPDATES AND SPECIAL
ANNOUNCEMENTS."></TD>
<TD WIDTH=100><IMG WIDTH=100 HEIGHT=51 SRC="A2.GIF" ALT="PLEASE SEND
ME YOUR EMAIL ADDRESS TO STAY INFORMED OF SITE UPDATES AND SPECIAL
ANNOUNCEMENTS."></TD>
<TD WIDTH=44><IMG WIDTH=44 HEIGHT=51 SRC="A3.GIF" ALT="PLEASE SEND ME
YOUR EMAIL ADDRESS TO STAY INFORMED OF SITE UPDATES AND SPECIAL
ANNOUNCEMENTS."></TD>


</TR>


<TR>


<TD WIDTH=16 VALIGN=TOP><IMG WIDTH=16 HEIGHT=19 SRC="B1.GIF"
ALT="PLEASE SEND ME YOUR EMAIL ADDRESS TO STAY INFORMED OF SITE
UPDATES AND SPECIAL ANNOUNCEMENTS."></TD>
<TD WIDTH=100 VALIGN=TOP><INPUT TYPE="TEXT" NAME="FROM"
SIZE="10"></TD>
<TD WIDTH=44 VALIGN=TOP><INPUT TYPE="IMAGE" SRC="B3.GIF" BOR-
DER="0"></FORM></TD>


</TR>


</TABLE>
```

Notice that the table's bottom row contains the form field within its middle column and has been set to `SIZE="10"`. When designing form fields, make sure that
you test the results on both Mac and PC platforms. Form field widths do not display consistently between platforms and browsers. You must compromise on a size
that fits within the table boundaries on all platforms and browsers, based on your
particular table width design.

Examples of Form–Field Containers

The following figure demonstrates how seamlessly the form-field container fits
within the page's design and conforms to the look and feel of the site without
looking like a boring HTML form element.

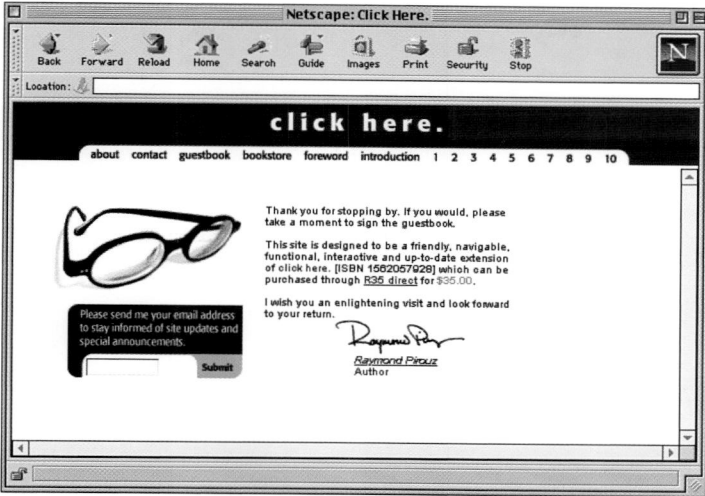

The click here. *site with table borders set to 0.*

Another example of a form-field container that conforms to the overall look and feel of a Web site can be found at `http://www.r35.com/direct`. The following figure demonstrates the R35 direct updates form-field graphics file that is sliced up into 11 final pieces and are then saved as GIF files and placed within a table on the R35 direct Web site.

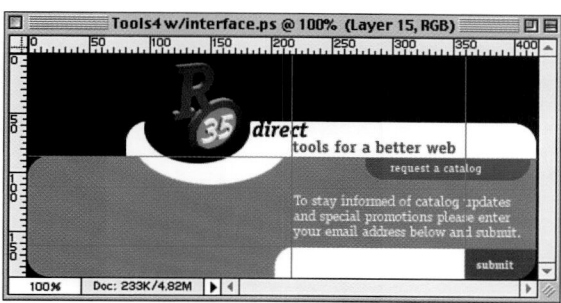

The R35 direct updates form-field container.

If you count the divisions in this figure, there are 12. However, the white area next to the Submit button graphic in the lower-right area is not saved as a file because that spot is reserved for the form field that gives this graphic part of its functionality.

271

The R35 direct updates form-field container within a visible table structure.

The preceding figure demonstrates all the pieces of the R35 updates graphic within the table structure coded here:

```
<TABLE WIDTH=420 BORDER=0 CELLPADDING=0 CELLSPACING=0>

<TR>
<TD WIDTH=218><IMG WIDTH=218 HEIGHT=86 SRC="A1.GIF" ALT="R35
LOGO"></TD>
<TD WIDTH=202 COLSPAN=2><A HREF = "products/r35d_all.htm"
onMouseOver="window.status='check them all out.'; return true"
onClick="xscreen()" Target=X><IMG WIDTH=202 HEIGHT=86 SRC="a2.gif"
ALT="R35 direct - tools for a better web - show all products" BOR-
DER=0></A></TD>
</TR>

<TR>
<TD WIDTH=218><IMG WIDTH=218 HEIGHT=26 SRC="b1.gif" ALT=""></TD>
<TD WIDTH=202 COLSPAN=2 ALIGN=LEFT><A HREF="register.htm"
onMouseOver="imgOn('img1');window.status='get your very own....';
return true;"onMouseOut="imgOff('img1');"><IMG NAME=img1 WIDTH=202
HEIGHT=26 SRC="b2off.gif" ALT="request a catalog" border=0></A></TD>
</TR>

<TR>
<TD WIDTH=218><A HREF = "spread.htm"
onMouseOver="window.status='enter for your chance to win!'; return
true"><IMG WIDTH=218 HEIGHT=50 SRC="c1.gif" ALT="" BORDER=0></A></TD>
<TD WIDTH=202 COLSPAN=2><IMG WIDTH=202 HEIGHT=50 SRC="c2.gif" ALT="To
stay informed of catalog updates and special promotions please enter
your email address below and submit."></TD>
```

```
</TR>

<TR>
<TD WIDTH=218 VALIGN=TOP><IMG WIDTH=218 HEIGHT=27 SRC="d1.gif" ALT=""></TD>
<TD WIDTH=142 BAKGROUND="d2.gif" ALIGN=LEFT VALIGN=TOP><INPUT TYPE="TEXT"
NAME="from" SIZE="15"></TD>
<td width=60 valign=top><INPUT TYPE="image" SRC="d3.gif" BORDER="0"></TD>
</TR>

</TABLE>
```

Please note that in the preceding code (fourth row down and middle table data cell) a background image is used for the white bar that attaches the first table data cell across to the right data cell containing the Submit button. In this case, a background color could not have been used because the <FORM> field information forces the data cell to be longer vertically than specified (as you can see in the preceding figure). In this case, if a background color were specified for the middle data cell, it would fall below the graphic borders created within the first and third data cells. Because HTML tends to behave differently on different platforms and browsers, there is no way to really know the outcome of certain code unless you actually test it on a browser. Welcome to advanced Web design with basic HTML!

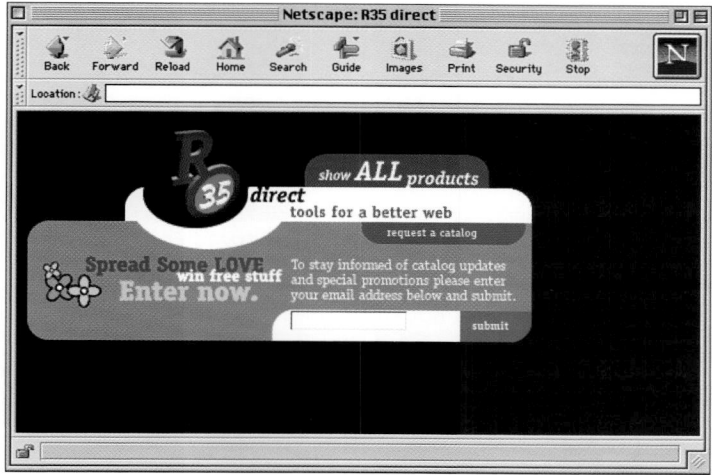

The R35 direct form-field container with table borders turned off.

As you can see in the preceding figure, the result of our haphazard HTML code is a seamless graphic that incorporates a form field within it. ●

273

Align Forms with Text and Images

Use this technique to:

- **Make your forms easier to use.** Organizing your text, form fields, and any images within an underlying structure enhances the usability and overall layout of your forms.

- **Group information into blocks.** Grouping text and form fields makes them easier to fill out and interact with.

- **Section off your form data.** Using the <HR> tag, you can create separate sections out of one long form. This causes your viewer to visually stop and pause between sections, making more lengthy forms digestible.

When it comes to usability and accessibility, forms must always perform at a superior level in order to be filled out. Nobody likes to wade through pages and pages of forms that are not well structured, not well designed, and not cleanly incorporated within the page's overall visual look and feel.

Designing Forms

Because form elements should be considered as important as graphics and text, they need to be *designed* into the page so that they are not a burden on your users.

Go to http://www.r35.com/direct and click order online. When the order form appears, take a look at the organization, use of white space, attention to detail, and categorization of form elements. To design forms with maximum impact, consider the following points:

- Follow each query on your part with an entry field, radio button, or check box and group each query and response together.

- Do not run form fields and text into one another; this causes confusion for the viewer, who might not know which question goes along with what form field.

- Use white space to house any images that will enhance the form. In the preceding figure, notice how the shipping symbols are placed next to the section that discusses shipping options.

- Use horizontal rules (<HR>) to section off different areas of your form. In the preceding figure, horizontal rules section off personal information, products ordered, and billing/shipping.

- Create long forms rather than multicolumn forms, as it is easier to navigate down a form than it is to navigate across it. This might not be true in print, but it's true on the Web.

- To create shorter forms, right-align your text to the left of your form fields, as in the following figure.

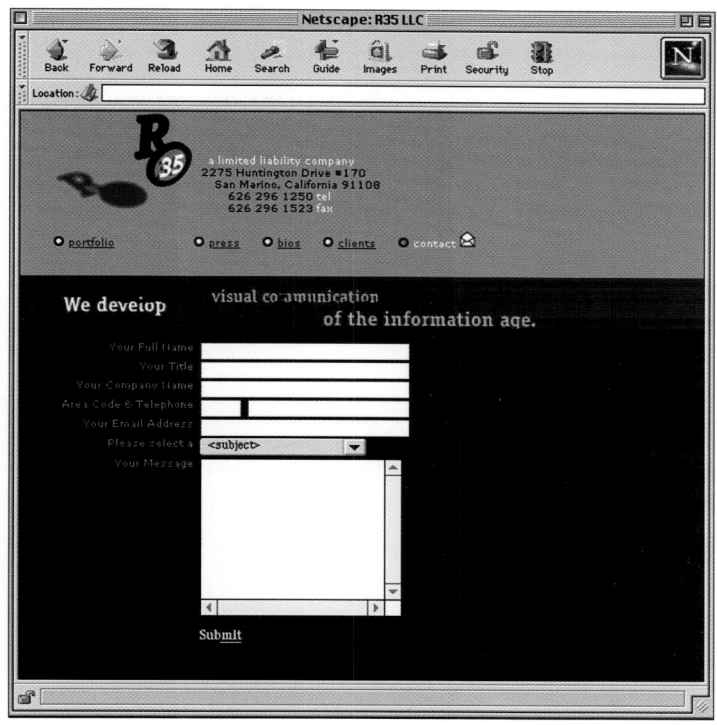

The R35 Web site contact page.

- When incorporating pull-down menus into your forms, flow query text into your form field—this creates a more seamless effect (see the preceding figure).

To learn more about designing with forms, check out Webmonkey's very informative article at:

    http://www.hotwired.com/webmonkey/html/97/06/index2a.html •

Create a Visual Submit Button

Use this technique to:

- **Overcome the limitations imposed by HTML buttons**. Do not limit yourself to the standard oval "Submit." Other options *do* exist.

- **Compel users to click by using creative "call-to-action" messages, graphics, and colors**. Create visual Submit buttons out of animated GIFs and draw your user's eye to that final step.

You have your form layed out and looking good. It's harmonious with the rest of your Web site, and you integrated graphics and colored background data cells to make it look sharp—nothing like the typical HTML forms you see out there. But wait, way at the bottom, you have that gray "Submit" thing trying to be oval 3D but failing miserably to look like a real button.

What's a Web designer to do? It's actually quite simple. Take a look at the following figure and you'll see a Submit button at the end of that form that's neither oval nor 3D.

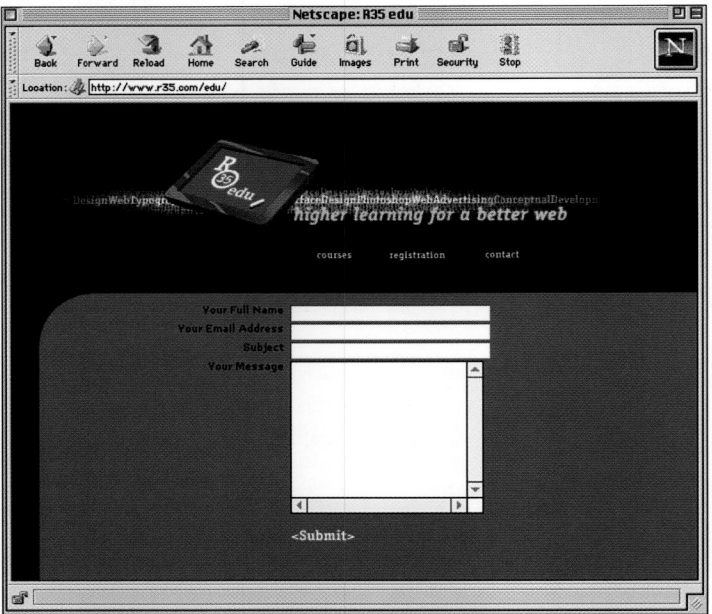

The R35 edu Web site's visual Submit button.

Designing the Submit Button

To create your visual Submit button, here's what you have to do:

1 Design an image within Adobe Photoshop or other visual creation tool. It can be any image, as long as your audience knows that it's meant to be the Submit button. You don't want to get carried away here—a screaming head might look cool, but unless people know it's a Submit button, you won't receive any form replies.

2 Save your image as a GIF or a JPEG graphic or go to step 3.

3 Create an animation sequence and save your file as an animated GIF.

That's all there is to it. You can use static JPEGs, GIFs, or animated GIF images for your visual Submit button, and there are no size restrictions for the image.

Inserting the Submit Button

As soon as you create your image, place the following code where you want your button to appear:

```
<INPUT TYPE="image" SRC="YourSubmitImageFile.gif or jpeg" BORDER="0">
```

Generally, when inserting a Submit button to a form, you use the <INPUT> tag with the TYPE="Submit" attribute. (This is what makes the default oval Submit button.) When we replace TYPE="Submit" with TYPE="image", we tell HTML to insert an image file (GIF, animated GIF, or JPEG) instead of its default (and plain looking) oval button. The SRC="" attribute tells HTML where your button image is located. Be sure to specify BORDER="0" as opposed to 1. Specifying BORDER="1" will result in a border around your Submit button, which often looks quite unattractive.

The R35 edu Web site in the preceding figure is an example of this technique put to the test. The visual Submit button on this pace is called by using the following simple piece of code:

```
<INPUT TYPE="image" SRC="submit.gif" BORDER="0">
```

277

Check out some other Web sites that use this cool technique:

Lycos (http://www.lycos.com)

GoTo.com (http://www.goto.com) ●

Create Wrapping Text Fields

Use this technique to:

- **Force text to automatically wrap.** Text within your TEXTAREA form field will automatically wrap to the next line, based on the field's width property.

- **Enhance data entry**. Data entry and editing is simplified when text wrap is enabled.

When integrating text entry fields within your forms, it's much more user friendly to force the fields to wrap. Although this is a simple technique to employ, many sites do not make use of it, often leaving users frustrated and begging for its implementation.

Wrapping occurs when a line of text that is entered in a field automatically flows down to the next line without the user having to press the Return key.

Using WRAP Property

In particular, this technique applies to the <TEXTAREA> tag, which is formatted by using ROWS and COLS (columns) attributes. (ROWS is a measure of its height and COLS is a measure of its width.)

The following figure illustrates the TEXTAREA field within the R35 direct order page. Notice that the text has automatically wrapped down to the next line; this is a function of having added the WRAP property within the <TEXTAREA> tag.

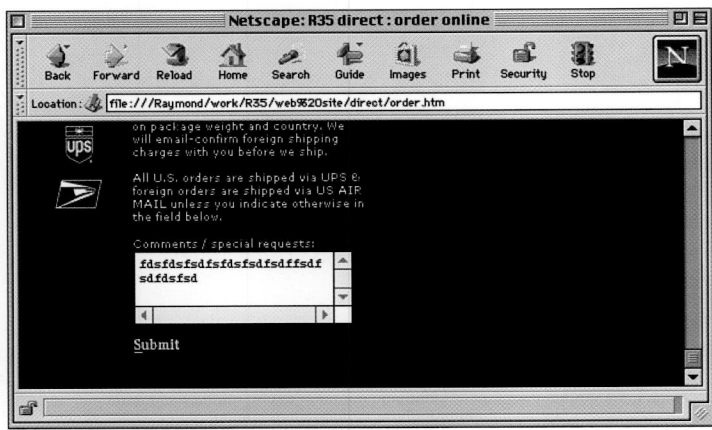

R35 direct's TEXTAREA *field.*

To cause your TEXTAREA fields to wrap, code your tag like so:

```
<TEXTAREA NAME="body" ROWS=3 COLS=25 WRAP></TEXTAREA>
```

Notice that all you need is the word WRAP within your <TEXTAREA> field. You may also code WRAP=VIRTUAL, which basically means the same thing, but both versions work fine on the Internet Explorer and Netscape Navigator browsers.

What if you don't use the WRAP property within your <TEXTAREA> tag? How bad can the result be? Well, it's not a matter of "bad"—it's a matter of aesthetics. For instance, take a look at the following figure. The following piece of type was keyed into the "Comments" field:

```
This is a long piece of text that is meant to wrap without having to
press the keyboard's "RETURN" key.
```

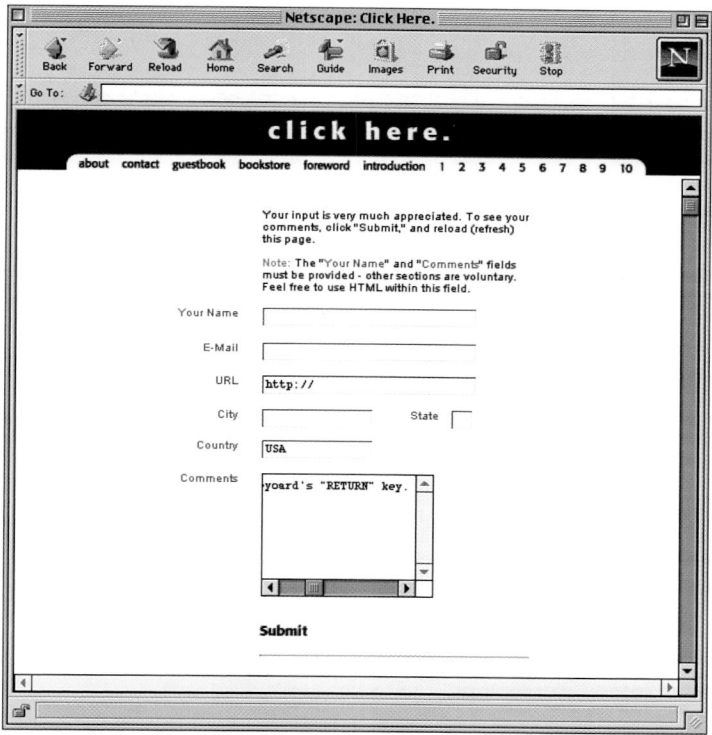

The click here. *guestbook with no text wrap.*

As you can see in the preceding figure, because the WRAP property is not utilized, the entire line of type does not wrap, forcing the text field's scrollbars to appear, leading the viewer across a maze of type within a small text entry box.

Take a look at the following figure for a much more appealing alternative to this visual eyesore.

279

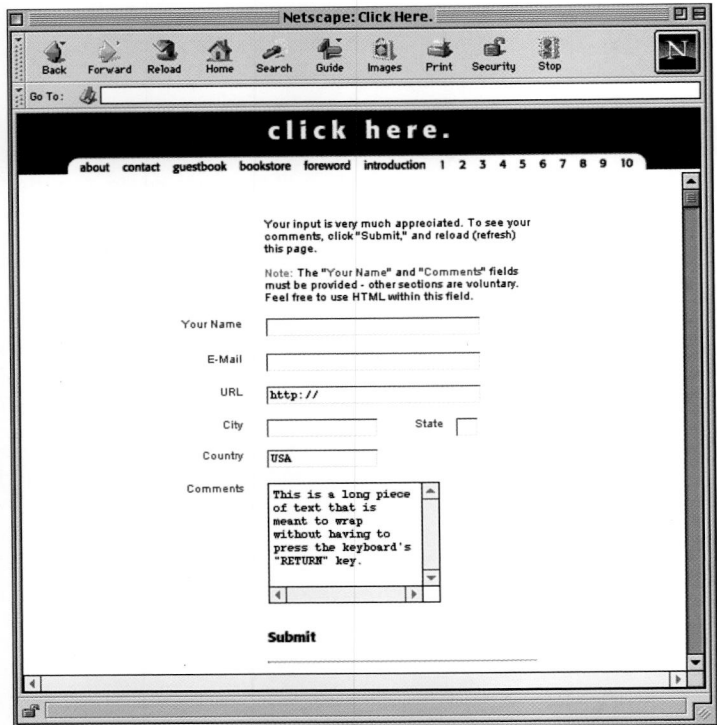

The click here. *guestbook with text wrap enabled.*

As you can see, this figure's use of the WRAP property within the <TEXTAREA> tag causes the text to automatically wrap within the confines of the established text field's dimensions. Of course, as more and more type is keyed into the field, the vertical scrollbars will appear, but at least the user does not have to scroll both vertically and horizontally.

The WRAP technique enhances the look and feel of your text entry fields, allowing your audience to focus on typing instead of scrolling.   ●

Design Pull-Down Menus with JavaScript

Use this technique to:

- **Create menu-driven options.** Present viewers with a familiar selection tool.

- **Provide an alternative to graphic navigation.** Without the need for images or rollovers, you can create an easy-to-use alternative to traditional forms of navigation.

- **Painlessly enhance your site's navigation.** Add a pull-down alternative to a graphic navigation for those who prefer the quicker route.

One of the most popular form elements is the pull-down menu. Using JavaScript, you can cause your pull-down menu to jump to a page within your Web site or to an anchor within the same page, as illustrated in the following figure.

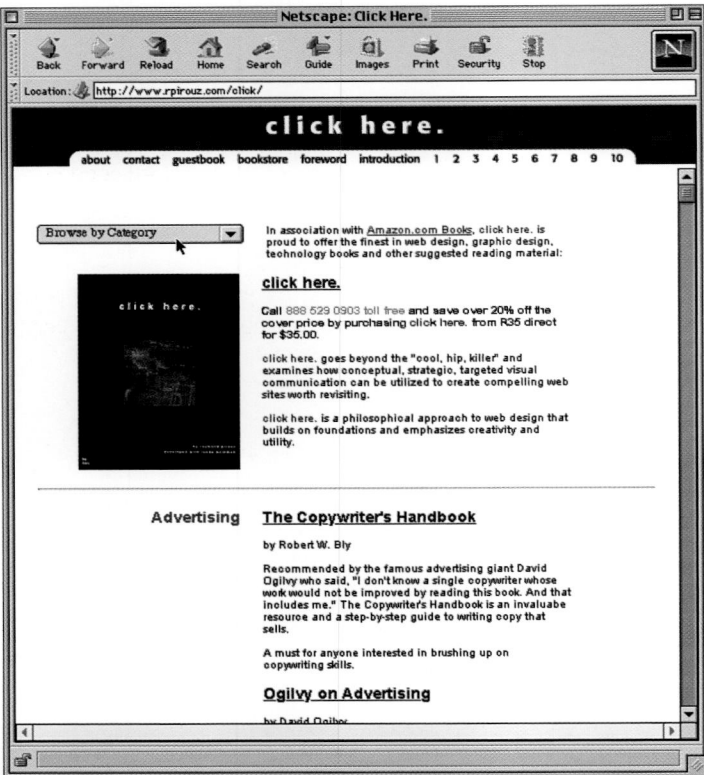

The click here. Web site bookstore uses JavaScript and a pull-down menu to ease navigation within the page.

This figure illustrates how a pull-down menu has been integrated into the *click here.* Web site bookstore page in order to give users quicker access to the page's content. Upon clicking the pull-down menu, viewers get an overview of all the books available, categorized by topic and in the order in which they appear on the page. Hence, the pull-down menu serves as a quick and easy way to navigate down the page without having to literally scroll down and wade through all the book titles and descriptions.

Define the Function

When coding such a menu for your site, begin by defining your JavaScript function within your HTML's <HEAD></HEAD> tags:

```
<SCRIPT LANGUAGE="JavaScript">
<!--//

function gotobook(book) {
    if (book != "") {
        self.location=book
    }
}

//-->
</script>
```

The preceding code tells JavaScript that when the gotobook function is called, it should jump to the location of the selected book.

Create the Pull-Down Menu

Once you have defined your function, lay out your page and code your pull-down menu by using the following HTML code as an example:

```
<FORM>
<SELECT NAME="url"
ONCHANGE="gotobook(this.options[this.selectedIndex].value)">
<OPTION SELECTED WIDTH=100>Browse by Category
<OPTION>
<OPTION>===================
<OPTION VALUE="#advertising">Advertising
<OPTION>===================
<OPTION VALUE="#tch">The Copywriter's
<OPTION VALUE="#tch">Handbook
<OPTION>
<OPTION VALUE="#ooa">Ogilvy on
<OPTION VALUE="#ooa">Advertising
<OPTION>
<OPTION>===================
<OPTION VALUE="#animation">Animation
```

283

```
<OPTION>===================
<OPTION VALUE="#dca">Digital
<OPTION VALUE="#dca">Character Animation
<OPTION>
</SELECT>
</FORM>
```

As you can see in the preceding code, each book title has a VALUE to which an
anchor is attached. When a particular book is selected by the viewer, JavaScript
jumps to the selected anchor, which resides within the HTML body of the document:

```
<TABLE WIDTH=550 CELLPADDING=0 CELLSPACING=0 BORDER=0>

<TR>

<TD WIDTH=180 VALIGN=TOP ALIGN=RIGHT><FONT FACE="ARIAL,HELVETICA"
SIZE=2 COLOR="#333366"><H3><A
NAME="ADVERTISING">ADVERTISING</A></H3></FONT></TD>

</TR>

</TABLE>
```

Although the preceding code is a truncated version of the original, it illustrates
how the anchor is used within the table data row. To place an anchor, simply give it
a name and place it around a word to which you want to anchor. Here's an example:

```
<A NAME="STUFF">some stuff</A>
```

For other uses of pull-down menus and JavaScript, check out BUILDER.COM's
"Menu Maker" tool at http://www.builder.com/Programming/Kahn/123097 and
WebCoder.com's Scriptorium at http://www.webcoder.com/scriptorium/
index.html. ●

<deconstructing web graphics>
Web Design Case Studies and Tutorials

Deconstructing Web Graphics profiles top web designers and programmers in order to demystify and analyze how they make decisions, solve complex issues, and create exceptional web sites. Adding her own voice and digital design teaching experience to the book, best-selling author Lynda Weinman selects from her list of favorite designed web sites. She walks you through how to read and understand the source code for each page, breaks down all of the technical elements, and describes the inside details straight from the designers and programmers who created the pages.

This conversational and information-rich guide offers insight into web design that is not found through any other means. Profiles of successful web designers, programmers, photographers, and illustrators allow them to share their tips, techniques, and recommendations. You'll bring your own web design skills to a higher level through studying their experiences and the step-by-step tutorials and examples found in *Deconstructing Web Graphics*.

In this book, you'll learn about:

- Low-bandwidth graphics
- Scanned imagery for the web
- Cross-platform colors
- Custom Photoshop brushes and patterns
- Artwork using ASCII
- Copyright issues
- Animated GIFs
- LOWSRC animation tricks
- Tables for alignment
- Invisible GIFs for spacers
- Frames for navigation
- HTML tricks and workarounds
- Java
- JavaScript
- CGI
- Forms processing
- Server push
- Client pull
- Shockwave and Macromedia Director
- Sound and video files
- VRML

Product and Sales Information

Deconstructing Web Graphics by Lynda Weinman
ISBN: 1-56205-641-7 ▪ $44.99/USA ▪ 250 pages
Available at your local bookstore or online
Macmillan Publishing ▪ 1-800-428-5331
- http://www.lynda.com
- http://www.mcp.com/newriders

<coloring web graphics.2>

Master Color and Image File Formats for the Web

The purpose of this book is to help artists, programmers, and hobbyists understand how to work with color and image file formats for web delivery. Web browsers and different operating systems handle color in specific ways that many web designers aren't aware of. This updated second edition includes information about Photoshop 4.0, Illustrator 7.0, DitherBox, and DeBabelizer Pro.

A color palette of 216 browser-safe colors is identified and organized to help web designers confidently select successful cross-platform color choices and combinations. The book includes sections on color theory and understanding web color file formats, as well as step-by-step tutorials that explain how to work with browser-safe colors in Photoshop 4.0, Paint Shop Pro, Photo-Paint, Painter, FreeHand, and Illustrator 7.0. The cross-platform CD-ROM includes hundreds of suggested color combinations for web page design, as well as hundreds of palettes and browser-safe clip art files.

In this book, you'll learn about:

- Creating colors in your artwork that won't shift or dither across multiple platforms
- Choosing web-appropriate color schemes for your page designs
- Creating browser-safe hybrid variations
- Using Photoshop, Paint Shop Pro, Photo-Paint, FreeHand, Illustrator, and Director to manage web-specific color

The cross-platform CD-ROM includes:

- Browser-safe color palettes
- Browser-safe color swatches for Photoshop and other imaging programs
- Browser-safe colors organized by hue, value, and saturation
- Browser-safe color clip art for web use
- Electronic versions of color swatches grouped as they are in the book
- Sample HTML pages with recommended color groupings
- Sample patterns, backgrounds, buttons, and rules

Product and Sales Information

Coloring Web Graphics.2
By Lynda Weinman & Bruce Heavin
ISBN: 1-56205-818-5 ▪ $50.00/USA ▪ 314 pages
Available at your local bookstore or online
Macmillan Publishing ▪ 1-800-428-5331
- http://www.lynda.com
- http://www.mcp.com/newriders

<designing web graphics.2>

How to Prepare Media and Images for the Web

Completely updated and expanded to include the latest on file formats, file sizes, compression methods, cross-platform web color, and browser-specific tehcniques, *Designing Web Graphics.2* is the definitive graphics guide for all web designers. If you are already working in the digital arts, in print or video, looking to transfer your skills to the web, this is the book for you. Step-by-step instruction in a conversational and easy to read style from a fellow artist/designer will help you understand the best methods and techniques for preparing graphics and media for the web.

Written in a conversational and user-friendly tone, *Designing Web Graphics.2* has received rave reviews from both experienced web designers and newcomers to the field. It's the bestselling book on this subject and is being used by web designers all over the world, including those from Hot Wired, Adobe, and Discovery Online.

In this book, you'll learn about:

- Creating small and fast web graphics
- Browser-safe colors for cross-platform use
- GIFs, JPEGs, and PNGs through the use of comparison charts that help you pick the best compression method
- Scanning tips (Photoshop 4.0 techniques)
- Sound, animation, and interactivity
- Creating navigation bars, rollover effects, and linked graphics
- Step-by-step tutorials for programming Photoshop 4.0 action palettes
- Practical applications for JavaScript, Shockwave, CGI, and plug-ins
- Embedding inline music, animation, and movie files
- Animated GIF creation techniques (how to control size, speed, and color palettes)
- Creating GIF and PNG transparencies for the web
- Web TV specs and authoring tips
- Updated typography section

Product and Sales Information

Designing Web Graphics.2 by Lynda Weinman
ISBN:1-56205-715-4 ▪ $55.00/USA ▪ 500 pages
Available at your local bookstore or online
Macmillan Publishing ▪ 1-800-428-5331
- http://www.lynda.com
- http://www.mcp.com/newriders

<creative html design>
A Hands-On HTML 4.0 Web Design Tutorial

It's easy to make web pages with today's new WYSIWYG editors, but those programs don't teach you how to make fast-loading graphics, write accurate HTML that will endure for future browsers, or the necessary techniques involved in preparing your site for the web. Written by two of the industry's foremost experts, this definitive tutorial teaches you not just how to make a web page, but how to design web sites that are cross-platform compatible and work effectively within the web's distinct constraints.

Creative HTML Design walks you through all the phases of site design—from selecting an ISP and uploading files, to more advanced techniques like adding animation and rollovers. Step-by-step tutorials for Photoshop 4.0 and Paint Shop Pro teach how to design using "safe" colors, make distinctive background tiles, align your graphics, use tables and frames, include JavaScript rollovers, use CSS, as well as numerous other design and HTML features.

In this book, you'll learn about:

- How to build a finished web site with real-world examples and exercises
- How to write and read HTML
- Choosing an Internet service provider or presence provider
- Creating speedy GIF, JPEG, and PNG files
- Working with safe, cross-platform colors that will not shift in web browsers
- Designing distinctive background tiles, with and without visible seams
- Typographic principles and type tricks for the web
- Cascading Style Sheets
- Creating artwork and code for JavaScript rollovers
- Using tables to align text and graphics
- How to use frames aesthetically and effectively
- Using forms aesthetically so they fit the look of the rest of your site
- Adding animation and sound
- Organizing your pages on a server using relative URLs and SSI
- Troubleshooting automatically generated WYSIWYG HTML
- A complete HTML 4.0 reference

Product and Sales Information

Creative HTML Design
By Lynda Wienman and William E. Weinman
ISBN: 1-56205-704.9 ▪ $39.99/USA ▪ 434 pages
Available at your local bookstore or online
Macmillan Publishing ▪ 1-800-428-5331
- http://wwwcgibook.com
- http://www.mcp.com/newriders

The cross-platform CD-ROM includes:

- All the necessary files for the tutorials in this book
- JavaScript rollover code and many other customizable scripts

HTML Artistry: More Than Code

by Ardith Ibañez and Natalie Zee

HTML Artistry: More Than Code combines the latest and most popular uses of HTML 4 along with practical, real-world design advice to help you achieve sophisticated page layouts through the use of innovative typography, animation, and interactive effects that work on both Netscape Navigator and Microsoft Internet Explorer.

Authors and professional Web designers, Ardith Ibañez and Natalie Zee, make knowing what's hot in the Web design industry their top priority. Their discoveries will keep your sites on the cutting-edge of technology and will catch the eyes of everyone.

This hands-on, full-color, Web design guide clearly illustrates all aspects of HTML design, from the simple table layout to full animation with Dynamic HTML. Case studies and inspirational design models will teach you a variety of design principles and how to apply them to your site design. *HTML Artistry: More Than Code* will inform and inspire you to create innovative cross-browser Web sites.

Ardith Ibañez has designed Web sites and Web content for Macromedia, Sony Pictures Entertainment, California Pizza Kitchen, PhotoDisc, and MGM.

Her studio, Akimbo Design, has created work on the forefront of dynamic HTML Web site development, and Hewlett-Packard recently featured Akimbo in a commercial for their innovative use of computer technology. Ardith has also co-authored *HTML Web Magic* and *Creating Killer Interactive Web Sites*, both from Hayden Books.

Natalie Zee is a Web designer whose work can be seen on such Web sites as Macromedia, Visa, RankIt, Dynamic HTML Zone, and Student Advantage. She was awarded the 1997 Communication Arts Interactive Design Award for "Best Business Web Site" for her work on Macromedia's Web site.

Natalie is also the co-author of *HTML Web Magic* from Hayden Books.

ISBN: 1-56830-454-4   **$40.00 USA/$56.95 CAN**

Inside Adobe Photoshop 5

by Gary Bouton, Barbara Bouton, Gary Kubicek

You can master the power of the world's most popular computer graphics program! Easy-to-follow tutorials, in Gary's famous style, teach you the full spectrum of Photoshop's powerful capabilities. The most comprehensive book available on Photoshop 5!

ISBN: 1-56205-884-3   **$44.99 USA/$63.95 CAN**

Dynamic HTML Web Magic

by Jeff Rouyer

Explore innovative DHTML techniques that you can combine, tweak, and apply to your own pages to create stunning designs and graphics. With step-by-step instructions, full-color illustrations, and the popular recipe-style Magic format, you'll be inspired with new artistic and technological know-how.

ISBN: 1-56830-421-8   **$39.99 USA/$56.95 CAN**

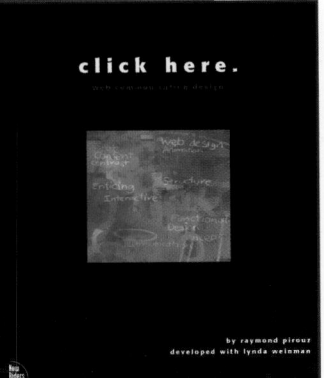

Click Here

by Raymond Pirouz

Written by an award-winning Web site designer, Click Here presents an expert's unique point of view on successful Web design, and teaches through hands-on tutorials how to think about, and implement, these designs. Topics covered inlcude: color, file size limitations, animation, load time, looping restrictions, and how to use popular design tools such as Photoshop, Illustrator, and GIFBuilder.

ISBN: 1-56205-792-8   **$45.00 USA/$63.95 CAN**

Photoshop 5 Type Magic

by Greg Simsic

This is the perfect resource for typographers, designers, and Photoshop users looking to spice up their work. Every page makes a visual promise: you will be able to create this exciting artwork! The book's highly effective, recipe-style approach walks you through the procedures of creating special effects with type, and the stunning four-color illustrations are sure to inspire any designer.

ISBN: 1-56830-465-X   **$39.99 USA/$56.95 CAN**

Photoshop Web Magic, Volume 1

by Ted Schulman, Renée LeWinter, and Tom Emmanuelides

This 4-color book provides numerous examples of dazzling Web graphics, textures, backgrounds, buttons, and animations in a recipe format with simple step-by-step instructions. Specific graphic techniques for customizing Web design to fit client needs and expert advice for print designers moving to the Web is included.

ISBN: 1-56830-314-9 $45.00 USA/$63.95 CAN

Photoshop Web Magic, Volume 2

by Jeff Foster

This companion volume to Photoshop Web Magic, Volume 1, includes 45 all-new techniques and provides step-by-step directions to create dazzling effects for the Web. A new section covers Java rollovers, animation tools, and WYSIWYG HTML editors.

ISBN: 1-56830-392-0 $45.00 USA/$63.95 CAN

Photoshop 5 Web Magic

by Michael Ninness

An all-new collection of animations, textures, edge treatments for images, buttons, and backgrounds! The companion CD-ROM will be filled with demos and live software for creating buttons quickly and easily!

ISBN: 1-56205-913-0 $39.99 USA/$56.95 CAN

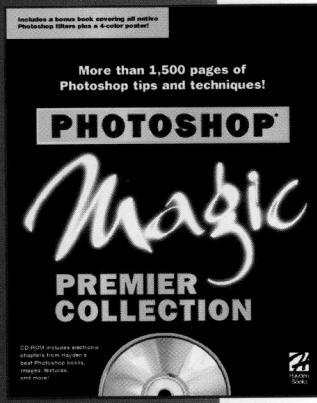

Photoshop Magic Premier Collection

Save over $50 on five of the most popular Magic books and get *The Complete Guide to Photoshop Native Filters*—complete coverage of all 97 of Photoshop's filters—and a poster showing the effects of all of them.

The boxed set includes *Photoshop Web Magic, Photoshop Type Magic 1, Photoshop Type Magic 2, Photoshop Effects Magic,* and *Photoshop Textures Magic.* It's the perfect way to achieve special effects for the Web, create amazing type treatments, design stunning graphics and illustrations, and appkly eye-catching textures.

ISBN: 1-56830-442-0   **$149.99 USA/$214.95 CAN**

Illustrator Type Magic

by Greg Simsic

Every page of *Illustrator Type Magic* makes a visual promise: you will be able to create this! The book's highly effective, recipe-style approach walks you through the procedures of creating special effects with type, and the stunning four-color illustrations are sure to inspire any designer.

ISBN: 1-56830-334-3   **$39.99 USA/$56.95 CAN**